# Quiet
# Kingmaker
## OF LAS VEGAS

*E. Parry Thomas*

# Quiet Kingmaker
## OF LAS VEGAS

### E. Parry Thomas

*E. Parry Thomas* (signature)

## BY JACK SHEEHAN

Stephens Press ∾ Las Vegas, Nevada

Editor: Geoff Schumacher
Jacket/Book Designer: Sue Campbell
Publishing Coordinator: Stacey Fott
Publishing Assistant: Kristina Hawkins
Cover Photo: Tom Donoghue

Cataloging in Publication Data
Sheehan, Jack.
Quiet kingmaker of Las Vegas : E. Parry Thomas / Jack Sheehan.
368 p. : photos ; 23 cm.
ISBN: 1-935043-05-6
ISBN 13: 978-1-935043-05-8
This presents the life E. Parry Thomas, one of Las Vegas's banking cor-
nerstones who helped finance much of the growth in the area over the
past forty years.
1. Thomas, E. Parry. 2. Las Vegas (Nev.)—History. 3. Bankers--Nevada—
Biography. I. Title.
[B] dc22 2009 2009921793

STEPHENS PRESS, LLC
A Stephens Media Company

Post Office Box 1600
Las Vegas, NV 89125-1600
www.stephenspress.com

Printed in Hong Kong

## Dedication:

*To my longtime partner and best friend, Jerry Mack.*
*Our friendship was closer than any brothers could be.*

— E. Parry Thomas

# CONTENTS

# ACKNOWLEDGMENTS

MUCH THANKS TO THE THOMAS FAMILY FOR THEIR TOTAL COOPERATION through the two years of working on this book. Particular thanks to Parry Thomas, for his patience and incredible recall of events going back eight decades, and for overcoming his initial reluctance to the project because he understood that it was important to get the record right for his family and friends and the students of Nevada history.

Tom Thomas served as a great point man on the book, enlisting cooperation of subjects, keeping our efforts on course, digging out family photos, and explaining some of the intricacies of banking and finance to someone poorly versed in the field.

Kathy Jackson is the best interview transcriber I've ever employed, and her ability to return interviews within a day or two is greatly appreciated.

Thanks to the four women of the Mack family, who enjoy a relationship with the Thomases that is closer than most biological families.

And to Steve and Elaine Wynn, who have never failed to mention the importance of Parry Thomas's friendship and guidance as they achieved one milestone after another in the building and shaping of modern Las Vegas.

No college course could ever have taught me more about how our city and state rose to its current heights than the time I was privileged to spend in the company of the subjects of our interviews. My thanks to them all.

As always, my greatest thanks go to my wife Carol, and children, J.P. and Lily, who put up with my frequent preoccupation with a writing project when they are deserving of my undivided attention.

—Jack Sheehan

# INTRODUCTION

IT'S A GOOD TWO-HOUR DRIVE FROM THE BOISE AIRPORT TO THE bucolic setting of Hailey, Idaho, a quaint little burg set in a valley surrounded by hills and mountains most notable for the world-famous snow-skiing resort Sun Valley.

The neighboring town of Ketchum is where Ernest Hemingway finished writing *For Whom the Bell Tolls*, and where he was laid to rest when life became too much for him.

At the time of my visit in autumn, Hailey was just dismissing summer and the leaves were turning a delicious golden brown and maroon.

Although Idaho is just one state removed from Nevada, if a person were to measure the distance by electrical wattage and human energy, this farming community of 6,000 full-time residents is more than a million miles away from the blinding glow of Las Vegas at night.

You can barely hear yourself think on a sidewalk jaunt down the famous Strip, with its erupting volcanoes and pirate battles and dancing waters with Ol' Blue Eyes on backup vocals, but during a long morning stroll down a dirt road in Hailey, I could hear a robin's song fifty yards away.

Yet it is in this pastoral setting, where the skies are big and the air pristine and the implementation of a new stoplight makes the front page of the morning paper, that the distinguished gentleman who spent his career "turning on the lights of Las Vegas," as one national magazine phrased it, has chosen to retire.

But you won't find E. Parry Thomas in an easy chair, poring over scrapbooks or memorabilia from his decades of guiding Valley Bank of Nevada, and in the process providing working capital and sage advice to every dreamer and schemer who migrated to Las Vegas from the mid-1950s to the mid-'8os. No, Parry Thomas, at eighty-seven, has spent the better part of the last quarter-century actively engaged in the world of horses, specifically the sport of dressage.

The same competitive drive that took him to the top of the business world finds him traveling to Germany once or twice each year to purchase the Hanoverian line of show horses. Parry learned early in the game that for Americans to compete at the top international level of a sport that requires horses to dance and prance—forward and backward and sideways—the process begins with acquiring animals whose DNA is genetically suited to the discipline.

The Thomas family is so well known at these German auctions that when Parry recently registered the top bid for a prize three-year-old, the orchestra immediately broke into a stirring rendition of "Viva Las Vegas."

The sixty-acre ranch that he calls River Grove Farm, and which was purchased as a gift to his bride of more than sixty years, Peggy, is as fine a dressage training facility as you'll find anywhere in the United States. The indoor training arena where his prize horses go through their daily routines has large chandeliers overhead, and the surface they move so gracefully over is composed of materials meticulously selected to prevent the turn of an ankle or the twist of a fetlock. River Grove is home to the Thomases' internationally famous mare, Brentina, the most acclaimed American dressage horse in history.

Parry explains his decision to forego his earlier passion for boating in his leisure years, and embrace horse country: "It was a mutual appreciation of horses that first brought Peggy and me together on a blind date. We've both always loved horses, and watching these magnificent animals work out each morning on the farm is the best part of our day."

As I first turned my car into River Grove, for several days of interviews leading to this book, I was greeted by a breathtaking bronze sculpture of a dressage-performing horse, which was commissioned by

Stephan Weiss, the late artist and husband of designer Donna Karan. An identical re-creation welcomes guests near the front entrance of the Wynn Resort in Las Vegas, 1,100 miles away. But we'll get to that part of the story later.

∞

I'd been hearing of the legend of Parry Thomas and his extraordinary influence on the growth of Las Vegas since I first got to town in the mid-1970s.

A Las Vegas city magazine I edited did a cover story on Thomas in 1978, but it was a fairly general profile, chronicling Parry's influence on the gaming sector and detailing his and his business partner Jerry Mack's enormous influence on the development of UNLV and their many philanthropic contributions to the community.

Another writer did the article, and it just skimmed the surface. The same story had been told with a slightly different spin many times through the years, as though all communications about Parry Thomas had been filtered through the same chamber. And it's likely they were. Yet I knew there was so much more to be told.

This was a man who structured the financing and served as chief adviser and go-between for all of Howard Hughes's hotel acquisitions in Las Vegas; who had recognized the brilliance of a young Steve Wynn when he first arrived in town in the mid-1960s and had guided him like a wise father on his ascent to fame and glory; had, with Jerry Mack, almost single-handedly seen to it that Nevada Southern University would have the vision, and the land, to grow into UNLV, a respected state university that would become the cultural heart of the city; and had worked individually with a diverse and motley assortment of casino owners and political bigwigs to help Las Vegas transition from an easily stereotyped Mob town in the 1950s and '60s to a darling of corporate America in the 1980s.

"Parry Thomas and Jerry Mack were legitimate guys who understood how to operate in an edgy environment," says Steve Wynn. "They always maintained their legitimacy and dealt with edginess professionally. There is no question that they moved gracefully and profitably on the edge. By that I mean they always knew where the line was and they didn't cross it. But they stayed right up against it because that's the only way they could have pulled this industry into the modern era.

"I don't think they ought to apologize for it, or sugarcoat it, or pretend it was anything else," Wynn says. "Pulling the gaming industry out of the post-bootleg, corrupt-politician, Italian-organized-crime era into a legitimate industry was an operation requiring major delicacy and only for people who possessed tremendous balance. And Parry had that balance. Yeah, Parry went to the stevedores' convention [Ed: *an allusion to the Teamsters, whose pension funds Parry used to package loans to casinos*], but he wasn't one of them. He was a guest, not a member of the club.

"I was allowed as a young man to hang out in the meeting rooms and watch him work," Wynn says. "I was given permission to listen in, and I heard the appeals and the proposals. When those guys would float ideas that were on the wrong side of the line, I would watch Parry shake his head and say, 'Oh, these guys are somethin'.'

"'Of course that's not gonna work,' he'd tell me afterwards, 'but they can get where they want to go in a different way, and I'll get them there.'"

"I wouldn't use the term 'puppet-master' to describe Parry," says Elaine Wynn, Steve's wife of forty-five years and herself a dynamic civic leader sometimes referred to as the First Lady of Las Vegas. "Because that word implies manipulation. But there's no one who had a broader view of what Las Vegas could become than Parry, nor is there anyone who had better intentions for the direction the city might go."

Another casino owner, asking not to be named, said, "Parry Thomas was the perfect man for the perfect time. With his intelligence, distinguished looks, Mormon background, and instant likeability, all the boys back in the day knew they needed Parry's loyalty to achieve their dreams, and if they crossed him, their long-term chance of success in Las Vegas was minimized."

A compelling argument can be made that no single individual has done more to direct the growth and maturation of Las Vegas in the last half-century than E. Parry Thomas. Every source we spoke with, many of whom would make a short list of Vegas' most important power brokers themselves, placed Thomas in the top five of their most influential people.

"If it's unquestioned that Parry ranks as a ten in terms of importance, the next closest person is a five," says Steve Wynn, who certainly belongs in that conversation whenever the subject comes up.

"He was the guy who made the selection on who stayed and who left, on who grew and who didn't, and on who bought and expanded and who sold. The cover of *Business Week*, with Parry's picture, said it well. 'Frank Sinatra Gives Las Vegas Its Glitter, Parry Thomas Gives It Its Gold.'"

On top of it all, with Peggy, who Parry says deserves "ninety-nine percent of the credit," the Thomases raised five children who all excelled in their own right to help Las Vegas achieve its current prominence.

Employing the understatement that characterizes many of his reflections, Parry says simply, "We didn't raise any dumb children."

As curious was I was about all those important dealings that Thomas had with gaming giants, business-builders, and politicians, I had never been able to find an in-depth profile on the man. I found it curious that someone involved in so many high-level decisions could keep his affairs so quiet.

It is well known that throughout his career Parry Thomas had shied away from reporters and writers. He shunned publicity and attention in all forms and had to have his arm twisted to accept awards or public recognition for everything he accomplished in transforming the Bank of Las Vegas from a six-month-old, nearly bankrupt enterprise in 1955 into Valley Bank of Nevada, the most important lending institution in the history of the state, and eventually into a billion-dollar acquisition by Bank of America.

Thus, when I had my first sit-down meeting with him in July of 2007, there was apprehension on both sides. Parry had been encouraged for years by his family and friends to put on the record the compelling story of his life, but it was just not in his nature to talk in detail about business affairs. He had always maintained that the relationship between a banker and his clients was every bit as sacred as attorney-client privilege. Since early in his career, he had even shunned keeping notes or calendars recording business meetings, having learned the hard way through some early subpoenas that the documented activities of some of his more notorious banking clients could become fodder for grand jury investigations. He trained his mind, and that of his long-time secretary, Belle James (whose value was so great she was made a vice president of the bank), to retain important matters in their heads.

Yet having just turned eighty-six weeks before our meeting, and with a memory still as sharp as a laser used to cut diamonds, Parry sensed that the time was right to put it all out there. He would consider cooperating on a book primarily as a legacy to his children, grandchildren, and great-grandchildren, but also as a gift to Las

Vegas history aficionados, who he knew would not be able to get these stories from anyone else.

In chronicling those years from the mid-1950s to the end of the 1980s and the paradigm-shifting opening of The Mirage resort, as Las Vegas evolved from a funky Western gambling town that no one took too seriously into the fastest-growing city in America, which was twice profiled on the cover of *Time* magazine and has been the subject of countless movies, books, and television series, Parry Thomas was the one person who could talk about nearly all of it. He, more than any single individual, lived those years in the eye of the hurricane.

Parry knew all the important players because he loaned money to most of them, and when you're the guy with your hand on the purse strings, you see people at their most exposed, their most vulnerable. His lending decisions often determined the success or failure of an individual's career. And make no mistake, when an entrepreneur with a gaming license, or even a small-business man with a good idea, needed money through those decades, the first call he made was usually to Parry Thomas.

The other banks in town were initially opposed to doing business with casino owners, and by the time those lending institutions realized that it was ludicrous not to make loans to the keystone industry in the state, Parry and his Bank of Las Vegas had cornered the market.

There's so much more to Parry than his business dealings that when you start hearing the stories, you wonder how he found time for it all. Parry had learned early in his banking career in Salt Lake City that it made good business sense, and was good for the soul, to give back in abundance any benefits derived from his work in a community. So he quickly became involved with the Las Vegas Chamber of Commerce, the Boy Scouts, United Way (which he totally restructured), and the groups that evolved into the Nevada Development Authority and the Las Vegas Convention and Visitors Authority, to name but a few.

Raised in a strong Mormon family, Parry had been a devout church-going Mormon until the age of fourteen, and although he hasn't participated in the rituals of the church since his teen years, he credits the religion with providing him the moral and ethical fundamentals that have guided him through his life. He has consistently answered calls from the church since then, whether it be for financial assistance or helping a brother in the faith through a difficult time. Two of the Thomas sons, orthopedic surgeon Steve and lawyer-businessman Tom, are bishops in the Mormon Church.

When I entered the room in the U.S. Bank Building for that first meeting, both Peggy and Parry Thomas were there, as was Tom Thomas, who had agreed to be our point man on the book were it to actually transpire. The project was entirely conditional on Parry and Peggy's consent, and the jury was still out as we started to talk.

"This is my sons' idea," was the first thing Parry said after giving me a firm handshake. "I've always taken the view that business dealings with clients were to be kept private. That is my policy, and that was always our policy at the bank. I told my people that they weren't ever to discuss banking matters even with their husbands and wives, and we never waivered from that policy. It's one of the reasons we had such customer loyalty."

"But most of the people we're going to discuss are dead," Tom said, injecting some levity into the proceedings.

"Yes, but they have children and grandchildren," Parry said.

"Investigative reporting is not my first calling," I assured him. "Certainly we want to put into a book all the interesting details of your life and the lives of the people around you, but this will be more of a biography, perhaps even an oral history, so that readers can learn

18

of so many important events in this city's history that haven't previously been disclosed."

Patting his hand on the table, Parry gave me a good looking over, and after a long minute finally said, "Well, let's begin and see where it goes."

Eventually, our conversation turned to writing down the names of sources who might be able to comment on the events that would comprise the bulk of the book, and Parry grew more at ease. I think it was because through my thirty-five years here I had come to know personally most of the people he mentioned: people like the Wynns, Bob Maheu (who was Howard Hughes' point man both before and during his years in Las Vegas), financier Michael Milken, and long-time gamers such as Bill Boyd and Jack Binion, Parry grew more at ease and felt that my asking these sources for their thoughts and memories would be less of an intrusion than if a stranger were to barge in with a list of questions about important matters in their careers.

I eventually learned that even Steve Wynn, whom I'd written about a number of times, had assured Parry that doing a book on his life was a noble endeavor and one well worth undertaking.

Over the next year and change, I conducted dozens of interviews with Parry. Most sessions were held in the U.S. Bank building on Sahara Avenue in Las Vegas, where the Thomas & Mack Company keeps offices; some were at River Grove Farm; some were at the Del Mar International Horse Show, where Brentina and her rider, Debbie McDonald, were engaged in pre-Olympic qualifying for the games in China; and others were at the National Finals Rodeo, where not surprisingly the Thomases have excellent seats. After all, the building in which the rodeo is held is named for Parry and his late partner.

"Las Vegas has grown so much that about the only thing most residents here know about Thomas and Mack is the basketball arena," Parry says with a laugh.

It is our hope that this book will expand that knowledge.

—Jack Sheehan

## Postscript:

ALL OF THE INTERVIEWS IN THIS BOOK TOOK PLACE OVER AN EIGHTEEN-month period from June 2007 through November 2008. It was explained to all interview subjects that their comments and recollections would be woven into a narrative that would be pieced together by the author, and that I could include and omit as I chose. What was most remarkable in the gathering of these stories and anecdotes is how similar the recollections were of these individuals, many of whom were in their seventies and beyond at the time of our conversations. I think it leads to the credibility of those who cooperated in the assemblage of this book that there was so little disagreement about how these important events transpired. It is my hope that the book in sum will make a significant contribution to the collected history of the fastest-growing city of the twentieth century, and one referred to by more than one credible observer as "the last great Western American city."

## A Family Note:

ON MORE OCCASIONS THAN I CAN COUNT, THE TOPIC OF RECORDING my dad's stories of his early years in Vegas came up and was dropped. First, Dad didn't feel the stories were all that significant, and second, he was concerned about the confidences he had so carefully guarded. Maybe after many, many years of family prodding he weakened. Certainly the passing of his best friend and partner, Jerry Mack, had something to do with it. What sealed the deal was the comfort he had with Jack Sheehan and confidence that this work would capture the stories straight from the horse's mouth.

Our only regret is in not having pushed this work forward while Jerry was still with us. Jerry and Joyce Mack's impact on our family and the success of my dad cannot be underestimated. The family joke when the phone would ring every evening at six p.m. was, "Dad, it's for you, it's Uncle Jerry"! It's as if the two were attached at the hip.

One of my favorite Parry and Jerry stories is when Nate Mack, Jerry's father, sat my dad and Jerry down at the very beginning of their partnership and said, "I want you two to be partners from here on out. Parry will handle the banking and Jerry will handle the properties. And until Parry has enough money to cover his half of the deals, Jerry, you lend it to him." Jerry was always the quiet partner. Dad usually got the news stories and the accolades, but there wasn't an event in my dad's business life that didn't involve Jerry; there wasn't a community success or banking milestone that didn't have Jerry's fingerprints all over it. As I read through this history, I can hear Uncle Jerry in the background saying, "Parry, you forgot the most important part of the story!"

—Tom Thomas

# CHAPTER ONE

# Early Years

I WAS BORN ON JUNE 29, 1921, IN OGDEN, UTAH. OUR FAMILY HOME WAS at 925 27<sup>th</sup> Street. I had what by all accounts would be a wonderful childhood and a wonderful relationship with my parents and my siblings. My father's name was Thomas Edward Thomas and my mother's was Olive Parry Thomas. The Parry with an "a" is the Welsh spelling.

I was number three in the pecking order of the six kids. I had two older sisters and two younger sisters who were twins, and my brother, Paul, who is about twelve years younger than me.

Ogden was a good place to grow up. It was a small city then, about 40,000 people, and the surrounding area offered a lot of outing opportunities in the mountains and up in Ogden Canyon and Huntsville and Eden and other nearby towns.

I was involved in scouting in those early days, up until about age fourteen or fifteen, and of course my family was very involved with the Mormon Church. I'd say about ninety to ninety-five percent of the people in Ogden were Mormon. All of us children were involved and our social life pretty well revolved around the church in those days. We'd go to Sunday school, and then later on, after I turned twelve, I'd go to the priesthood meetings—all the men do—and my activities included scout training and even playing basketball and attending church dances most weeks. It was a structured and well-supervised social upbringing in all ways.

Generations of my family had been involved with the church back into the middle 1800s, from the time the church was formed. And as most people know, the church had very difficult times and its members were chased and persecuted wherever they went. So they kept going west until they ended up in Salt Lake.

Brigham Young was a colonizer, and he settled the areas in Utah, southern Idaho, parts of Nevada and so on. I found from my studies that he was a pretty bright guy. He kept the English people in Salt Lake. He sent the Welsh and the Dutch to Ogden, and he sent most of the Scots up in the upper country to Huntsville and Eden in the mountain area. And all the Norwegians and Danish and Swedes he sent to the Provo area, as I recall. That way he avoided a lot of classic infighting, so he was a pretty smart colonizer.

My childhood was closely aligned with my father, as I was the oldest son. My birth name is Edward Parry Thomas, but I was called Parry from birth because my mother's family and relations far outnumbered my father's and all the Parrys chose to call me Parry. I didn't even know I had a first name until I got a birth certificate to go into the Army.

My dad had quite a history behind him. His father had abandoned the family when Dad was about nine or ten years old. When he was eleven he got a job as a water boy with Sanford Plumbing Company in Ogden. The water boy's responsibility was to work with the ditch-digging crew and the like in those days. He learned various new aspects of the plumbing business through those early years and he stayed with the company in a variety of positions and became a journeyed plumber by the time he was twenty. So his early career was forged in the plumbing business.

My father's first great gain was when he married my mother. My mother Olive's father was named Chauncey Parry and her mother was Julia Parry. Chauncey Parry died at quite an early age, of pneumonia I believe, but he had done pretty well in real estate and left my grandmother in a relatively good position. As the story goes, my grandmother Julia left my father a wedding present, five hundred dollars worth of plumbing tools, and with those he quit the Sanford Company and opened his own business, Thomas Heating and Plumbing Company.

My father started his new business slowly, but he was a very bright fellow and he saw that there was more plumbing to be done in the many public schools that were being built in those days than in residential work, so he directed his energies toward that business. He also did the plumbing for the Salt Lake Depot and the Ogden Depot. And then he got the contracts to do some schools up in Idaho, including clear up north at the University of Idaho in Moscow.

From there he moved on to the field of plumbing work where the budgets in those days were the largest, and that was in hospitals, which became his new specialty. He did four or five of the big veterans' hospitals that were being built at the time to minister to the health needs of the many vets of World War I.

When he would land these big hospital contracts, the family would move with him. We moved to Tucson, and then to Arkansas, and finally the biggest one was in Sterling, New Jersey, just outside of Plainfield.

I went to the first grade in Arizona and the second and third grade in New Jersey. I don't remember those moves as being particularly difficult for me. The only problem was that being Mormon in New Jersey subjected me to some insensitivity from the other students. Some of the kids would yell at you and make fun of you and call you

25

names. I did get in a couple of fistfights over that. There would be references to polygamy and growing horns on our heads when we grew up and things like that. It was just dumb stuff, but it helped me learn how to fight pretty good and how to defend myself.

I don't know if those experiences of moving and meeting new people helped me later on or not, but it probably didn't hurt. You learn to adapt to new situations and so that might have been helpful, but we eventually moved back to Ogden and I finished my grade school at Quincy Grammar School, around the corner from where we lived.

I did well in school and the work came fairly easy to me, and I played most of the sports as a kid. I played soccer and baseball, and I was comfortable with horses. It was a different time back then and most of the people who lived around us had a horse or several horses, so a love of horses was ingrained in me early on.

A lot of my time outside school was spent helping my father on his various jobs. I picked up all sorts of skills and knowledge just watching him do his business and helping where I could. I became his chief maintenance man and mechanic through those years and I really enjoyed doing whatever my father asked me to do, and doing it the best I could.

Of course the Depression started in 1929 with the stock market crash, and I was just eight years old at the time. Everything tightened up considerably after that, and one positive result is that families became closer because each family had to fend for itself and watch every dime that was spent. You just couldn't incur any expense.

I think my allowance in the first part of the Depression was fifty cents a week, and any work that had to be done you just pitched in without getting any additional payment for it.

I'll never forget one time I was invited by a neighbor kid up to the state fair in Salt Lake City. I was just ten or eleven years old. My friend's father owned a dairy farm and he used to exhibit cows at the state fair. I'd never been to Salt Lake and I'd heard so many times what a great city it was, so I really wanted to go badly. I asked my father at about noon, and my friend and his dad were leaving at three o'clock. My father reached in his pocket and all he had was two dollars and fifty cents. He gave me fifty cents and said that money had to last me for the three days I was in Salt Lake. Of course when we got there we performed odd jobs for the exhibitors, who would pay us nickels or quarters to run errands for them. The Depression was severe, and that's how you lived. You just did whatever you could to make ends meet.

As I said, nearly all of the families in Utah then were involved with the Mormon Church. I would say our family was semi-involved with the church, but not too close to it. All us kids went to the church functions. That was our main entertainment in those days, because those activities didn't cost any money, and nobody had any money. We'd also go to a movie on Saturdays. It was about a forty-five-minute walk from our house to the movie theater, and we'd make that walk with a quarter in our pocket. The movie would cost a nickel and a candy bar would cost another nickel and then you'd have fifteen cents left over for the rest of the week. One job I had at the age of ten or eleven was as a box boy for the corner grocery store. It was owned by Aaron Rubenstein, who surprised everyone years later when he finally joined the Mormon Church. He never paid me with money, but would let me eat all the ice cream I wanted and even take pints of it home to the family.

One thing I learned from my father during those lean years was the advantage of staying out of debt. That was a big difference between our family and many others during the Depression. Whatever property my dad owned, he owned free and clear, while other families couldn't make enough money to pay the mortgage or the light bill or any other darn thing.

In hindsight, my reluctance to ever borrow money probably kept me from making a lot more money on good deals. If I would have borrowed and used leverage, like as a banker I was always preaching to others, I might have been a rich man today (laughing).

∞

As I mentioned, my father was a brilliant man, and even though his formal education went only through the sixth or seventh grade, he was self-educated. He was a voracious reader and he not only read the basic textbooks, but books on business and self-improvement. He was also a tireless worker, with a mind that was always searching for better and more economical ways to run his business.

While he was working on hospitals, my dad noticed that in addressing the various illnesses that people had, some hospital rooms had to be kept colder or warmer than others, depending on the patient. He saw the need for an air-conditioning system that would set the temperature in the room automatically. He came up with an invention called the double-armature air-conditioning unit. It's a motor that could run either forward or backward. And he made them in small enough sizes that they would work in a hospital room. In those days everything was controlled by radiators, so either you turned the valve up or you turned it down. If you had a double-armature motor put on the radiator valve, it worked fine, but the problem was that the thermostats in those days were so sluggish that it defeated the purpose. It took too long to activate the motor.

It was ingenious the way he created the thermostat. It was based on the theory of the bi-metallic expansion of metal. The bi-metallic expansion for brass and copper would be different than for steel, for instance. So he laminated steel and brass in thin strips. He laminated them together with electro-contacts on the end of them, and he then put them between a dual-electric contact field, so that when the temperature would change just the least little bit, it would move that temperature-controlled arm and it would snap it over and make contact.

With a lot of work and study he addressed that problem and worked through it and invented the first true thermostat. His invention works on the same principle we have today.

He patented his thermostat, but then got in a legal wrangle with Honeywell over the patents and that started a helluva legal fight. He eventually sold his patents to American Radiators. And he did pretty well on the sale, although he could have done a lot better without the litigation.

After my dad had completed that big job in New Jersey he wanted to go to school and pursue several other ideas he had for inventions. He enrolled in the University of Southern California, and I believe he rented a house down in Pasadena. This was in the fall of 1929. But then a month later the stock market collapsed and the Depression was on, and our lives took a distinct U-turn.

The second biggest bank in Utah at that time was the Ogden State Bank, and it was run by the Bigelow family. By that time, my father was probably the biggest plumbing contractor in the country, and because of his success with the government hospitals, he was possibly the largest single depositor in that bank when it went broke. And he was just trapped.

I was only eight or nine years old at that time, but I have a pretty good memory of what happened because it had such a dramatic effect on our family. We knew we were facing some pretty lean years ahead of us.

After the market crashed, the state banking commission took over the banks, and they sent up some bank examiners to take over the failed bank. What those men did when they got to Ogden was to set themselves up like they were living in a country club. At least that's what I remember my dad saying about them. And they started selling off some of the best assets of the bank at bargain prices. Dad was watching them closely because he had somewhere between six hundred thousand and a million dollars in that bank, and in those days that was a helluva lot of money. So he complained to the examiners bitterly and was getting nowhere, so he finally went down and had an audience with the Utah governor, George Dern.

My dad complained to the governor that the way this bank crisis was being handled was going to leave no money for the depositors. But the governor didn't have an answer for him. So Dad ran some ads in the Ogden Standard Examiner asking that all the bank's depositors meet with him in the tabernacle. Ogden didn't have a Mormon temple, but there was a tabernacle out on North Washington Street. And at the meeting he got up and told all these depositors exactly what was happening, and that the solution was to bring all their energy collectively and put pressure on the governor to change this situation, which would mean putting an instant freeze on all bank assets until they could be managed correctly.

When that happened, the governor turned around and pointed at my father to be the liquidating agent of the bank. So Dad took over what was left of the old Ogden State Bank. And that was my first introduction into banking.

I remember that my father just did a terrific job with that bank. He put a freeze on selling anything because the factories were down, the flour mills were down, and the canning factories that the bank had had to repossess were down. One by one, or even collectively, he would get these plants running and get them going to where they would show some economic value. Then he'd sell them for the best offer. I guess there were only about forty-six percent of the assets left by the time he got in there to run the bank, but he built them up to where he made profits out of them and returned around seventy to eighty percent back to the depositors.

My father was only thirty-five or thirty-six when he was forced to take over that crisis and manage it, and he worked at it full time for about twelve years. In hindsight, it really aged him, with all that worry and stress and having to provide for six children while the country was going through a Depression. But he was a thousand percent honest, and everyone knew it, and he had a terrific reputation when it was all said and done.

∞

During those years, Dad became very close friends with George Eccles and the Eccles family, who owned First Security Bank. George was a wonderful man, just terrific to our family. He had no children of his own, and he took a liking to me and he used to follow everything I was doing and he used to talk to me a lot about his career in banking. I pretty well knew before I left high school that I wanted to go into banking as a career.

I went to Central Junior High School in Ogden, where I participated in a lot of sports and other activities, and then I went to Ogden High School. I was involved in ROTC there and a couple of scholastic societies, just small things. And I became even more interested in horses and riding and learning how to take care of them. Dad had two or three horses, and I remember how excited I was when I got my first horse. It was a mare called Bess. Then I had a thoroughbred named Bees and Honey. He was an excellent horse. I also started playing polo then, although a more fair statement would be that I was playing at polo, because we didn't really know what we were doing. But that early practice allowed me to make the varsity polo team at the University of Utah my freshman year. We had intercollegiate competition and we traveled a lot, with games or exhibitions in Texas, Arizona, New Mexico, and Southern California.

I want to mention some other experiences I had helping my dad with his banking challenges at Ogden State Bank, which would prove invaluable years later after I'd moved to Las Vegas.

I was given a couple of assignments by my dad to go out and try to collect loans or collateral on loans. I'll never forget one time I had a big old Dodge truck, a cattle truck. And I chose my friend Spencer Peterson to go with me because he was the biggest kid on the football team. We were sent out to pick up half a dozen dairy cows out by Syracuse, Utah, which is right on the border of the Great Salt Lake. This was in the depths of the Depression.

I went out there to this old shack where a poor old farmer and his toothless wife were living, and I said, "I'm awfully sorry, but I have orders and sheriff's papers with me and it's my job to pick up these cows."

And I'll never forget what he said to me. "You won't believe it, young man, but those cows got up one day and walked out and floated away in that lake," he said. "And I haven't seen them since."

Of course, the farmer had been forced to sell them to live. I felt so damn sorry for him. If I'd had any money, I would have given it to him, whatever I had. But those were the difficult times we were living in.

I learned a lot that day, but I remember telling myself that when I became a banker I was never going to loan money on cows. I would take any chattel over cattle.

Another thing that stuck with me from those early years in Ogden was that the Eccles family and the Hemingway family were the main bankers in Ogden, and they lived in the biggest houses and drove the biggest cars. That made an impression on me.

When I started at the University of Utah in 1940 I naturally took all the core curriculum and some business classes. But about a year after World War II broke out for the U.S. in December 1941, our entire ROTC class was taken into the Army. We were shipped to Camp Roberts, in Paso Robles, California, for basic training. From there we were going to go to officer training school. In the meantime, a couple of us decided we'd like to go into the Air Corps. So we made application and were accepted to go to cadet training in Santa Ana, and from there we were sent to Victorville for flight training. That didn't go well for me. My eardrums just kept bursting every time I flew above five or six thousand feet. I couldn't take it. I just had a terrible time with my ears, so they washed me out. I've been hard of hearing ever since that time.

From Victorville I was sent to a replacement center, and then from there I was sent to Fort Lewis, outside Tacoma, Washington.

I was there for about three months as they were forming a new hospital, the Eighth Field Hospital. Then I was sent for more training to a big Army hospital in Denver for a couple months. And then we were shipped overseas and we got there in September, a few months after D-Day in 1944. We landed at a port called Fecamp in France, near Normandy.

I was just an enlisted man in the Army, but I got to be a sergeant. In France I was assigned to intelligence work, but I don't want it to sound more important than it was. All it meant was that we'd keep records, and if we had prisoners, we would try to interview them. We had a bunch of side duties in addition.

Shortly after D-Day, I was sent with approximately a dozen other people down to Munich and to the Zugspitz, which is Germany's highest mountain. It's three thousand meters in elevation and has sensational snow skiing. The skiing takes place on a small glacier just below the main peak. A guy named Sergeant Bergen and myself were down there. We spent about a month there and it was good duty, skiing every day.

Then my whole outfit was sent to Marseilles. We were to be reactivated and regrouped and we were going to be sent to Japan. I'll never forget it because we got everything loaded on the troop ship and we were going to sail the next day, and then we got orders in the middle of the night that the Enola Gay had dropped the bomb on Hiroshima [*August 6, 1945*], so our orders were canceled.

Our outfit was broken up and about half of us were sent to a place called Saint Jean de Luz. It's on the Bay of Biscay, a beautiful little fishing port city in France, right on the border of Spain, up against the Pyrenees. We set up a hospital there because the government had a lot of agents and people living in Spain. We took care of those who needed medical care and then we'd get them out of Spain. We'd also go to a place in the Pyrenees where we'd get information from Spain that the agents would give us and we'd bring it back and get it to Paris. So the hospital doubled as both an intelligence and medical service. That lasted until I was discharged and came home in June of 1946.

I had come from a very small community, and kind of a sheltered situation, and I learned so much in the Army. The education I got there was probably more important in my development than my years in college. I just learned so much about people. I was in the Army with guys from Rhode Island to California, and learned all about their attitudes and their religions and their economic situations and their regional biases. I remember teaming up with a guy named Schwarz, and he and I started playing bridge and beating everyone around us, playing a quarter a game or fifty cents a game. That was about the most I ever gambled for because I surely wasn't interested in gambling in the casinos years later in Las Vegas. But it was just such an eye-opener for me in the Army, to learn how to read people and make friends with different personalities and learn how to anticipate their likes and dislikes. It really helped me to become a people person.

When we disembarked from the ship in the United States, we were sent to Fort Dix in New Jersey, where we stayed for two days. I called my fraternity house at the university and talked to a couple of my fraternity brothers, and my good friend Dick Stein. I told Dick that I'd be home in two days, and he said, "Good, we're all going to a dance out at Salt Air," which was a big dance floor out on the lake, the Great Salt Lake. It's all washed away now, but it used to be quite popular for big bands and things like that.

I said, "Great, get me a date." And one of them knew a girl named Peggy Chatterton, and knew that she was into horses, and they kept throwing to her that I was a polo player and that we'd have horses in common. Peggy was scared to death because she'd never had a blind date in her life, but then neither had I.

## Peggy Thomas

I REMEMBER IT WAS A FRATERNITY BROTHER OF PARRY'S WHO CALLED me and mentioned this blind date. Parry was a Beta Theta Pi at the University of Utah and I was a Chi Omega. A blind date was out of the question for me then, but this boy explained to me that Parry had just gotten out of the Army and that he had been a polo player. And I thought, well, the party sounded fun and if he was a rider, that would make him interesting to me, so I agreed to go.

## Parry Thomas

THE DATE WENT WELL AND WE GOT ALONG, BUT WE DIDN'T START dating each other exclusively for a few more months. But once we did, things moved along rapidly and we were married the following year, on September 12, 1947.

I still had two and a half years of college remaining, so Peggy and I had some lean years after we were married. I had declared my major as business, but what I really wanted was to get a degree in banking and finance. Unfortunately, the University of Utah didn't offer that degree. So I got a bright idea and went to Dr. Roland Stucki, who was the head of the business school, and I said, "Why don't we create our own banking school?"

His first reaction was to say no. But I pushed the case that the state of Utah, and particularly Salt Lake, was noted for their famous bankers. At the time we had the Eccles family, and Marriner Eccles was chairman of the Federal Reserve Board. Another Utah man named Kennedy had been chairman of the FDIC, and there were others very prominent in banking, including one that was head of Chase Manhattan Bank. So the state really had a strong banking fraternity.

I suggested to Dr. Stucki that we look into all the banks and get the best banker in each field of banking and operations, and all the different types of loans, all the trust work, and every category of banking imaginable. We could then invite them up to the university to give lectures at seven in the morning. We'd then tape those lectures and make a textbook out of it.

By golly Dr. Stucki loved the idea and that's what we did. We created the School of Banking for the university.

Although Dr. Stucki did all the work from there, they gave me the credit for it. He had the courage to take a student's idea and implement it and I am forever grateful to him for doing that. He was a wonderful man and a wonderful teacher. The *Wall Street Journal* gave a couple of awards each year around the country to outstanding finance students, and they named me one of the recipients. It was clearly that idea to form the banking school that got their attention.

Peggy had graduated that previous spring of 1947, and she was working as a secretary to the head of the English Department. We basically lived off her salary until I graduated in December. As I recall our monthly rent was fifty dollars for a one-room apartment. When you pulled down the Murphy bed, that was the end of the room, but we managed, as young people do.

When it came time to get my first banking job, it's important to realize that the talent pool was overflowing with millions of young men recently returned from the war, and they all were looking to start careers. There's probably never been a more competitive time to find a good job in America than in those post-WWII years.

As I've said, my dad and George Eccles were partners on many ventures and very close friends, and given that equation it was fairly assumed that I was going to go to work for First Security Bank, owned by the Eccles family. As much as I loved George Eccles and the family and everything about it, I realized there was a downside to it. I knew in my heart that if I went to work for First Security, I'd do well, that I'd have a good life and a good secure job. I knew I'd become a top officer of the bank and maybe even become president of it. But that would be it. That would be the ceiling. And I knew even at twenty-six years old that I wanted to own my own bank. I wanted to be my own person, in my own business, and call my own shots. So I turned away from that certain opportunity.

My best friend in college was Larry Higgins, and Larry had a job as a night-time bookkeeper at the Continental Bank, which was one of the smallest banks in Salt Lake. So I asked Larry if I could get a job down there, and he told me they were hiring people in their installment loan department, which they'd just opened up.

Larry got me an appointment for an interview with the manager of that department. I couldn't help noticing on the morning of that appointment that as I walked into the bank there was this platform on the first floor where all these gray-headed guys—vice presidents— were sitting. But the installment loan department was on the second floor, so I went up there. The manager was sitting in his glass-enclosed office while I was in the waiting room outside. He was playing footsie with his secretary at the time. I could see this going on. So I had time to look over the room, and I noticed about twenty young guys, every one of them better looking than me, out there working their tails off. And in the moments I sat there I thought, this isn't for me.

I got up and walked out, went downstairs, and walked up to a big tall guy with the nameplate, "G.S. Murphy, Cashier."

I reached out my hand and said, "I'm Parry Thomas and I just graduated from the University of Utah, where I received high honors and won the *Wall Street Journal* Award as an outstanding finance student because I helped organize the School of Banking for the university while I was there. The school didn't have one, and I wanted to graduate with that degree so I organized it."

If I was hoping that Mr. Murphy would be impressed, he wasn't, because he told me they didn't have anything for me and that I would have to go upstairs to the installment loan department where they were hiring.

I knew Mr. Murphy was an old-time banker and a man who looked like he took pride in his work, so I looked him right in the eye and said, "Mr. Murphy, I don't want to be an installment banker. I want to be a commercial banker like you."

He paused for a second and then pulled a sheet of paper out of his drawer, and said, "Well, there's an opening as an assistant trainee bookkeeper in our booking department. It pays only one hundred twenty dollars a month, and you'll have to get up at two in the morning because you post the books before the bank opens later that day."

I said, "I'll take it." And that was one of the best decisions in my life. That's the day I officially became a banker.

I got up just after midnight each day to go to work at the Continental Bank, and I noticed in our department that all the young employees were wearing Levis and sweat shirts, you know, because at that hour they weren't dealing with the general public. I also noticed that Mr. Murphy was a good storekeeper. He'd walk through that department just like clockwork at seven o'clock every morning, near the tail end of the shift. With all the eager young employees, I decided one day that I had to do something to get noticed by him. So I started wearing a vest suit, with a nice shirt and tie to go to work.

They used those old Burroughs adding machines in our department, and you really had to have great dexterity in your fingers and hands to work them well, and I was terrible at it. I really was. So I needed to use every advantage, so I figured the suit and tie was one way.

Of course, I stood out like a sore thumb, but at least I stood out. So I'd been there about four months and Mr. Murphy called me into his office. I thought maybe I was going to get fired because I was a lousy bookkeeper, and I was lousy on the damn adding machine. But he surprised me. He said, "Keith Christensen is sitting on our new accounts desk, but he's goofing off. He's taking too long for lunch, so I'm going to put him back on the teller line, and I'm going to give you the job." Those were his exact words.

Well, he put me into new accounts, and I sat there. And I sat there some more. I opened one account the first day. The second day I opened two accounts, just sitting there watching the clock creep by all day. On the third day I went to Mr. Murphy's office and told him that I needed a secretary.

He gave me a surprised look, like I'd lost my marbles, and he opened up that same middle drawer where he kept all his records that he'd opened when he first hired me. He ran his finger down the page of his records and said, "Well, yesterday you opened two accounts and the day before that you opened one. You've opened a total of three accounts in two days and you're telling me you need a secretary?"

I said, "Mr. Murphy, I really don't need a secretary, but you've got that pretty girl with long red hair up on the third floor, and she's smart as a whip. I want her to handle the business I bring in because I want to go out and ring doorbells and get us new business, and when I have new customers rushing through the front door I want someone who can handle all the paperwork. If it doesn't work out, and I don't generate a whole lot of new business, you can fire me. But I can't just sit there and wait for people to come to me. It's not going to work. I've got to go find them."

Over the next several months I think I rang every damn business doorbell in Salt Lake City, and we took the bank from $33 million in deposits up to about $80 million in five years. But I'll never forget Mr. Murphy's surprise when, as a new young employee who hadn't done much, I told him I needed a secretary.

Anyhow, that's when I really started to learn about what it took to become a salesman. Keep in mind, twelve million soldiers had just come back from the war, mostly young men, all finishing their education, all of them looking for jobs. And there were no good jobs, so you just took any damn thing you could get and you had to prove yourself and fight your way through. Salt Lake was certainly no exception. The universities were jam-packed with veterans coming back.

By the way, when I was in the bookkeeping department, I couldn't help but notice that it was helter skelter the way the machines were placed in the departments. There was no logical flow to the operation, and it was hard to know what was going on. They had the sorting machines in the middle of the bookkeeping machines and vice versa, and the general bookkeeper in the corner and so on. So I measured the room and I measured all the equipment and I redesigned and laid out the whole floor as to the normal flow of the work. I designed it so the flow would go to the sorting machines, the sorting machines to the booking entries, and then to the mail room, so that everything flowed smoothly. I think George Murphy and the other executives appreciated an employee taking the initiative to do that.

I tried to be as organized as possible when I went out to sell the merits of our bank. I'd get a map of the business district and I'd quarter off the map into sections, and I had an index system listing every business in that section. I'd phone every single business in that quarter, and then move on to the next section. Then after a few days I'd come back and repeat my calls to the first group.

I kept very good records and wrote down the names of the children of the business owner or manager, and the names of the wife or husband, inquire whether they played golf—anything I could think to talk about, like any good salesman would do.

Also, the Chamber of Commerce was controlled by the Walker Bank and the First Security Banks and they were getting most of the business and we weren't. So I volunteered to become a member of the Chamber of Commerce and to serve on their membership committee. That was an easy position to get because no one wanted to be on that committee; it was a terrible committee to be on.

I remember they gave a hat to whoever got the most new members to sign up in a month. After about a year I had more damn hats than I had closets, because I was able to bring that chamber membership from 156 members to several hundred new members. And nearly every one of those new members I brought in became bank customers at Continental.

And other Continental Bank employees followed me onto the Chamber of Commerce and the membership committee because we saw that as a great way to network in the business community.

I also learned at the Continental Bank the importance of being involved with charities, and how to give back to my community. Those lessons stayed with me later in Las Vegas, when I found that giving to charities was not only its own reward, but could be an asset for business as well.

At Continental I got channeled into working with the National Foundation for Infantile Paralysis. At that time, polio was a devastating disease, particularly in Utah. There were all kinds of theories, some of them about impurities in the drinking water, but the incidence percentage-wise was far higher than in other states. They weren't raising much money for the cause, so I volunteered to be the drive chairman. It occurred to me that rather than just asking people for money, we would collect it involuntarily. The first thing we did was raffle off a car. It was important to get the right car and the right location to display it and the right people to work on the raffle, and then we could raise a significant amount. I got some of my fraternity brothers and Peggy got some of her sorority sisters and we manned the ticket booth around the clock. We had people we could trust and strict procedures on how to handle the money, because we were dealing with cash.

I got the city of Salt Lake to let us put up the car on a nice display stand at South and Main Street, which got a lot of car and foot traffic. Everyone asked whether we were going to get a Ford or a Chevrolet, but I told them that wouldn't cut it. We had to get a car with a little more moxie. So I went to a local Pontiac dealer who was a good guy, and he gave us the car for cost. We auctioned off the car at a dollar a chance, and we raised more money for infantile paralysis than they'd ever raised before. That first year we raised about $170,000. The second year we got two Pontiacs and sold chances for five dollars apiece, and we raised $400,000. We were very organized, and we got permission to use bullhorns on the street corner. When the auction was over and they totaled up the money, they gave me a medal.

After that, the bank volunteered me for the heart association and every darn thing you could think of. I learned the important lesson that charity and banking have to go together. And I've always instructed my people that way, and I always volunteered people who worked for the bank. As a banker you're dealing with the top people in the community, and it's imperative that you're involved in community service.

After a couple of years working at the bank in Salt Lake City, I was getting a good education in banking, but you couldn't make any money there. As a banker, they'd give you titles but they didn't give you any money, and you can't buy groceries with titles. I was married and we had two children by 1952, Peter and Roger, and I needed to make some good income.

I had seen the potential of Las Vegas as far back as my time in the Army, when I visited the gunnery school there in 1943. I was only twenty-two at the time, but I was amazed to see all the money on the gaming tables there. Even though the town was very small and there were only the casinos downtown—nothing to speak of on the Strip—I said to myself at the time that if they could ever perfect air-conditioning, Las Vegas might really become something.

There was plenty of water at Lake Mead, and the city was nicely located halfway between Salt Lake and Los Angeles, and the train came through here, and there was just so much action around the place. Although we didn't gamble, and never were gamblers, I knew that many people did and that Las Vegas was the only game around. I just knew that Las Vegas was going to experience terrific growth. There wasn't a doubt in my mind, even back then. So I started coming down from Salt Lake to speculate in real estate down here.

It was in late 1952, I believe, that I first started coming down here. I had a customer at the Continental Bank in Salt Lake named Al Manning. He was a wonderful old guy and a loan shark on top of it. A funny character. And he used to come to Las Vegas and loan money at high interest rates, and he used to talk about the city a lot and he really started to get my attention. I made a few trips here with Al Manning, and we made a few personal loans down here, and I eventually hooked up with a guy named Al MacPeck, who owned MacPeck Realty. My father had left my brothers and sisters and me with some money from his estate, and so these investments I made benefited the entire family, so I was extra careful about anything I did with that money.

On the northeast side of San Francisco Street, which has long since been renamed Sahara Avenue, there was a shallow little piece of land that had been left in an estate to the American Legion. The Legion wouldn't sell the land, but they leased it to MacPeck and me for seven hundred dollars a month, that whole block. And for about

$100,000 that I was able to scrape together, we built fourteen stores on it. We had a dress shop called Mary Ann's on the corner, and a beauty parlor, and the main tenant was a restaurant called Foxy's, which did pretty well. It was a Jewish delicatessen owned by a guy named Abe Fox, and everyone loved the food there. [*Author's note: Years later, a small casino called Foxy's Firehouse Casino was built on that same corner.*] We found tenants for all those stores immediately. And we went from zero to about $15,000 a month in income in no time. The money I invested from my father's estate was divided by all my brothers and sisters, so we did pretty well with that. That shopping center was my first big financial score in Las Vegas, and further enhanced my idea that Las Vegas was a rapidly growing area and a great place to do business.

We had to high-grade all the materials we put into the shops in that center. The Korean War was still going on and I had to scrounge for materials because they were so hard to find. We just had a heck of a time getting the thing built. It was probably the cheapest-built building in the history of Las Vegas . . . probably the worst building ever built in Las Vegas.

About three years after opening these shops, we sold them off to a fellow from New York named Schwartz, and MacPeck and I split up about a million and a half off it.

There was only about thirty thousand people living in Clark County in the mid-'50s, but even then the area was starting to grow pretty fast, and I was realizing more all the time that Las Vegas had enormous potential. My opportunity to move here occurred late in 1954 when Charlie Canfield, who was running the Bank of Las Vegas, which had received its charter in January of that year, was diagnosed with prostate cancer. The bank was owned by Walter Cosgriff, whose family owned the Continental Bank of Salt Lake, where I was working. The family owned lots of small banks through Idaho and California and several in Utah, and so they opened a small bank in Las Vegas.

Even before Canfield got cancer, he was having some problems with the bank down here, and Ken Sullivan Sr. had sent me down a few times to assist Canfield. Of course, after Charlie got sick it was clear that he couldn't carry on running the bank, so it was decided by Cosgriff that he would send me down to Las Vegas along with Jim Clifford, who was working with me at Continental Bank, to take over the bank. With my growing interests in real estate in Las Vegas, and my knowledge of the area, it was just a natural for me to take that opportunity when it came along.

We had two children at the time and Peggy was pregnant with Steven, and she wasn't exactly sold on the idea of moving from Salt Lake to Las Vegas. I told her we would be down here for just two years. I lied, [*he laughs*] because I knew it was very likely going to be a permanent move. But Peggy's a good scout and she was wonderful about it.

## Peggy Thomas

PARRY PROMISED ME THAT WE WOULD BE IN LAS VEGAS FOR TWO YEARS at the most. This was not the place I would have chosen to raise a family at the time. But our children all turned out very well. I think they've developed a few immunities from growing up in Las Vegas. They weren't interested in gambling, for one. And we were able to get away in the summers, to Newport Beach for many years. We also spent a lot of time on our boat out at Lake Mead, so that was helpful.

## Parry Thomas

WHILE I WORKED IN LAS VEGAS, PEGGY STAYED IN SALT LAKE UNTIL Stephen was born in September of '55, then came down here. So we had three little boys, Peter, five, Roger, three, and the baby.

We stayed in a bank customer's tract house on Torrey Pines and Evergreen, right on the border of the desert, and then I bought a little house over on Ellen Way, a little street one block south of Oakey and two blocks east of the Strip.

I got along well with Jim Clifford, who was an outstanding fellow. He had been the head of the credit department at the Continental Bank, and had great experience with credit issues, and I specialized in business development and managing people. So we made a pretty good team running the Bank of Las Vegas. Three years later, in 1958, Walter Cosgriff and Ken Sullivan Sr. and I, with a little bit of money I'd saved up, bought the Bank of Encino in California. We sent Jim Clifford down there and I stayed in Las Vegas. That's when Jim and I split, and from that point on I had complete control of the bank here.

The Bank of Encino was a much bigger bank at that time than the Bank of Las Vegas. We had grown to about $5 million in deposits by then, and the Bank of Encino out in the valley there was about a $15 million bank. We eventually put branches in Sherman Oaks, Granada Hills, and finally in Thousand Oaks. There was never a question that Jim would be the one to move, because his wife hated Las Vegas, which was the main reason he moved down there. I would never have moved down there because I looked at California as being mature and developed, whereas the potential for growth in Las Vegas was unlimited and I loved it here.

Sadly, Walter Cosgriff died shortly after that. He was a terrific golfer and had won the state amateur championship in Utah, and I think another state title somewhere in the Southwest. After one of these tournaments he was driving back to Salt Lake, and he came to a railroad trestle at Wells, Nevada, that goes over a big gorge. Somehow he drove over the side of that bridge and was killed. It was a horrible thing to happen. He was a young man, just in his early fifties. He had inherited these banks from his father and had done a great job overseeing them.

When we started at the Bank of Las Vegas in '55 it was a very small bank. We had only about $3 million in deposits, so we didn't have many loans. We had some small commercial loans, a few little real estate loans, a ma-and-pa shop here and there.

The biggest obstacle for us then was the lack of money. Loans were tight. The two banks that existed in Las Vegas were paying, I think, just one percent on savings accounts, which is virtually nothing. And in that post-war era, you had to put up so much collateral, and this and that, that by the time you got through you really didn't need the loan anymore. The lending policies weren't just conservative, they were very restrictive. In my opinion, they were stupid and silly, which actually worked to our bank's advantage.

Also, the prevalent thinking throughout the whole country was that gambling was illegal and immoral. It was everything bad. It was classified right in the same group as criminal networks. And the existing banks would not loan five cents to any gaming people. My feeling was that gambling was a legal industry in Nevada, and I thought a good bank should service all legal businesses.

The two banks that existed in Las Vegas prior to ours were First National Bank and Bank of Nevada. They were both owned by Western Bank Corporation, which was a bank holding company that had spun away from Transamerica.

The famous banker A.P. Giannini had formed both Bank of America and Transamerica and as they got bigger, he made them split. First National, I believe, was the only bank in Nevada that didn't go broke during the Depression.

Anyway, Western Bank Corporation owned ninety-five percent of First National Bank and eighty-five percent of Bank of Nevada in the '50s. Spence Butterfield was running Bank of Nevada when we moved here and a big Italian guy, Harry Manetti, was running First National. The policy on all their banks nationwide was set from San Francisco, and that was that gambling was illegal in forty-seven of the forty-eight states, and so they wouldn't allow their banks to deal with gamblers. That was an issue only in Nevada, because back then we had the only legal gambling in the country.

Their policy was that they simply were not going to do business with bootleggers or gamblers or madams in whorehouses. It was all just taboo. The people working in those banks in Las Vegas were just following orders, to stay in line with their company's policies. So when we came along we were looking at an open playing field, and I was given a lot of freedom to do what I wanted to do.

Now, being a newcomer to the area and therefore not infected by the past histories of these gambling people, all you had to do was look around and see that all of the major payrolls in Las Vegas were from gambling. The major industry was gambling, and of course there was Nellis Air Force Base, but everything about the community, with the exception of the railroad, was dependent on gaming. So in my mind, although I was determined to be damned careful and conservative with the loans we made, I was determined that our bank was going to cater to the gambling industry.

It's important to explain a little about the gaming situation when I first moved down in the mid-'50s. The city and the community were growing and seemed to be healthy. But there was one struggle after another as these hotels were being built. By 1955 the Strip had the El Rancho Vegas, the Last Frontier, the Thunderbird, the Desert Inn, the Sands, the Flamingo, and at the north end they were just starting a conversion from the Bingo Club to the Sahara Hotel. And the financing for these hotels was full of oddities.

For instance, Jake Katleman, who started the first hotel, the El Rancho, had previously run a gambling operation in Palm Springs. And he started the El Rancho during the war and the way he did

48

it was by applying for and getting FHA housing for bungalows. The government had no idea he was building a gambling joint. I was told later on that when the government found out about it, they were too embarrassed to do anything about it. So the first casino here was financing on FHA money.

The Last Frontier Hotel was financed by a family out of Texas, but then when Jake Katleman was killed in an automobile accident, his nephew Belden Katleman took over the El Rancho. Belden owned the property that the Last Frontier was on, and he retained a twenty percent ownership in the Frontier.

Then the third hotel, the Flamingo, which opened at Christmas time 1946, everyone knows was financed through New York Mob money. Bugsy Siegel was killed for misappropriating or misusing that money.

I have a pretty good idea who killed him, but I'm not going to talk about it with a tape recorder going.

Marion Hicks and Cliff Jones started the Thunderbird, and they thought they could run out and get loans but found that they couldn't, so they turned to Meyer Lansky for money and through his connections they were able to finish construction.

Wilbur Clark started the Desert Inn. He was from San Diego, where he worked on gaming boats down in the San Diego area. Now Wilbur thought he could raise enough money from Southern California business connections, but he couldn't. So he had to turn to the Cleveland-Detroit Purple Gang. Moe Dalitz and Morris Kleinman and Sam Tucker and that group, to get the DI financed.

The Sands Hotel was financed by New York mainly. The first fellow they chose to run the place couldn't get licensed, so they got Jakey Friedman, who had run gaming in Houston and Galveston, to come and head up the Sands. So they got that property finished.

The Sahara was more legitimate than the others, and that was the hotel where our little Bank of Las Vegas arranged its first big loan, which I'll talk about later.

In those first years, I would say that ninety percent of the gaming loans we made were to existing establishments that had, in my opinion, proven themselves. I was scared of start-up operations. Also, I would never finance independent bars or restaurants, and I took a lot of heat for that. There were two reasons I avoided those businesses: Basically, there were on leased property, and secondly, they'd borrow the money for furniture and fixtures to open their doors, and if you foreclosed on bar equipment or restaurant equipment, what the hell were you supposed to do with it? You just had to pay to haul it to the junkyard. Restaurants and bars had the highest casualty rates of any businesses I could think of.

I was even threatened once for my refusal to loan money to a restaurateur. The guy wanted to open a restaurant down at Commercial Center, on what is now East Sahara. He pestered me for a loan and put pressure on me every way he could. But I just wouldn't loan him any money because I didn't give loans to those types of businesses. The guy eventually got so mad he took out newspaper ads criticizing me and he passed out fliers all through my neighborhood and downtown criticizing me and saying that I was a bad banker and a bad person. I had to figure out a way to shut him up, and so I called this little guy who worked at the Sands. His name was Aaron Weisberg. He was a wonderful fellow. I knew that Aaron had a lot of clout with some important tough guys, so I asked Aaron if he could do anything about this guy who was threatening me. All the hassling just stopped cold the next day.

Incidentally, the guy's restaurant finally opened, and it closed six months later. I'm glad our bank didn't do loans to restaurants.

## Peggy Thomas

IN THOSE EARLY YEARS I WASN'T THINKING DECADES AHEAD, BUT FROM the very beginning I was impressed with Parry and his abilities. I knew he had a lot of plans and he had a way of accomplishing what he intended to accomplish. I didn't anticipate the success that would come, but I'm certainly grateful for it.

## Herb Jones

I WAS ON THE BOARD WHEN PARRY CAME DOWN FROM UTAH TO BE A co-president of the Bank of Las Vegas. My wife, Sara Jane, met Peggy and the kids and helped them get adjusted in schools and all that.

My first and lasting impression of Parry is that this guy is a strange genius because he has a brilliant mind, and yet he's a regular guy. Some geniuses are way out there, but he was so charming and so personable. This was a man who was thinking about business twenty-three hours a day. Some people daydream, but I think Parry thought all through the night. He was a night-dreamer. And his thinking was always progressive—how to do things better and more creatively. He was never satisfied with the status quo.

My father was employed by Shell Oil and had been living in Sumatra, but in passing through Kingman, Arizona, one time he saw a sign that said a dam was going to be built in Las Vegas, and he sensed right then that Las Vegas was going to be a good place to live. We moved here in 1931, and my older brother Cliff [*who went on to become the lieutenant governor of Nevada, a hotel owner of the Thunderbird, and an influential man in early Las Vegas whose nickname was "The Big Juice"*] actually worked as a laborer on the dam.

My sister Florence Jones Cahlan returned to journalism school at the University of Missouri before she came here and became a well-known reporter in Las Vegas. I also attended Missouri and then the University of Arizona Law School before starting a law practice here.

Parry obviously had so much going for him, you could see that right away. He was very good looking, but looks only go so far. He was extremely personable. He just exuded personality and likeability, and he was accepted very quickly in Las Vegas.

Parry went out looking for business. He was smarter and more aggressive than the other bankers in town. He made it happen. I sat on the senior loan committee of the Bank of Las Vegas and we were making big loans at the time, and somehow Parry would go out across the country and find partners in those loans. He was incredible that way. Just imagine the ability of this young man to go out and sell Las Vegas the way he did and put together these big loans. There wasn't that much money around in those days. It was incredible what he did. He got the money from Texas and from everywhere. He allowed our bank to make loans that the other banks just couldn't make.

Those of us on the bank's board never said no to him. But there was one time where Parry wanted to make a loan and there was some discussion about it. It wasn't unanimous by any means. So Parry walked into the room where the senior loan committee was meeting and said, "Okay, gentlemen, we're going to take a vote on this loan. Those in favor of making it, say 'Aye.' Those opposed, say, 'I resign.'"

We all got a laugh out of that one, but it gives you the idea that we were never going to really turn down one of his loans because his judgment in those matters was impeccable.

Parry was, above all, a banker. He understood banking better than anyone I ever saw. And he understood loans. And he understood people. He had an innate ability to analyze people and size them up, to determine whether he wanted to do business with them.

I remember we made a $500 loan to a particular customer, which was one in a long line of small loans we'd made to him, and he'd always paid them back on time. Anyway, one morning this gentleman got in a fight with his girlfriend and threw her out the front door of his house naked. Well, she went to his car and got a gun and when he wouldn't open the door she shot straight through it. The bullet went directly into his heart and killed him instantly. That was one loan that I recall was never paid back. But it wasn't a bad loan. He'd been a good customer.

Parry was so far-sighted, always looking into the future. He saw a small village and he envisioned a metropolis, even back fifty some years ago. He believed in the potential of Las Vegas more than anyone else at that time.

## Bill Boyd

I FIRST MET PARRY WHEN I WAS IN MY EARLY TWENTIES, RIGHT AFTER he came to Las Vegas. My dad, Sam Boyd, owned some stock in the Bank of Las Vegas and I'd go into the bank with him. At the time Dad was working for Nate Mack, Jerry's father, and of course Nate owned the Jackpot Casino downtown on Fremont Street, in partnership with Bob Kaltenbourne. Parry was running the bank then with Jim Clifford.

After years in the industry as first a dealer then a shift manager and casino manager, my dad got a big break when he was offered a one percent ownership in the Sahara Hotel by Milton Prell. My dad knew Al Winter, who was the largest stockholder in the Sahara. Al was a lawyer by education but he never practiced law. He was always in the gaming business. At one time my dad was working in gaming up in Portland, Oregon, and he met Al Winter, who was running a place up there. It wasn't legal up there then, by the way. And Al asked my dad if he would like to come into the Sahara. That one percent cost him sixteen thousand dollars, six thousand of which my parents had save up in cash, and the other ten thousand came from a family friend. Dad was forty-two years old at the time and that was a very big deal for him, because that was the start of his investing in the gaming business. Later on he purchased three and a half percent of the Mint. And on most of those early loans, and much bigger loans later on, Parry was the one who made the loans.

Dad knew Jerry Mack even before Parry because Jerry grew up here and was around the Jackpot a lot. I know our family moved here in 1941 and Nate Mack had been here a number of years already.

When Parry got here the existing bankers looked on the gaming industry as something to be wary of. Because the people in gaming were not solid citizens. They had histories, is a nice way of putting it. Even though when we moved here the gaming industry was more important overall than it is today—because today we have so many more things in Las Vegas—the attitude was still that you were a second-class citizen if you were in the industry. But Parry never expressed that opinion. With him you always felt like he supported you and respected you. He was a partner of yours and he wanted you to succeed, and he would do whatever he could to help you succeed. He was in a business that was in business to make loans, and that's what he did.

## Irwin Molasky

MY FIRST INTRODUCTION TO PARRY WAS MADE BY NATE MACK, JERRY Mack's father, who called me one day and asked me to meet this bright young man from Utah whom he was bringing in to run what was then called the Bank of Las Vegas. I was a borrower of the bank, and the first time I met Parry we hit it off and became close friends.

We had a lot in common. He was a family man and so was I, and our children were about the same ages. We also shared a personal like for Las Vegas and I think we both understood even back then that the city had real potential and was going to experience terrific growth. We had some good conversations about where this community could go and what challenges existed in getting there. I was surprised by how many questions he asked me, and how intently he listened. This was someone who was formulating some big plans for Las Vegas, and I appreciated that.

I built a small motel on the Strip, which opened in December 1952, called the Pyramids. It was the first pyramid before they built the Luxor [*laughing*]. It was just eighteen rooms to start out with, but it grew to about sixty rooms. It was located next to the Flamingo where Harrah's is today.

My little motel opened the same day the Sands Hotel opened, and I remember their first act was Danny Thomas. Danny was in rehearsals at the Sands just before the opening and he would take walks in the morning. He stopped by my place a couple of times on his walks and we'd visit, and he actually invited me to his opening show.

During the next few years I got a contractor's license, number 3174, which was a general building contractor's license. In those days, the existing banks didn't loan any real money on projects. If you were fortunate they might loan you thirty to fifty percent of your costs. It was my father and mother's life savings that they invested at my request in that first project. I was newly married, just out of the Army, and it was impossible for me to envision anything except continued growth and opportunities here. So I was very bullish. I didn't look at Las Vegas as a gambling mecca then. I just saw the opportunities that existed with people coming to these hotels, and it was a wonderful place to raise children. The climate was terrific if you could stand the heat. But I knew that once people would get used to it, they would become desert rats like me.

For the next three or four years I was doing room additions and garage enclosures. And then I started building spec houses, and that's when I met Parry. When I did meet with him, I didn't look at it as only an opportunity to borrow money. I wanted to have a relationship with him because I could see right away we had a lot in common and that he had similar family values to mine. I learned that he is a man of immense virtues and honor. If Parry Thomas told you something, you could literally take it to the bank, no pun intended.

We had lunch together downtown quite often, and we exchanged a lot of ideas about Las Vegas and what could be done here. I didn't do any real banking with him until a couple of years after I met him.

Parry believed in more than balance sheets. He believed in a person's character. I know today that sounds trite in regards to bankers, but that's the way it was with Parry. He would look you in the eye and talk about other things than the loan you were requesting. He would find out pretty quickly what your character traits were. In that way he created relationships that surpassed the normal lender-borrower status. With other bankers I'd go to for loans, I'd have to jump through hoops with them because I didn't have a big balance sheet back then. But with Parry you'd give him your ideas, he'd talk to you for fifteen or twenty minutes, he'd ask you what you thought your project would cost, he'd listen carefully, and he'd usually approve the loan.

The relationship between Parry and Jerry Mack was one I admired greatly. It's so rare to see a partnership like that, that endures for a lifetime with so much success. Jerry was a personal friend of mine and we spent a lot of time at each other's houses, and our kids grew up together.

I think Parry felt a fierce loyalty to Jerry's father, Nate, for his help in bringing Parry down to the Bank of Las Vegas and getting him started on the right foot here, and I know Parry had great respect for Jerry's ability in business matters, especially in real estate matters. It was just an amazing partnership, and they went into all kinds of things together and it was a binding relationship. Parry was the front man, the salesman, the pitch man, if you will, to sell ideas and vision, and Jerry was equally effective behind the scenes.

## Parry Thomas

HERE'S THE STORY OF HOW I MET JERRY MACK: AS I SAID EARLIER, Walter Cosgriff owned probably a dozen small banks, and he was always looking to start another bank. His mode of operation in the 1940s and '50s was to get a small young bank, then try and put in reasonably good management and build it up. Then he'd sell it and get the capital gains. Income taxes back then were impossible. The rates were so high that the only way you could make any money was to own something at a certain price and sell it at a profit and keep it over a year and get a capital gain on it. Tax-wise, you just had to go the capital-gain route. That was Cosgriff's mode of operation. He'd get a small bank, build it up, then milk the hell out of it for dividends.

Walter found out through an attorney in Beverly Hills named Sam Kurland that there was an opportunity to put a bank in Las Vegas. Sam Kurland's brother Bill owned the Pioneer Club in downtown Las Vegas, so Sam came here a lot and he was friends with Nate Mack. Sam and Nate were both Jewish, and Nate was without question the most influential of all the Jewish people in Las Vegas.

Nate had an interesting history. He owned a grocery store in Los Angeles and he went broke in the Depression. Because he knew there was a payroll on the Boulder Dam [*later renamed Hoover Dam*], he moved to Boulder City and started a junkyard. And with the dam came all that equipment, busted out materials and left-over, sawed-off pieces of steel and so forth, and Nate went into the junk business. That business did well, and then he started buying and selling real estate in Clark County and he became by far the most prominent man in the real estate business during that period. And Bob Kaltenbourne was his partner in most of those ventures in the early days.

About six months after I'd moved to Las Vegas and taken over the bank, Nate came to me and said that he'd been watching how I operated and that he liked the way I'd been able to move into the gaming business, which he understood very well. Nate had been a minority partner in the Flamingo with Bugsy Siegel—he owned just one or two points—and he'd owned the El Dorado Club downtown, which was the predecessor of the Horseshoe Casino. He also operated the Jackpot Casino on Fremont Street. He told me he liked how I was handling things at the bank and that he'd like me to become partners with his son, Jerry.

I'd met Jerry a few times and I liked him, but that thought had never crossed my mind and it probably hadn't crossed Jerry's either. I told Nate that I couldn't be his son's partner because I didn't have the resources to invest alongside him. I just didn't see how I could become an equal partner with him. Jerry was Nate's only child, and this was obviously very important to him. He said, "Things like this have a way of taking care of themselves. Don't worry about it."

About two weeks later Nate sat down with Jerry and me and he said, "You guys just bought eighty acres on San Francisco Street [*later renamed Sahara Avenue*] almost from Paradise Road down to Maryland Parkway on the south side of the street. Now you take it from there."

Nate had gone through the Campbell Real Estate Company and put the property in escrow. He selected the land for us, got it at a good price, which we then paid for. I had to scramble for some money, but I was able to do it. This was right at the end of 1955 or the beginning of 1956. So that's how Jerry and I started a partnership that would be carried on between our children and grandchildren. And no man could ever have had a better partner than I did with Jerry. He was just outstanding in every way.

## Joyce Mack

I CAME HERE IN 1949, TWO YEARS AFTER JERRY AND I WERE MARRIED, and we already had two baby daughters. Nate and Jenny Mack lived here already. They had come to Southern Nevada in 1930, when the country was in the Great Depression. Nate said the only payroll he heard of in those times was in Boulder City, where Hoover Dam was under way. And he thought, well, this might be the best place to go to make some money. So they went to Boulder City and he opened a junkyard, which dealt mainly in old cars and tires and things like that. That's where Jerry, who was their only son, learned so much about cars and engines. He was always playing with cars and car parts.

So Nate and Jenny ran that business and did well with it, and eventually they moved down to Las Vegas where Nate and his brother Lou opened up a clothing store. He wasn't real active in that—it was mostly Lou who ran it—but Nate started speculating in real estate. He also owned a produce truck and a liquor distributorship. He'd buy a small property here and a small property there, and he was never afraid to make an investment. He would buy a piece, then sell it at a profit, then buy the same piece back later on and sell it again. He owned the land that the Desert Inn was on and sold it three different times and made money each time. He bought and re-bought a lot of properties up and down the Strip.

Nate was first in a lot of things in the Las Vegas community. He actually started the first temple, Temple Beth Sholom, and before that he organized meetings for the small Jewish community that had settled here. They had trouble early on getting nine people assembled for Jewish ceremonies.

In 1948 Nate went to Israel and actually spoke with Jewish leaders there about a plan to help Holocaust survivors settle in southern Mexico. But the Orthodox Jews didn't want to leave the motherland, and so that eventually didn't transpire. Nate would do anything to help the Jewish cause when Israel was formed, and that passion for Israel and the Jewish people was certainly inherited by his only son.

One day, as a new bride and mother who wasn't so sure about living in Las Vegas, I was told by Nate that we were going to take a ride around town. I had been here only a few months. Only the Flamingo and the Last Frontier and I think the El Cortez were here, and a small residential community around the Strip.

Nate drove me out to the middle of nowhere, and he said, "Look around, in every direction."

All I could see was yucky-looking desert with nothing there. Remember, I grew up in Los Angeles.

Then he said, "Honey, I want you to look out to where the mountains are and I want you to visualize this. One day, this whole valley here that you're looking at is going to be filled with homes and stores and temples and schools. The entire floor of this valley will be populated to the base of these mountains."

Although I thought he was just a big dreamer, that tells you what Nate had in his head. He believed in the growth of Las Vegas one hundred percent. Talk about a visionary. There you go.

And he passed that vision on to Jerry and Parry. They came to believe it as much as he did. Everything they did in business was directed to building the economy and directing the growth of Las Vegas and making sure that it grew in the right direction.

## Marilyn Mack

MY GRANDPA [NATE MACK] JUST HAD A STROKE OF GENIUS WHEN HE put my dad and Parry together. It turned into one of the most amazing partnerships you could ever imagine, lasting through the generations. He obviously saw something early on that would be good for both my dad and Parry, and so there was genius behind it.

60

Grandpa could talk to gangsters and waiters and get the same reaction. They all loved him, just like they do Parry. I don't know one person who doesn't like Parry Thomas.

I was a young girl, about ten and eleven years old, when my grandparents died. My grandmother Jenny went first, and then Grandpa about a year and a half later.

I'd spend two weeks in the summer with them. They lived in L.A. at the time, and Grandpa Nate would take me to Hollywood Park racetrack. He loved to play the horses. He had this little table there, and he'd lay out the tickets he bought on each race.

I always had a winning ticket in the early races, every single time. I never knew why until just a few years ago, when I found out that Grandpa would buy a two-dollar Win ticket on every horse in the race. So that way I always had a sure winner. Thank God I didn't get hooked on gambling, and form the notion that it was that easy to win.

I think Grandpa Nate was something of a daredevil. He was in his early seventies, I think, when he'd take me to Pacific Ocean Park in Santa Monica and he'd go on the roller coasters with me. We'd whoop it up and have a great time.

## Parry Thomas

I CAN'T TELL YOU HOW GRATEFUL I AM TO NATE MACK FOR BUYING that land and having that kind of trust in me, to put me in partnership with his only son. Nate became like a father to me, and he was certainly a role model in business. He was a small man in stature and he didn't say very much, but when he spoke people would listen, because he always knew what he was talking about.

You could certainly say that Nate was looking out for his son when he put us together, but he was also choosing a second son.

So one thing led to another in our partnership and we developed those eighty acres on Sahara Avenue and we made a lot of money on it. At least for me it was a lot of money. Then Jerry and I decided early on that the best way for us to operate was not get in each other's way and not do double duty on business matters. We each had our own area. Jerry would run anything to do with real estate, which he was an expert in because he'd learn at his father's elbow from the time he was very young, and I would run the bank.

## Tom Thomas

EITHER ONE OF THEM COULD HAVE DONE THE OTHER'S BUSINESS PRO-ficiently, but Dad and Jerry had so much respect for each other that they gave each other carte blanche to do their own businesses. Jerry understood the banking business inside and out and my Dad understood the real estate business. That trust they had in the other to handle his business well was a real key to their success as partners.

## Joyce Mack

IT WAS THE MOST AMAZING, PERFECT PARTNERSHIP YOU COULD EVER find. And the credit all goes back to Nate for seeing how good these two young men could be for each other, even with all the differences that were obvious on the surface.

One was Jewish, the other Mormon. One was Democrat, the other Republican. Parry was very social and outgoing and loved to be with people. Jerry liked people too, but he'd just as soon stay away from them.

Parry was the generous one, always leaving big tips, always going to the finest restaurants. My husband, on the other hand, would go to the slop joints, the hot dog places or delis. They would always kid about Jerry being so cheap, and not leaving a big enough tip.

Jerry was just more conservative than Parry, and how Parry got the way he was I don't know, because he was raised in a very conservative Mormon family in Utah.

When they had their apartment in New York and they were going out somewhere, to a business dinner or a play or something, Jerry would immediately go to Parry's tie drawer and get one of his ties, because Parry had the most gorgeous silk ties you've ever seen. And Jerry would laugh about what would happen when they would walk down the street. He'd tell me, "All the girls tag after Parry, and not me. I don't know why, but they just don't go after me."

And I would say, "Well, thank goodness."

## Peggy Thomas

ONE OF THE MANY THINGS I ENJOYED ABOUT OUR FRIENDSHIP WITH the Macks was that it was nice to have an introduction to the Jewish faith. It wasn't something I knew much about growing up in Utah. I had a couple of friends in Salt Lake who were Jewish, but I didn't have any real knowledge of their beliefs or anything. Both families had a mutual respect for the other's beliefs, and the bonds were just so strong in every area. Parry and Jerry just melded together so beautifully, and it carried right down through all the family members.

## Parry Thomas

NATE MACK DIED JUST FIVE OR SIX YEARS AFTER OUR PARTNERSHIP WAS formed, and he had been a founding director of the bank, so we immediately put Jerry on the board when his father died.

For any partnership to thrive, each partner has to bring an equal amount to the table, and more than anything else a mutual respect has to exist between the partners. There has to be a respect for the other's ability, and empathy for each other's problems, which inevitably arise.

Jerry was like his dad in that he was very strong-willed and definite in his thinking. He thought things out carefully, came to a decision, and then enforced that decision. And he could be very stubborn about things, like I was. He was more outspoken than his father, but not in a loud or obnoxious way. He was very much a good listener because he loved to learn things. You have to be a learner to advance. The minute you start thinking you know it all, you're headed for trouble.

Jerry and I were really closer than brothers could be because of the mutual trust between us. We had so much confidence in what we were doing, maybe it was just the confidence of youth, but we knew we were going to do well.

## Bill Boyd

I THINK NATE MACK SAW THE POTENTIAL THAT PARRY HAD IN THE banking business, and he knew the talents of his own son, Jerry, who was involved in real estate, and he thought they were a match made in heaven, I'm sure.

Their backgrounds were very different, with Parry being raised in Ogden and Salt Lake and the University of Utah, which was a very conservative school. And Jerry, who was raised in Las Vegas and went to UCLA, which had kind of a Hollywood flavor, if you will. And so despite their very different backgrounds, they seemed to immediately like each other and they could see that their different backgrounds put together could make a great combination. Marriages are hard, and partnerships are hard, and yet theirs seemed to be as seamless and without divisiveness as any partnership you'd ever encounter.

I know that people always consider Parry the salesman of the two, but Jerry was also a heckuva salesman. They were both very gregarious and they just got along so well. I know that Parry was the guy that made the loans and the final decisions about loans to the Sahara, the Sands, the Riviera, and so many other early places both on the Strip and downtown. And on that score Jerry was in the background. But he was so well-known and so well-respected in the Jewish community and that was very valuable to their partnership. When you don't hear negatives about people that have obtained stature and wealth, you know they're well-liked because people like to take shots at successful people.

## Parry Thomas

WE DECIDED EARLY ON THAT JERRY WOULD RUN ALL THE THINGS CON-
cerning property and I would stick to operations and run the bank.
You could not have overlapping authority in the banks. If you did,
several things would happen. Employees could play one of us off
against the other, and in the banking business, the fish stinks from
the head down. You had to have a direct line of command and it had
to be strong and it had to be definite. That's the only way to operate.

So I would run the bank and Jerry would run the properties, and
when later on we got into hotels, he would be responsible for those,
choosing the top officers in the hotels and whatnot.

After the Bank of Las Vegas had become Valley Bank, because of
its expansion into Reno and other Nevada cities, and we aggressively
sought out acquisitions of properties for opening new branches, Jerry
handled all of that, and he oversaw and managed all the construction
and bidding and so on. We ended up with over one hundred branches
for Valley Bank, so that was a big job.

I've been asked many times whether we ever did any deals separately, and I don't think we ever even discussed that. It didn't enter
our thinking. We enjoyed each other's company, we enjoyed doing
deals, and so that was the only consideration when an opportunity
would come up.

The first really big loan we ever made was to Milton Prell for the
Sahara Hotel. That one was for $600,000. That hotel started out as
the Club Bingo, and then changed its name to the Sahara. They
had only about one hundred rooms there then, and a small casino
with some lounge acts. No headliner entertainment. The $600,000
was loaned to improve the lounge area, make the casino bigger, and
add two hundred rooms. At the south end of the property they had

a string of rooms that was known as the E-Ring. Anyway, this was a controversial loan to make, as it was the first loan of any size our bank was going to make to a gaming operation. Our loan limit at Bank of Las Vegas was just $75,000. So when we made loans bigger than that, we had to scrounge around and get participation from everybody we could think of.

The first banks we went to were other banks owned by Walter Cosgriff, one in Ridgefield and one in Salt Lake, for instance. But it scared the hell out of me when we made that loan, I'll tell you that.

I'd only met Milt Prell a few times at that point. I didn't know him well, but I was familiar with him through my owning that shopping center across the street from his hotel. He was absolutely a top-notch man, a very bright fellow and exceptionally conservative. He was much more of a businessman than a gambler and he always impressed me because he stayed on top of his business and always knew everything that was going on.

Milt was originally from the Pacific Northwest, and he was running bingo parlors and whatnot up in Montana when he first came down and opened the Club Bingo. He was associated with an attorney up north named Al Winter, who was rumored to be mixed in with some unsavory guys, and he was part and parcel of the whole thing as well. The Del Webb people were going to do the construction on that tower and on those E-ring rooms as well. That came about because Del Webb had done most of the construction on the Flamingo for Bugsy, and his company was getting more and more involved with Las Vegas. Webb owned eleven percent of the Sahara at that time.

Ken Sullivan Sr. and I were handling that loan, and we met with Milt three or four times during the negotiation of the credit. In those days, loans went for around four percent. Savings accounts earned only one percent. We were worried about whether we were going to be able to get participation from partners to raise that $600,000, and

I explained to Milt the challenge of syndicating this loan out, and how we were going to have to get a pretty stiff interest rate from him.

I remember that he had a bad back and he was rocking back and forth in his chair. He said, "Well, what's it gonna be?"

I said, "It'll be at least six percent."

He said, "What'll I get if I pay the six percent?"

I said, "You'll get the loan."

He rocked two or three more times and said, "I'll take it."

But, boy, did we have to scratch to put that loan together. It turns out that was the first of a whole bunch of loans we made to Milt.

Anyway, after he built the first small tower—I think it was just ten or twelve stories—I got a call from Milt in Hawaii, where he'd gone on vacation. He'd recently had a serious heart attack and explained to me that he couldn't carry on, that his health was so poor that he'd have to sell the Sahara. He asked if I could possibly find a buyer for it.

I knew Dick Boondesar of the Sheraton Hotel Corporation back in Boston, and so I talked to him about possibly marketing the hotel to Sheraton. He set up a meeting in New York with the two Sheraton founders, Bob Moore and Earnest Henderson. They were interesting guys. They had been Navy pilots in World War I and after the war, being enterprising guys, they bought up a lot of stuff in Germany and brought it back to the U.S. and started marketing it and did very well. As their business interests grew, they bought a little hotel that had been named after the cabinet-maker who built it. His name was Sheraton. When they bought that little hotel, they didn't have enough money to change the name and that's why that large company still carries the Sheraton name today.

So the big day comes to negotiate the sale between Milt Prell and Sheraton. I think this was in 1964 or '65. A man named L.C. Jacobson, who was the president of the Webb Company, was there, as was Dick Boondesar. We met at their hotel on 7<sup>th</sup> Avenue and 55<sup>th</sup> Street, the old New York Sheraton, and we were on the seventeenth floor in a suite. Now the Sheraton group tried to avoid putting their own money into deals, and they therefore needed the deal to be financed.

We had to find $17 million to make the deal work. I was thinking really fast and the only guy I could think of who had that kind of money was the real estate mogul Harry Helmsley. The reason I knew him was that I was in on the deal when he bought the Desert Inn. A lot of people don't realize that Helmsley owned all the land that the Desert Inn was on. I was involved with Harry, and I'd stayed in touch with him through the years. He would visit me when he came out west.

So Harry comes up to the seventeenth floor of the Sheraton Hotel and we go over the deal with him and explain that Boondesar and the Sheraton Corporation would buy it if they could borrow the $17 million.

Harry turned to me and said, "You know what my formula is: I'll go any way you want to go. I'll buy it and lease it to you or I'll loan you the money. However you want to work it, but my formula is that I have to get seventeen percent."

So we had tentatively agreed to that when L.C. Jacobson, who drank bourbon by the bottle, stands up from his chair in a corner of the room and says to Helmsley, "You're the son of a bitch who sued us for fifty-five million and you're so damn cheap you settled out of court for a hundred and fifty thousand. Anybody who's that cheap, I don't want to do business with!"

He said it in just those words. It got real quiet, and then Helmsley, who was a tall man, stood up and walked over to me and said, "Thanks, Parry, for inviting me, but I think it's best I leave now." And he got up and walked out.

When we got into the elevator to leave, I turned to L.C. Jacobson and said, "You so and so, Del Webb just bought the Sahara Hotel. You're gonna buy it because you just blew the only deal we had or could possibly get."

68

We continued to discuss it on the elevator down from the seventeenth floor, and by the time we hit the ground floor we shook hands on it. And that's how Del Webb bought the Sahara Hotel. It was all because of a little bourbon and some ego. I've always had fun that I made a deal on the Sahara going from the seventeenth floor to the ground floor.

So anyway, that deal went well and we were paid back every cent, and we just continued to do big loans to gaming companies from there. We never lost any money on those gaming loans, and the reason we didn't was interesting. Remember, these people who were running casinos were all from different parts of the country where gambling was illegal, and they had come here and it was legal in Nevada. And almost all of them were connected to the Mob someplace. I don't like to get into it too much, but we knew they were wiseguys from where they came, but out here they were employed in a legal industry. I found out early on that the one thing these people craved more than anything else was respect. And if you would show them respect, you could do business with them and you would never lose any money. Although I never lost money to any gambler, I did have a few narrow escapes working with some of the old-timers. If they said they were going to pay back a loan on a certain day, they would pay you on that very day. They might go down the street and rob a bank to get the money, but they'd pay you.

There's an old line that a gambling debt is more sacred to a gambler than the note on his house. Well, those gambling people treated our bank with that same kind of trust. If we believed in them enough to loan them the money, they sure as hell were going to pay it back, and pay it on time.

∽

As I said, there were just the two banks in Las Vegas when I came down here in late 1954, the Bank of Nevada and First National Bank.

Gambling was illegal in forty-seven states back then, and their instructions to their branches in Nevada were that you don't do business with gamblers. They just didn't consider that to be a viable business to be in. But what I thought—and what I used to say to my superiors in Salt Lake at the time—was that it was very simple: We were a community bank and it was our business to serve the public in the Las Vegas community. We should serve all legal entities, and gambling was not only legal in Nevada, but it was the main industry. If we didn't do business with gaming, we were not being a good bank for our community.

Another principle that I held dearly through my entire career is that confidentiality between a banker and a client is a sacred trust. I tried to be the most confidential banker you ever met. I used to lecture my people at the bank that under no circumstances were they ever to discuss anything that goes on in this bank with their wife or girlfriend, because if they did, it would get all over town and it would destroy our business if we were not confidential. That was the number one rule of our bank: confidentiality. That's why I turned down hundreds if not thousands of requests for interviews through the years. It's even difficult now to talk about a lot of these things, because it's contrary to my nature. I'm doing it because as I get older and nearly all of these people I dealt with have died, I recognize there might be some value to people in Las Vegas from a historical standpoint, who might want to know about how our city grew as magnificently as it did.

We certainly didn't loan to everyone wanting to build a casino or wanting to expand their operation, and we were so small it was important that we not make big mistakes. We had more than $3 million in deposits when I first came down, and then it went right down to $1 million when Charlie Canfield got sick, because a lot of people pulled their accounts from us. Our loan limit, as I've said, was just

$75,000, so every time we made any big loans, I had to go find the money. I spent more than half my life finding money for Las Vegas.

I found that my biggest source came from the large number of small insurance companies in the Baptist belt. I traveled extensively through Texas and the Southwest finding these insurance companies to participate in our credit. My sales pitch to them was very simple. I told them I could get them much higher rates, and that they would earn a lot more money and have better collateral than in their normal loans. In addition, after a few years we could show them a great track record—that the Bank of Las Vegas had never had a default—and they would listen carefully to that.

I also used to tell them that when they really analyzed it, they would see that the gambling business is a lot like banking or making a loan in the insurance business. It is nothing more than an exchange of money for a percentage. The only problem was that in banking and with insurance companies, we exchange percentage per annum. But those casinos exchange percentages every few seconds. So it's a better business than either banking or insurance, and that made a lot of sense to them.

I'd often fly into Dallas on these sales trips. There were over one hundred and ten insurance companies headquartered in Dallas alone. There were about four big ones in New Orleans, like Pan American Insurance, but the one that really helped us break through was American National Insurance of Galveston, Texas. I had made a friend who had been in the Continental Bank building in Salt Lake named Bill Vogler, and he went from being a manager for American National to chairman of the board. Bill just gave me carte blanche, and his company was big enough that I could work with his people and they would help me bring in the other companies on these large syndicated loans.

I experienced very little rejection from American National. They were extremely careful with the money they loaned us. There was a fellow named Wallace who was head of the loan department down there, and he pretty well set me up with several other insurance companies. He gave us such a strong recommendation that it was pretty well established we'd get the money before I ever talked to them.

We had phenomenal success putting these loans together, and especially once we'd had some success it became much easier, because everyone wanted to make these good loans at attractive interest rates.

I remember a funny story about one of these loans, after Del Webb took control of the Sahara. They wanted to build a new tower at the Sahara and a big tower at the Mint, which L.C. Jacobson used to refer to as "the slab." At the same time, they wanted to build a high-rise hotel at Lake Tahoe. So this would be a major financing of over $50 million. That was big-time stuff for us back in those days. So we really had to get together and syndicate all the loans we could, bring all the companies together to raise this kind of money.

So we brought all these executives together down in Phoenix because we didn't want to bring them to Las Vegas. It just seemed easier to do it in the board room of Del Webb, down in Arizona. We had all these big insurance companies represented there and we were going through the details of the credit and we got down to the chattels and the question of how we were going to identify the chattels under our credit.

When we got down to gaming equipment, the question came up whether we were going to burn serial numbers into the tables, or should we put a brass plaque with staples onto them. In other words, how were we going to identify the chattels under our credit.

Anyway, we were debating this back and forth and an older attorney in the room named Burl Godfrey, who represented Service Life Insurance Company out of Fort Worth, which was taking a big chunk of the credit, raised his hand and asked if he could say something. He said, "You know, we're in the Baptist belt, and if our insurance customers think we've got chattels on this type of equipment, it might become an issue. I think we should write the mortgage so it lists the chattel as one bicycle and other incidental sporting equipment. And then we'll have to go out and buy a bicycle."

Everyone got a good laugh and that's exactly what we did. Here was a $50 million loan and we were listing it as a bike and other incidental sporting equipment. I explained to the guys that if they ever had to foreclose, the damn gambling equipment wasn't worth anything anyway. It would just cost more money to haul it off to the junkyard.

Another interesting story in the early makeup of the Strip involves the Stardust. It was built by Tony Cornero, who owned the Rex gambling ship off the coast of Long Beach. He bought a big piece of land on the west side of the Strip when things were starting to get going here.

Cornero's real last name was Strolla, and he came here from Napa Valley, the wine country of central California. His family were big farmers up there, and when Tony decided to go into gambling, I was told by his brother Lou Strolla that his relatives forced Tony to change his last name so he wouldn't embarrass the family.

Anyway, Tony Cornero was about the funniest character ever to hit Las Vegas. I didn't really know him, but I used to see him around town a little bit in the months before he died. I had just moved here when he was starting to build the Stardust in late 1954. Wherever you saw him, no matter what the circumstance, he always had this little Italian hat on. I think he wore it to bed at night. And he was an odd-looking little guy, but he was very persuasive. He talked Charlie Canfield at our bank into loaning him $120,000. He then printed up stock certificates for the Stardust and went down onto the San Francisco wharf and started peddling them. He had no filings with the SEC, no registration, no nothing, if you can imagine that.

Obviously, he was on a collision course with the law and was certainly headed to jail, just printing paper and selling it and using the money to buy the Royal Nevada, which was to become the Stardust. He was also shooting craps with some of the investor money. So shortly after Charlie had loaned him the money and right before I took over the Bank of Las Vegas, Tony was shooting craps at the Desert Inn—I believe it was on Easter morning—and he had a heart attack and died right on the crap table.

All hell broke loose after that because the Stardust was only about a third completed, and everything was in a shambles and there was no money. Lou Strolla came in to take over the operation. Now Lou was a nice fellow who was a grape farmer by trade, but he was totally out of his element in every direction.

Our bank had no security on the $120,000 Charlie had loaned Tony, so I had to think real fast. Lou had been in Las Vegas only three months or so, struggling along, trying to raise money and wheeling and dealing, and it was the corporation that owed us the money.

There were plenty of assets in the property, so I wasn't overly worried in the long run, but it was still a sticky situation. I went to the title company and pulled all the papers on it, and when I studied the title to the property, there were no trustees filed on it or anything. There were no liens on the property either.

So I met with Lou Strolla and I got another bank to go in with me on the loan and I told him we would loan him another $120,000, to make the debt $240,000, but that I would have to be the trustee. So by God I got to be the trustee on the whole thing. That made me the senior creditor, so then I could sit back and see what would happen.

The one thing we didn't want to happen under the Bankruptcy Act was to have anybody take security for a loan within a hundred and twenty days, because then we would lose our position. We would then have to share our collateral with all the other creditors. But if it goes for a hundred and twenty days under the law, then you're okay.

So I was sweating it out for four months, laying real quiet, in hopes that everything worked out. And it did. The four months went by, and then around two months after that Lou Strolla just threw in the towel at the Stardust and gave up. And so the place got thrown into bankruptcy.

A good friend of mine, Paul McDermott, who I'd known from school in Salt Lake, owned this big insurance agency in Las Vegas, and he was appointed the receiver for the Strolla estate. With the property in bankruptcy, the law steps in and nobody can do anything until the old assets are marshaled and adjudicated and all the debts come forward and a registry is made of the creditors. This has to be sorted out to see if there's enough assets to cover the liability. If there's not, then it becomes the secured creditors that get paid first and then what's left over goes to the unsecured creditors. And I was the only secured creditor.

Paul took over the receivership of the Stardust, and generally what happens in a case like that is they hold hearings and they let people bid on all the property and take it over. In this case, because there was gaming involved and licensing and everything else, it got complicated and it all came under the auspices of Judge John Ross up in Carson City. He was the only federal judge we had in Nevada at the time, and he was a damn good judge in my opinion. All this was happening in 1956 and '57, before the hotel had even been completed.

We estimated that it would take approximately $6 million to complete work on the Stardust. So we had to find someone with that kind of money, because under the Bankruptcy Act, when you submit a bid, it has to be supported by financial responsibility and business feasibility. You had to have somebody who could really run it and make it go.

I got Dick Boondesar, who I talked about earlier, to get the Sheraton Corporation interested in the Stardust. Turns out Sheraton was interested, but they would not run the gambling part of it. So I made a deal with Moe Dalitz and the Desert Inn people to come over and run the gambling, and Sheraton would run the hotel. So with those two, I had the operator feasibility and the gambling feasibility.

I certainly didn't have the $6 million to make the purchase, so I talked with a friend of mine, Irving Leff, who was a partner in the Last Frontier. I asked him if he knew anyone in Beverly Hills who would want to step forward, or even a group of people who would want to come in and put up the cash to finish the property, because that was a helluva lot of money in the 1950s.

Irving said that he had a guy, a good friend of his named John Factor, who might be interested. John was the brother of Max Factor Sr., the founder of the big cosmetics firm.

So I was introduced to and got to know John Factor, who we called Jack. He was smart as hell and to know him was to like him. He was the youngest of nine children and he grew up in Chicago. He told me that his family was very poor when he was a child and many a day he'd come home from school and there was no food on the table. Max Factor, the oldest brother, struck out on his own and opened a barber shop, and Jack Factor later worked for his brother in that shop. Most of the business in Chicago in their neighborhood was controlled by the Mob, under the leadership of Al Capone, and they gave out a lot of nicknames. Jack Factor became known as a young man as Jake the Barber. That was his moniker, but I didn't learn about all of this until later on.

Anyway, Jack Factor had made millions in the insurance business. He was really the guy who designed the whole mode of operation of health insurance, and after I got to know him a little he was interested in putting up the $6 million to purchase the Stardust and lease it back to Sheraton and the DI people.

It was a helluva tough situation because we had to get the place going and opened as soon as possible. There was a real sense of urgency there. So we went before the court and laid out our whole plan. There were four or five other groups also laying out their plans for taking over the Stardust, but ours was far superior because we had more feasibility and more money on our side.

This hearing went on for three days, from a Wednesday through a Friday, and we laid everything out as clearly as could be, that John Factor was our money source and that Sheraton and the Dalitz group from the DI would lease their ends of it from him.

So on Friday night when these hearings were coming to a close, four of the other groups got together and made a consolidated offer on the property. They wanted to knock us out, and the way they were going to do it was to call in reporters and announce that our financial partner was Jake the Barber, who had spent some time in prison and was affiliated at one time with Al Capone. Now even though Jack Factor had totally been rehabilitated and was an outstanding businessman and very charitable—later on he was even given a presidential pardon by John F. Kennedy—this was quite a bombshell. The next day the headlines clear across the country read, "Jake the Barber to Buy the Stardust." And here we had these wonderful gentlemen who had been war buddies and who had started the Sheraton chain, Earnest Henderson and Bob Moore, reading this in the paper. Remember, I had used some foresight and insisted that I hold all the documents on this deal, and I didn't learn until late in the negotiations about all this Jake the Barber stuff.

Earnest Henderson called me on Saturday morning, just after the story broke, and said, "Parry, I'm awfully sorry, but I cannot allow the corporation to go forward on this." He said, "Sheraton is a distinguished corporation in Boston. We have Cabots on the board, we have Lodges on the board, and we have all these other blue-blood gentlemen, and they'll never allow me to go forward with this Jake the Barber."

Earnest said he knew they would be subject to lawsuits because he had signed the leases and that Sheraton was liable for some damages, and he apologized again.

"Well, Mr. Henderson, I understand and respect what you're saying," I said, "but I want you to know there will be no lawsuits. I hold the only signed lease documents from both sides, and I'm going to tear up the lease agreement and mail you the pieces right now, both copies of them. I promise there will be no lawsuits."

Henderson couldn't get over the fact that I would do that. But I could see that if there was a lawsuit it was going to tie up in the courts for years, maybe even ten years, and the Stardust would never get open. And the legal expense would be far more than the damn place was worth. And I did tear up all the pieces of the documents and mailed them to him, with a note thanking him for all the courtesies and the hope that we would do business again in the future.

I then called Judge Ross at his home on that Sunday, and I told him the whole story. I explained how these other groups had ganged up on us and brought out the past history of John Factor, who had totally rehabilitated himself and was an exemplary citizen, and who had shown the courage to come forward with his $6 million to resurrect the property. I explained that what our competitors had done with their talking to the press was to ruin the chance to have Sheraton come into this deal and into Nevada. And I explained that the reason that Sheraton was going to take the hotel and not the gaming was because they couldn't get licensed, the way that licensing was done back then.

Ross was really upset when he heard the whole story and the background on it, and so the next day, Monday, we went back into court in Carson City at ten o'clock, and he pulled everybody in front of the bench and explained that he knew exactly how everything happened.

He told the other group that they had embarrassed Nevada and that the Thomas plan had been changed in only one regard, and that was that the Desert Inn people would now take all of the hotel and the gambling and bars and that he was now awarding them the offer. And with that he slapped his gavel, got up and walked out, and that was it. And that's exactly how the Stardust got finished with Jake the Barber's $6 million.

So Jake then owned the place. He bought the Stardust through the court. He bought the whole Strolla estate and the creditors all got paid and there was enough money left to finish construction. The DI people came in as lessee operators and paid Jake a monthly rent. Jake didn't have to get licensed because he was getting only a fixed rent. And Moe and his partners made a big success of the property after that. When the Stardust opened it was the biggest hotel-casino in the state, and had the most rooms. The opening review was the Lido de Paris, and that was a huge hit right away.

Jack Factor died about five years after the Stardust opened, and Dalitz and his partners bought the place. Howard Hughes wanted to buy it later on, but the SEC wouldn't allow it because of a monopoly statute. It was too bad that didn't happen, because what happened later on in the 1970s at the Stardust was suicide. [*The reference is to the Argent Corporation's takeover of the Stardust, and the infiltration of organized crime figures Frank "Lefty" Rosenthal and his Chicago boyhood friend Anthony Spilotro, which led to a massive skimming operation. The Stardust saga was immortalized in Nicholas Pileggi's book* Casino, *and a move of the same title directed by Martin Scorsese.*]

One of the funny things that happened prior to the Stardust's opening in July 1958 was the story about how they got all the expensive Lido costumes for free.

Allard Roen, who was a very good friend of mine, was overseeing the final stages of construction and he was doing an outstanding job. And as they were preparing to bring in the Lido show, they were designing and making all the costumes in France. We talked it over, and I believe it was Allard's idea to open an escrow account in

Switzerland and then when the costumes were finished, the escrow holder would pay for the costumes. The price as I remember it was $300,000. But the Stardust had the option to pay for them either in the value of francs or in dollars. The reason it was thought out that way was because of the fluctuation of either currency, and how it might affect the Stardust. Say they agreed to pay in francs and the value of francs went down, then it would take a helluva lot more dollars than what they had agreed to in the first place.

As luck would have it, right after that Charles de Gaulle came to power and the franc more than doubled in value. They'd already put the money for the costumes into francs, which were then evaluated and turned back into dollars. So $300,000 was paid for the costumes in francs, and then $300,000 was returned to the Stardust because of the valuation change, so they got the costumes for nothing. That's how it worked out. That's an arbitrage like I've never seen before, a helluva deal.

I also recall that the DI people brought a guy named Johnny Drew down from Reno to run the gaming for them. He was strictly a syndicate guy, and his wife, Jeannie Drew, was a madam. None of the other women would have anything to do with her. But she was also an excellent golfer, and Wilbur Clark partnered up with her several times in golf games and they beat up on everybody.

It's funny, but I've read time and again when these authors write about the Stardust, they say that upon Tony Cornero's death the Mob sent Moe Dalitz in to run the place. The Mob had no more to do with it than the Rotary Club. That whole transaction was handled by us at the Bank of Las Vegas. The approved purchase of the Stardust was even called the Bank of Las Vegas Plan.

Incidentally, later on, [*former Nevada Governor and U.S. Senator*] Paul Laxalt married the daughter of Federal Judge John Ross, who made the ruling on the Jake the Barber matter. Small world.

I'll never forget the first time I met Benny Binion. It was in 1959. At the time we had helped finance the Fremont Hotel for a guy out of San Francisco named Lou Lurie. At any rate, we used to sit at a big table in the back of the coffee shop at the Fremont about once a month. It would be Eddie Levinson of the Fremont, and sometimes Bucky Blaine, who ran the Golden Nugget across the street, and sometimes E.O. Barrick would come over. We would discuss various plans and developments and things we wanted to do. So this one morning the front-page headline in the *Las Vegas Sun* had just two words, in big bold letters: "Benny's Back."

Of course, Benny had been in the bucket, which is what he called prison. He'd served a stretch in a federal penitentiary in Texas for income tax evasion. I think he agreed to serve double time for tax evasion rather than do a shorter stretch for murder in the state prison, because he thought for sure he'd be murdered in the state prison. Whatever the case, the newspaper article went on to say that Benny was alleged to have killed seven men.

That very day I got a call from Benny saying he wanted to talk to me about a loan to buy back the Horseshoe, which the family had owned, but which had been under the proprietorship of Joe W. Brown, who was the wealthiest man in Las Vegas in those days.

Benny started calling me "Wall Street" that day, which is what he called me until the day he died. I liked him instantly and we became good friends. But that very first day I asked him if it were true whether he really had killed seven men.

He looked straight at me and said, "Well, I never killed anybody that didn't need killin' real bad." He also told me that he considered the actual total of victims to be five, because two of 'em were so worthless they didn't even count."

We got the Binions the loan they needed to take over the Horseshoe from Joe Brown, although Benny never did get licensed. Mainly his son Jack ran the place and his other son Ted worked there, and it became a huge success and the casino was known as the purest gambling joint in Las Vegas. That's because Benny was a flat genius when it came to running games and knowing how to treat customers well. All the biggest gamblers liked to play at Benny's place.

I think for the type of place Benny managed, he was unquestionably the best I ever knew, probably the best casino manager in the world. One time I was having lunch with Jack Binion and his sister Becky Behnen and they had a little argument going about redoing the furniture in the casino. They were discussing what type of covering they would put on the chairs at the 21 tables. Becky wanted some kind of brocade embroidered covering on it, and Jack said that wouldn't work, that he wanted something less sticky, and they were going back and forth when Benny interrupted and said, "I suggest you just cover those chairs with asses first."

Another time I set up a meeting between Bill Vogler and Benny because Bill had bought the Bing Crosby ranch up in Elko, Nevada, and he wanted to sell it. And Benny was a potential buyer. He had this big ranch in Montana where he raised prize cattle, and Bill thought he might be interested in buying a ranch closer to Las Vegas. I got some master suites up on the twenty-second floor of the Dunes Hotel and set it up for a dinner. And Bill and Mike Furbish, the president of American National, came along and I picked up Benny, who came with me.

In the course of the conversation, Bill said, "Benny, if you buy the ranch, you won't have to pay for everything in checks. We'll be glad to take some of that green money you gamblers have."

Benny looked at me and I looked at Benny, and he finally said, "Well, Mr. Vogler, it's true that cash and dead men tell no tales, but the problem is they usually go together."

Benny had too much street smarts to get involved with anyone who would make that kind of statement.

I also recall that when Benny designed the big house the family lived in on Bonanza Road, he designed it so the only way to get to the children's bedrooms was through his room. That was his way of ensuring security for his kids.

Another story with the Binions was that our bank supplied all those $10,000 bills that they displayed for years down at the Horseshoe. It was one of the big downtown attractions that drew people to the hotel, the chance to get their picture taken with one million dollars in cash.

In the 1950s the government circulated $10,000 bills. They were used by some big gamblers because it's a lot easier to pack a few $10,000 bills in a carry bag than smaller denominations. Benny liked the idea of a big horseshoe display with those bills in it, but he didn't want to tie up that much working capital, so our bank made him a loan for a million dollars and we got all the bills through the Federal Reserve. It was a wonderful deal for the bank because we charged Benny six percent interest on the million dollars and at the same time we got that counted as cash-in-till against our reserves. I won't get into all the technicalities of banking, but that was the net effect of it. It became part of our cash reserves, and the Fed never did come down on us about it.

It wasn't long after that the Fed called all those bills in and made them illegal currency, but that display of the million dollars remained at Binion's Horseshoe for over twenty years, and was a big drawing card.

CO

Another time, years later, my son Peter and I were having lunch at the Horseshoe and this was just after Benny had nearly died in the hospital. His heart had stopped and he was clinically dead until they revived him. Federal Judge Harry Claiborne was with us at the time, and he was one of Benny's closest friends. Harry said, "Hey, Benny, when you were dead, do you remember anything? Did you see anything?"

"Oh, yeah," Benny said. "I saw this great big long hallway. It was all bright and gold with big chandeliers, and it was unbelievably beautiful. And down at the end of it was standing the Man himself. And he was all dressed up like Liberace."

[*Author's note: Another time, for another book, Benny Binion told us in an interview that Jesus actually called to him at that moment. He heard Jesus gently mouth, "Benny," when suddenly the defibrillator brought him back to life. Binion described Jesus as being a young man, with long hair, "like you see in the pictures. But I wasn't there long enough to see much. You die longer than a second, you stay."*]

### Elaine Wynn

BENNY BINION WAS THE KIND OF A GUY WHO I DON'T THINK CARED IF he was respectable or not. He had enough confidence in who he was and what he could do that he just didn't worry about it. He associated only with people he liked.

### Larry Ruvo

Here's a story I've heard about Benny Binion: He was driving from Texas to Las Vegas, which he often did, and he was alone in the car as he drove through Arizona and pulled over to pick up a hitchhiker.

The man got in the car and he was quiet for a short while and then said to Benny, "What would you say if I told you I got a gun on me?"

Benny, calm as could be, said, "I'd say we're even."

He pulled the car over and the hitchhiker got out.

## Jack Binion

IT'S TRUE THAT MY FATHER CALLED PARRY "WALL STREET," WHICH WAS a perfect nickname for him, if you think about it. Parry was the most dynamic guy. He was blessed with movie star looks, had a personality and charm that was undeniable, and he was very decisive. When he came in he told you exactly what he would do and he was there to make deals. Looking back, Parry was an accommodator, not a ball buster. And I think that's kind of a key. He dove right in with Jerry Mack and they were perfect for each other. Jerry's father, Nate Mack, was here real early and so they were very established in the town, and they were equally good for each other and became great friends and partners.

The two banks that were here, First National and Bank of Nevada, would never loan money to Southern Nevada casinos. I know they did loan money to some Northern Nevada casinos, but they wouldn't loan one single dollar to Las Vegas gamblers. So all these places here were built basically with capital equity from the owners, or from any place they could get it. Before Parry got here, some of these guys would borrow money from some rich oil man, guarantee the loans, and give a good spread for the money.

As I recall I met Parry through Eddie Levinson, and Parry really liked Eddie. Him and a guy named Ed Torres. [*Torres' daughter, Dara Torres, recently became the oldest Olympic swimmer to earn medals in the Olympic Games. She won three silver medals in Beijing at age forty-one.*]

Joe Brown owned the Horseshoe when Benny Binion went to jail, and he sold the joint to Brown. That was in 1953. And it was in 1959 that Torres and Levinson built the Fremont across the street from the Horseshoe. And they brought in some new guys, some new partners, smaller partners. And in those days, instead of offering stock options, they might carry 'em even if the guy was strong enough for one percent of the company or two percent or whatever. Looking back,

Levinson was really a smart guy for the time. Torres was just a "No" man. No matter what happened, Torres would say no. He was only interested in cutting the nut. Every time someone came to him with a new idea or suggestion and said, "Can we do this?" or "Should we do that?" Torres would say no.

Let me sidetrack a minute and tell you a story of how Torres and Levinson got in trouble at the Fremont. It happened because Torres was so cheap. There was a girl who worked in the office at the Fremont and her husband worked at the phone company. So Torres brought him in to do something with the phones where the hotel wouldn't have to pay a service charge to the phone company. It was a cheap move to save a few bucks. There were a lot of guys there like that. They didn't have much of a sense of humor and they went out of their way to squeeze a dollar. One of the guys at the Fremont, who was considered the funniest of the bunch, used to use this line: Someone would ask to borrow money, and he'd say, "You know I have a reputation in this town for not giving a guy the time of day, but in your case I'll make an exception. It's ten minutes to twelve." So that's about as funny as those guys got.

Anyway, one day Torres is on the phone and he sensed that something was wrong. He noticed that there was an extra line hooked up. And that's how they discovered that the guy who'd installed the device, to save money, I guess, had been hooked up with the FBI to tap the phone. And they knew that all sorts of business had been discussed that could cause problems.

But rather than lay back, they got the Sands lawyer, a fellow named Brian Burton, and they threatened to press criminal charges against the phone company and against the local FBI agent in charge because what they had done was completely illegal. And then they went out and got Edward Bennett Williams, who was the best lawyer in the history of the world, and he negotiated the deal, and the only one who

86

would face any kind of conviction or anything was Eddie Levinson, and he was pretty well along in age at the time anyway.

But back to Parry and the Horseshoe. Joe Brown bought the hotel when Benny Binion left town in '53, and the Torres and Levinson bunch came in with a small piece, and another guy nicknamed Dobie Doc [*Author's note: real name was Robert Caudill*] had some. I had twenty-five percent, and when we bought it back for the family, we borrowed the money from Parry and the Bank of Las Vegas.

## Parry Thomas

THERE'S A STORY ABOUT JOE W. BROWN THAT MANY PEOPLE DON'T KNOW, but it's a beautiful story. Joe had made a fortune in gambling and real estate in New Orleans. His longtime friend and partner Jakey Friedman had made his money in gambling in Houston and Galveston. Joe Brown ended up owning several hundred thousand acres of land in the Delta and the bayous south of New Orleans. And it became probably the richest gas and oil field in America, or one of the richest. It was operated by Standard Oil of New Jersey. A friend of ours named Matilda Street, a dear friend from Sun Valley, was in a family that was very close to Joe Brown. Matilda's mother owned several hundred thousand acres and large tracks of oil and gas leases in New Orleans, and like Joe she ended up being one of the richest people in America at one time.

Anyway, when Benny went to the bucket, he got Joe Brown and his wife, Josephine, to come up and take over the Horseshoe. Now Jakey Friedman was the chairman of the Sands Hotel at the time because the first guy they put in to run the place couldn't get licensed. His name was Max Cumperman, and although as a Jewish fella he was not a "made man," because he wasn't Italian, he was still pretty heavily connected back in New York.

Although there was no Nevada Gaming Control Board back then— there was just the Gaming Commission—and although it was very lenient, this guy Cumperman was so notorious that they wouldn't give him a license. So they brought Jakey in, and he was just wonderful to me. Friedman had run most of the gambling down in Galveston and Houston and the southern part of Texas, and he was an experienced operator. He was very wealthy when he first came to the Sands, and quite elderly as well, probably in his late sixties or early seventies. But I was fortunate in that he put his hand on my shoulder shortly after I got here, and he helped me every way he possibly could. He was a really short man with a gravelly voice, and he was just wonderful to me.

As the years went on, Jake started shooting craps, and although he would win big at times, he'd lose even bigger. After a while he'd lost a few million dollars, and this is some forty-five years ago. Imagine what that would mean today. So one day I get a call from Joe W. Brown, and he says that he's told Jakey Friedman and Jakey's wife, Sadie, to meet me in my office at ten o'clock that morning. They arrive, and just after that Joe Brown walks in. He didn't say too much, but he sat down and wrote out a check for $3 million. He handed me the check.

Joe said, "Put this to work with the best municipal interest you can get, and give the money to Sadie. Don't give it to Jake, cuz he'll just blow it."

As he got up to leave, he turned to Jakey and said, "I just paid you back for that twenty-seven-dollar and forty-nine-cent bus ticket."

Obviously, this was a pretty dramatic moment, and of course I was wondering what it all meant. Here's the back story:

What I found out was that Jakey Friedman and Joe Brown were raised in an orphanage together in Houston in the early 1900s. The rule in that orphanage was that when the kids turned fifteen years old, they had to leave the orphanage and go out on their own.

While they'd been in the orphanage, Jakey and Joe had learned to gamble like crazy, which would serve them well later on in their casino careers. Now Jakey being Jewish, some of his Jewish friends bought him a produce stand or something, but Joe's only contact was a distant aunt who lived in New Orleans. So Jake gave Joe enough money out of his earnings to buy a bus ticket to New Orleans. And the ticket cost twenty-seven dollars and forty-nine cents.

That was a humbling moment in my office, humbling for Jakey Friedman for sure to have to face the reality of his gambling problem, and humbling for me to be privy to it. But at the same time it's a beautiful story of friendship.

Jakey died about six months after that meeting in my office. The poor guy had an oversized aorta and it burst and he died of a massive hemorrhage. And just as Joe Brown had instructed, the money went to Sadie Friedman.

The Sands was the second big hotel-casino loan we made at the Bank of Las Vegas, after the Sahara. The hotel opened in 1952, right after the Desert Inn opened, and it was successful right away. In addition to Jakey Friedman, they brought in Jack Entratter from the Stork Club in New York, who was just outstanding in the world of entertainment. I think it could fairly be said that Entratter was the man who invented the early days' headliner entertainment policy of Las Vegas, which is still in place today.

Entratter was one of the managers at the Stork Club, and he had a great sense of what people wanted in their nightclub entertainment. Shortly after coming to Las Vegas he was able to attract big stars like Danny Thomas and Nat King Cole and Frank Sinatra to perform at the Sands. I saw all the great entertainers in the early days, and I went to shows about once a week. The guy I liked best, who I thought had the best voice and was the overall classiest, best entertainer was Nat King Cole.

Entratter deserves all the credit for creating the Rat Pack. It was his idea to put Sinatra and Dean Martin and Sammy Davis and Joey Bishop together on stage at the same time and let them just be themselves and wisecrack around. I was right there, in 1960, when those first appearances happened. The chemistry between those guys, and the humor they would express when they were together, just made a terrific show that everyone in the country wanted to see. I saw dozens of those performances, and I'm not surprised that the Rat Pack is now thought of as representing a golden era of entertainment in Las Vegas.

Entratter also raised the bar and stepped up to the plate when it came to paying big-name entertainers. While most of the early hotels might pay $5,000 a week for a headliner, or $10,000 for the biggest stars, Entratter and the Sands would pay $25,000 and up. By doing that, he established the Sands as far and away the place for entertainment.

Carl Cohen was the casino manager at the Sands, and he and Entratter were the property's two most important elements. I believe Carl had come over to the Sands from the El Rancho Vegas, where he'd been working for Beldon Katleman. Carl was a well-respected guy and he had a wonderful personality. You just felt good around the man, and an owner could have full confidence that he was a great manager. He was also a pretty tough guy. He became something of a legend around Las Vegas after he took on Sinatra that one time.

Frank had this bad habit of going into a casino he was playing at—I know he did this at both the Sands and Caesars Palace later on—and he'd play craps or blackjack, and if he lost, he'd say he was a shill for the house and wouldn't pay off his debts, and if he won, he'd keep the money.

If Carl wasn't working the evening shift, Frank could get away with it at the Sands, but one time Frank got a little drunk in the casino and was mouthing off to Cohen and Carl stood up to him. I think Sinatra threw the first punch. Carl just reacted and decked him right there, in front of everybody. Carl used to be a boxer and I guess it was a helluva punch. But that incident solidified Cohen's reputation as a guy who wouldn't take flak from anybody and a guy who ran a tight ship.

It's funny, but about two years after that, Sinatra was gambling at Caesars and the shift boss was Sandy Waterman, who was a protégé of Carl Cohen's before he got a better offer at Caesars. Now Sandy was just a slight, frail man, and when Sinatra tried to get out of paying a gambling debt, Sandy got on him and Frank sicked a couple of his bodyguards on him. Sandy just pulled a six-shooter out of his pocket and said, "Guys, I have no qualms about shooting all three of you."

And that put an end to that.

Jerry Mack and I financed and built a health club for the Sands around 1959 or '60, when the Rat Pack was in its prime. Jack Entratter asked us to build a well-appointed club that was to be only for Sinatra and Dean and those guys. It was a place where they could relax and not be bothered by anyone. Jack told Jerry and me that we were the only other guys who could use that club, other than himself and Carl Cohen.

I didn't use it very often but Jerry used it quite a bit. He liked that stuff, and he enjoyed being in their company. Who wouldn't? I got to know all of them a little bit, Dean Martin better than the others, but as far as banking went, I never wanted to have anything to do with entertainers. They were a lousy credit risk. I always had good business instincts, who to lend money to and who not to lend money to. I just didn't want to be taken advantage of by celebrities because they were such a terrible credit risk. Believe me, they're worse than a house painter who drinks his own paint thinner.

I did like Shecky Greene a lot, although if he got two drinks in him he became a different person. Jerry Mack became good friends with Shecky. They had a Jewish thing going. And I did like Dean Martin. He was a nice guy, but he could be a little scatter-brained. When we were involved with the Riviera, we decided we needed an entertainer policy and I guess it was Ed Torres' idea to give Dean five percent of the place if he would start bringing in the right entertainers. But that never worked out.

So then the darnedest thing happened. We made the same offer to the Broadway producer David Merrick. He was the biggest of the big at that time. David came in and he booked *Pajama Game* and *L'il Abner* and those kinds of shows. They were good shows, and they brought new people in, but they didn't bring gambling people. So finally we mutually agreed to separate out. But in the meantime, Jerry and Harvey Silbert, who was our partner in the Riviera, and I bought sixty percent of Merrick's enterprises, twenty percent each. We didn't buy all of his productions, but some of them. One of them was *Hello Dolly*, so we were involved in the production of that. But then he asked us to sell out. David was very honest about it. He said he was going to sell the movie rights to the play and that he was going to make a lot of money, but that he had to do it by himself, that he couldn't take any partners with it. We agreed, and sold our interest, and he subsequently got something like $8 million for the movie rights on it, which we were happy to see him get. Of course, Barbra Streisand was great in the movie and it was a huge hit. We enjoyed being associated with Merrick. He was a damn tough producer and a tough businessman, but he was honest and a square-shooter and I really liked him.

The only time I broke my own rule was with two entertainers, one was Shecky Greene, and the other was Sammy Davis Jr. And both times when I loaned them money, the Sands Hotel guaranteed it. I distinctly remember that Shecky paid back his loan, but the hotel had to pay back Sammy's, which they later recovered from his appearances.

## Barbara Mack, the eldest of Jerry Mack's three daughters

MY FATHER JUST LOVED JACK ENTRATTER. HE CALLED HIM YONKEL, which is Yiddish for Jack. At the Sands health club they would take schvitz baths [*steam baths*]. It was very private, only for special guests of the Sands and celebrities. So when Dad would go there with Jack, he would see Sammy Davis and Sinatra and Dean Martin, and I know he enjoyed those times. It wasn't that Dad was enamored with celebrities, it was just that he liked the camaraderie and having a place to really relax and enjoy conversation.

I remember one time we were having dinner at the Sands, and I had just graduated from high school. Sammy Davis stopped by our table to say hello, and Dad told him we were celebrating my graduation. A few minutes later Sammy came by again and gave me this beautiful gold-coin necklace with pearls. I still have it. That's a special memory.

## Parry Thomas

ANYWAY, THE SANDS WAS ADDING ANOTHER TWO HUNDRED ROOMS OR so to the hotel and they needed to borrow $800,000 from us when we made that big loan. I had to syndicate it, of course, because our limit was $75,000. I called my father's best friend, George Eccles, who was the president and chairman of First Security, and he came in with $250,000. We also used all of the Cosgriff banks, and Continental Bank, my former employer, put in $250,000 and we made the loan. Everybody was surprised that the little Bank of Las Vegas could do anything like that, and it got a lot of attention up and down the Strip. It allowed me to gain a position with properties like the Desert Inn and other hotels, and I picked up a number of accounts because of the success of that loan.

Jakey Friedman was the chairman of the board of the Sands and Jack Entratter was then the president of the hotel, and they were drawing the biggest players in town. And Jakey would always invite me to lunch or dinner with any big-shots he was meeting with, and our network really began to grow from those introductions.

Jakey set up two different dinners for me with Howard Hughes. They had been friends going back to Houston, where Howard was from. Howard would often stay at the Sands in the early 1950s, when he was more social. So I went to dinner a couple of times with Jakey and Howard, but Hughes wasn't very talkative. As I recall those nights, Jakey did all the talking and Hughes and I would do all the listening.

I had actually met Hughes some years before, in the late 1940s when I was employed at Continental Bank. I had met him through Glenn Brewer, who was a great high school pal of mine and in our first years at the University of Utah. As the war got nearer, Glenn married a girl by the name of Joan Cannon, who happened to be the daughter of a famous general in the Air Force who was known as Uncle Joe Cannon. Through that connection, and with all the work that Hughes Aviation was doing for the military, Glenn landed a job with Hughes Aviation.

Glenn was a great-looking guy, and Mormon, and Hughes really liked him a lot. Hughes told Glenn that he could use a young Mormon guy to work for him in finance, and so I was invited down to Hollywood, on Roxbury Drive, to meet him at his office. I just met Hughes briefly on that occasion, and I remember being aghast at a chance to meet this legendary man who was reputed to be the wealthiest man in the country. The actual interview was conducted with Noah Dietrich, who handled all Hughes' affairs at the time, and Glenn Brewer sat in with us. When I was offered the job I told Noah I was very flattered and I sure appreciated the opportunity they were giving me, but that I wasn't qualified to do that kind of work and it was important for me to try and proceed in the banking world, where I could end up owning my own bank one day. I told him that was my goal, and that, win or lose, that was what I had to shoot for.

I made the right decision because that would have been a dead end for me, but it turns out that years later I would be involved in some important dealings with Hughes in his purchase of Las Vegas hotel-casinos, so those early meetings in a way set the stage for those later transactions.

I should add that Hughes' great working relationship with Glenn Brewer was the genesis of his connection to all the Mormons he would hire later on to take care of him. That's the group that has come to be known as the Mormon Mafia.

<br>

There just wasn't a lot of money in Las Vegas in the mid-'50s, or even the availability of money to grow businesses, when we got here to run the Bank of Las Vegas. There were some pioneers who were well off, and they were the backbone of the community. People like Big Jim Cashman, whose family is still a large part of the fabric of Las Vegas, and a man named Bob Griffith, who owned lots of land in the area, and the Von Tobel family. There was also a man named Bob Kaltenbourne, who created the Rancho Circle neighborhood where we ended up living for years. Bob also owned a lot of downtown property, and was involved in several civic organizations.

I don't want to create the impression that our bank just grew by leaps and bounds every year. Actually, we went through a series of ups and downs from the day I got here. Real estate prices would get up, and then they'd fall. Then they'd get up again, and then they'd fall. The only place where I could see that the Mob had a real effect on the economics was when they'd skim so much money from a place that there wasn't a heck of a lot left for expansion and improvement.

We had to be creative in finding new ways to create business and accelerate growth, for both our bank and the community. One of the ideas I came up with—and I don't mean to be braggadocio or anything—was an offshoot of something we'd done in Salt Lake City at the Chamber of Commerce. A group of us in Utah would make trips to all the little cities around the inner mountain country to explain Salt Lake and its importance as a hub of commerce and agriculture and so on. I made dozens of those trips for the chamber. And so I got the idea that we should do something like that down here to promote the image of Las Vegas on a non-gaming basis. My thinking was that if some of our community and state leaders would go out to various important cities in the country and explain all the attractions of Las Vegas, with its great weather, great livability, attractive tax structure, and a growing business core, without even talking about gaming, that we would be supporting gaming indirectly without even mentioning it.

I came up with the idea to form the Southern Nevada Industrial Foundation, which we called SNIF. That organization was the forerunner of the Nevada Development Authority, which is so effective today in attracting new businesses to Las Vegas.

I had two guys help me do it. One was Julian Moore, who had been a lieutenant colonel in the Army and was stationed here and married a local girl named McNamee. He was from Florida and just a terrific guy. Later on, I put him on the bank's board. And the other guy who helped me a lot in forming SNIF was Jim Rogers Sr., who was president of the telephone company. He was really an outstanding local citizen, very involved in the community. [Author's note: His son Jim Rogers Jr. is the current chancellor of the state university system in 2009, and owns a chain of television stations through the West.]

The three of us formed that foundation and we made Julian the president of it. He was an excellent speaker, really good at the podium, and he did a great job. We usually had a contingent of about thirty people along on those trips. We'd have business leaders and the chairman of the county commissioners and the mayor. We even brought our governor, Grant Sawyer, along on several of these trips. We went all over the country, to San Francisco and Denver and Cleveland and New Orleans.

I remember one time we had a big show in Dallas, and I sat next to the billionaire H.R. Hunt, who was thought to be the wealthiest man in America. We had this big luncheon with an incredible menu, and Hunt sat next to me and ate his lunch out of a paper bag that he'd brought. I don't know whether he didn't trust people to prepare food for him or what, but that made quite an impression on me.

At these meetings we'd talk to manufacturers and industrial people and small-business owners. We would stress to them that Las Vegas was becoming a hub for the West Coast, that it was a free port with a great tax structure and the best climate in the country. After these gatherings we'd always get a lot of calls from people asking us to make hotel reservations. Whether they decided to move their business or build a plant here was incidental to the fact that we were creating more good customers for Las Vegas.

The biggest thing I was looking for on these trips with SNIF was to develop more sources of money for Las Vegas. So I'd invite the principal insurance company and the biggest bankers in the area to these luncheons, and I'd always try to sit where the money people were. I was pretty successful at it and I made some important contacts to help raise money out of those excursions. I had my eye on mortgage people, insurance company people, lending departments, and commercial banks. In Dallas, for instance, I was able to get the Republic National Bank of Dallas to participate with me. Another important one was the First National Bank of Dallas.

When I used to structure the big loans for the hotels and casinos, the way I'd do it was to divide the loan into short-term and medium- and long-term loans. I'd try to get enough banks to take the short-term credit and insurance companies to take the longer end of the credit. So I'd get a full structure, because banks were sensitive about long-term lending. For these commercial banks, one or two years, or three years at the most, was about the limit of where they would lend money. But insurance companies were long-term lenders. They just wanted to get interest rolling and compounding and compounding and compounding. And that way of structuring the credit really worked well.

Republic National had a fellow by the name of Bill Stevens, a senior vice president, who was my first contact. At large banking conventions Republic would always have first-class hospitality suites, and they would put on a show. Bill Stevens had a terrific singing voice and he would always break into a song, like "Yellow Rose of Texas." Stevens and his bank became a great lending source for Las Vegas.

Another big deal for us in the 1950s was the Riviera Hotel. They first started building it in 1953, when I was still living in Salt Lake and making frequent trips to Las Vegas. It was the first high-rise built on the Strip, with nine stories and three hundred rooms originally. The only other high-rise in town was the Fremont downtown.

The Riv was built by a consortium of five partners from Miami. There was Sam Cohen, Meyer Lansky, and three Ginsberg brothers, I believe. They'd all been successful in their various businesses and they'd all moved to Beverly Hills. Their attorney was Harvey Silbert, and then they hooked up with a guy named Morey Mason, who owned the Taylor Construction Company in Miami, which was the builder of the Riviera. Taylor had previously built some major hotels in Miami, including the Fontainebleau.

The Riv opened in April of 1955, shortly after I'd moved here to run the Bank of Las Vegas, and they had quite a grand opening. Liberace opened the main showroom, and played there for some twenty years afterward, and was the biggest draw in town for many of those years.

Once the place was finished, the owners owed a ton of money in every direction, mainly to the vendors. Through some hidden ownership and mismanagement, mainly I think from Meyer Lansky, a lot of skimming started to occur and eventually busted the joint. The Riviera still had several million out in debt to all types of vendors, and so we had creditors' meetings. Through these I got to know Harvey Silbert very well and liked him a lot. He was an outstanding man in every way.

There were creditors all over the place, both local and national, and finally Harvey produced a tenant, Gus Greenbaum, who would come in and lease the place. Greenbaum had previously operated the Flamingo after Bugsy Siegel was killed in '47, so he had experience running an operation like that.

I'll never forget the lease payment they agreed to: It was $144,444.66 per month.

We needed to get to the creditors to give their permission to let us stay out of bankruptcy, which was no easy feat. The creditors included big companies like National Cash Register and IBM and various movie companies and so on. Their initial reaction to the situation was just to say hell with it, throw in on a bankruptcy, take what they could, and then go on their merry way.

But the local companies would in turn have gone bankrupt if that happened. These were the plumbing contractors and painting and plastering contractors. And if they went into bankruptcy it would break several more small companies down the line and our bank had a lot of loans out to these guys, so we certainly didn't want that to happen.

So after carefully examining the options, I made a little speech and said, "Why don't we do this democratically and take a vote, and if we get fifty percent or more by dollar amount to vote for an extension agreement, which I personally will promise I'll see is handled right, then we'll go to an extension agreement. But if we get less than fifty percent, we'll go into bankruptcy."

I knew the national creditors would go for this resolution, because they assumed they had more than fifty percent of the dollars outstanding. So the resolution passed. So then we took the vote in the creditors' meeting. I'll never forget it as long as I live, even with my poor memory. I was smart enough to put myself on the ballot committee to count the votes. And Harvey Silbert, of course, was there representing the Ginsbergs and himself. I could see real fast as we were counting the votes that we were in trouble.

It was going to be real close and the bankruptcy option looked like it was going to win. I raised my hand and said that we had to take a break, that I had to go to the bathroom. I kicked Harvey in the shins and nodded to him to go with me.

We got in the bathroom and I said, "Harvey, you know that $360,000 bill that Rupert the plumber has put in for that you wouldn't allow because you said he's crooked and cheating you?"

He said, "Yeah, I remember."

I said, "Well, you're going to have to pay it."

"I'll never pay that SOB ever, he cheated me!" said Harvey.

I said, "You're gonna pay him or you're going to go into bankruptcy, because the extension ballot needs those $360,000 to get over fifty percent."

We went bank in the room and counted the ballots, and submitted the Rupert claim, and our side came to fifty and one-half percent.

So we went into an extension agreement and I personally handled that $144,444.66 monthly lease payment for the next three years that was paid out for the Riviera.

∞

Gus Greenbaum and those guys had a helluva crew. There was Ben Goffstein, and Ross Miller, and Davey "The Man" Berman, and "Ice Pick" Willie Alderman.

One thing is for sure: Nobody would mess with those guys or try to steal from them. They were connected to the Outfit, no question about that, but they knew how to run a gambling joint, and they paid that monthly check religiously.

That agreement worked well for those three years, but then Gus Greenbaum, who was a serious cocaine user, got to drinking heavily to go with it. One thing led to another, and he started wasting people's money he shouldn't have been taking. He had his wife living in Phoenix at the time—she never did move to Las Vegas—and he would go down there on weekends to be with her and his family. And on one of those weekend visits they cut his throat and his wife's throat.

They never did catch the killers. That was a professional job. Real professional.

Harvey Silbert was named as a pallbearer at the funeral. All that time he had been handling the entertainment policy for the hotel, and doing all their legal work and writing their contracts and he had gotten pretty close to Gus.

I've read in several books where it is said that after the Greenbaums were murdered, the Mob put Ed Torres in there to run the place. That's totally fabricated. The Mob was in there behind Gus and his partners, but when he got his throat cut it was chaos. Ben Goffstein maintained a little semblance of order for a while, and tried to keep things together, but it was absolutely chaos.

So eventually Harvey came to me and said, "We're going to lose the place and all the property and everything if we don't do something."

It was then decided that Harvey Silbert, Jerry Mack, and I would buy the Riviera. We had long discussions about it, and we decided that no outsider would buy a corporation that was operated by these people for the simple reason they wouldn't be able to determine how much debt there was and other side deals that went on. I was the only living person who knew that corporation inside and out because I had been handling the distribution of the $144,000 lease payment for three years. I knew exactly what every nickel was for and what was old debt and what wasn't. We had the confidence that we could go in and take over this corporation, and that we could buy it very, very cheaply.

We knew that we had to have a sharp operator, because this would not be an easy property to manage. We had been heavily involved in the financing of the Fremont Hotel and my partner Jerry had long been a large stockholder in it. In our observation, Ed Torres, who had run the Fremont, was the meanest, toughest, best operator we knew. He paid attention to detail and he watched every penny. So we called up Ed, had a meeting with him, and asked him if he wanted to join us in a four-way partnership and run the Riviera.

Jerry and I decided for several reasons that we wouldn't go into the partnership personally. We'd do it in our children's trust, for two reasons. The most important reason was that we wanted to do our estate planning early, have a trust for our children that if it made big money, the money would go to them. And secondly, we didn't want to be in competition with our other banking customers. We wanted to stay at arm's length from them, the best we could anyway.

So Jerry put his interest in the Center Trust, which would go to his three daughters, and from my side we established the Peter Trust, after our oldest son, who was just twelve years old at the time.

## Tom Thomas

IT WAS VERY UNUSUAL FOR MY DAD AND JERRY MACK TO SET UP THOSE trusts when they did, in the early '60s. That was not a common thing for people to do at that time. I believe the first trust he set up for us, which was called the Peter Trust, is now a limited partnership that we still use today.

My understanding was that Dad had to get a hold of one of the Ford Family Trusts as an example of how to set up that kind of trust. There weren't a lot of trust attorneys around at that time. Dad's reasoning was that if he set aside a little bit of money whenever he could, it would eventually amount to something. Whenever he saw deals here that had a lot of risk to them, but risk he felt he could manage, he'd put his kids' trust into those deals.

The best example of a deal with high risk that he thought he could manage was the Riviera. When the Greenbaums had their throats cut, and he put together that partnership with Harvey Silbert, Dad put a lot of his blood and sweat and probably some tears into it as well, along with Jerry. They had some very difficult people they had to deal with back then. But that turned out to be a very good deal with a lot of upside for the trust, and sort of established the pattern for future trust deals he engaged in.

## Parry Thomas

Once we had established our plan, then we had to go to the state and get a gaming license. We were told by the Gaming Commission that we had to have $800,000 for bankroll. So the four groups, the Center Trust, the Peter Trust, Harvey Silbert, and Ed Torres, each put up $50,000. That made $200,000. Then I called my friend George Eccles in Salt Lake and borrowed $600,000 from him.

We told Harvey we wouldn't complete the deal unless we got an option from the Ginsbergs to buy the place for $12 million, which included the whole plant and the property it sat on. So we got that option.

Ed Torres went in to run the place. We got rid of the counting room, and we put in other procedures and safeguards against skimming that we thought would work best.

Within ninety days I had paid off the $600,000 to Eccles, and by the end of that first year we exercised the option and bought the property for $12 million. Then we had a policy to just keep the money piling up and years later we sold the Riviera for $84 million. So for every $50,000 each of the four partners got back $21 million. Which wasn't really that good a deal, because if we'd kept it longer, we'd have gotten a lot more [*he says with a smile*].

But it did establish a great platform for our family trust. We put Jerry in as president of the hotel during those years, Ed did a marvelous job running the place, and Harvey Silbert continued to do a good job on the entertainment policy.

### Barbara Mack

I have this distinct memory of seeing my dad and Parry and Harvey Silbert walking down Fifth Avenue. This was in the time they were in New York a lot, running their tanker company. And Parry was always dressed perfectly, in elegant suits, and Harvey Silbert had this beautiful white hair like Parry, and they looked like celebrities. Parry worked with my father and taught him to dress more stylishly, because it wasn't a real priority for Dad.

Another vivid memory is of Parry walking in New York and carrying a large stack of thin boxes, the kind you use for neckties and scarves. He would buy maybe a dozen Gucci scarves to give as gifts to employees of the bank or wives of his friends. Back then, designer scarves weren't as common as they are today. They were a luxury item. But that's the way Parry is, always doing nice things for people and making gestures they would always remember.

### Marilyn Mack

I remember Daddy telling me this story about how he and Parry and Harvey were walking down Park Avenue one day and a couple women, I think he said they were call girls, came by and tried to get Parry and Harvey to go with them. Dad would laugh and say how the women totally ignored him because the two guys he was with looked like movie stars.

## Elaine Wynn

I THINK WHAT PROBABLY STARTED THE INCREDIBLE BOND BETWEEN Parry and Jerry was Parry's enormous gratitude to Nate Mack for putting him in the spot that he was in. And because Parry is such an honorable man, he was going to honor the conditions of the arrangement that established their partnership. And Parry wound up falling in love with Jerry. Yet they were so quirky and opposite in so many ways.

Jerry was a hypochondriac. People will tell you he used to travel with a medicine kit with a pill for every little ailment. If he sneezed, it was hubba-hubba. Now with Parry, I don't remember Parry being sick a single day in his life. He was always healthy, vital, active, vigorous, and still is. I'm sure people had reported that Parry would ski every day for the number of years he had lived. And I believe he did that up until he was about eighty.

Certainly, regarding politics, Parry was inherently more conservative, Jerry far more liberal. But Parry didn't wear his political beliefs on his sleeve the way Jerry did.

Most importantly, there was so much mutual respect for one another. I think Parry thought that Jerry was really, really smart, and obviously Jerry felt the same way about Parry.

They also had a mutual love of leisure activities, with their interest in boating and snow skiing. The families also played tennis together. Definitely, the two families were married in a sense, which was highly unusual given the religious affiliation. So it's quite a remarkable story that the force of the fathers and the nature of the wonderful wives would pass on to the families.

## Karen Mack

I HAVE HEARD THE TERM "CLOSER THAN BROTHERS" COUNTLESS TIMES when people have talked about my father and Parry. And that's true, for a reason. When two men are brothers, there's all that growing-up baggage that is very complicated psychologically. There are the inevitable rivalries, the "who does Mom like best" and the "which one is going to be more successful" issues to deal with.

But in two friends and partners who greatly respect each other, without all those layers of rivalry that exist between brothers, the relationship is more pure and untainted.

Dad never questioned Parry's judgment or loyalty, and Parry never questioned my dad's. There just weren't the kind of ego problems that come into play like in relationships between brothers. And there was never a hint of jealousy between them. They both had their talents and areas they were comfortable with, and they allowed each other to do what they did best. While Parry was more social and would attend all the functions and social activities, Dad was entirely comfortable with not getting out there, with staying in the background with the numbers. When I was in college, *Business Week* magazine called Dad a financial wizard. He would always be penciling out deals on a little piece of paper. He just loved doing that.

Yet they both had the financial gift. Both of them knew how to work deals. So it wasn't like one was carrying the load and the other wasn't; it's just that one preferred to be in the background and one preferred to be out front. And so it worked out perfectly. The stars were clearly in the right place when these two guys came together, with their personalities and the way they looked at life.

## Parry Thomas

ONE OF THE STRONGEST FRIENDSHIPS I MADE IN THOSE FIRST YEARS in Las Vegas was with Hank Greenspun, the publisher of the *Las Vegas Sun*.

Nate Mack was the one who introduced us. But before I get to that, I have to say that Nate was the most perfect bank director I ever knew. Not only did he never interfere with management, nor try to impose his will or judgment on us in our decision-making, but he actually took it upon himself to go out and round up depositors for the bank. He used to bring in four or five a day, to help our young bank grow faster. Nate recognized that the biggest contribution he could make was to get us new business, and that's what he did.

Being a leader in the Jewish community, and having gotten to know and respect Hank Greenspun, Nate told me many times that it was very important that the bank help keep Hank's newspaper alive. Nate said to me, more than once, "Without Hank all we have is the *Las Vegas Review-Journal*, and I know Don Reynolds and I know how they operate and how they feel about Jews."

He told me that while Hank was a maverick and was volatile, he was very important to the Jewish community and the Las Vegas community as a whole. He said that there would come times when Hank and the newspaper might be low on money, and that he would probably not be able to get credit from other banks, and that if we would take care of him and use good business judgment, we would never lose any money on him. Nate even went beyond that and said that he would personally guarantee anything we loaned to Hank Greenspun. That's how important he felt that newspaper was to this city.

Later on, Hank got in a legal tangle with Senator Pat McCarran, and they tried to indict him for inciting a riot against a U.S. senator. That was a very famous fight. Hank had written that McCarran was a crook and said he was notorious for taking money from anyone who would hand it to him.

Hank Greenspun was just fearless, the most fearless guy I ever knew in Las Vegas, including all the Mobsters. He didn't give a damn who he took on. He even wrote scathing articles about Moe [*Dalitz*].

Later on he owned a small piece of the Desert Inn, maybe one or two percent, but Moe's people treated him like a skunk.

Eventually they became friends, but it was the funniest damn thing. They were friends, and yet they were enemies.

I remember one time at a dinner party at Dalitz's house, a purely social affair, Moe and Allard Roen pulled me into a bedroom. Allard said, "You're keeping Hank Greenspun and his newspaper in business and he keeps hammering us. We want you to stop supporting him."

It was customary of Moe that he told Allard what to say and Allard did all the talking, because Moe was too smart to ever have his words caught on tape. He was a shrewd son of a gun.

"Look, fellas," I said, "I never as long as I live will talk about your business with anybody else, and I'm not going to talk about Hank Greenspun's business with the bank, any more than I'll talk about your business to him or anybody else. That's the way I run the bank, and that's the way it's going to be and the way it has to be. Our bank has to be independent and autonomous to its own judgment."

That was the end of the conversation. You had to stand up to Moe. If you backed down, you were going to get run over.

I remember the *Review-Journal* poked some fun at me later on in an editorial for some things I was doing at the bank.

In those early days at Bank of Las Vegas, the highest interest rates you could get on bank loans was about 4 or 4.5 percent, and I was making loans out on the Strip at 6.5 up to 8 percent. That was damn near usury in some people's eyes, I guess, but I was making a lot of money for the bank. I was getting all the business, too. But because the other banks were getting such a low interest rate on their loans, they paid out very small interest on savings accounts. First National and the Bank of Nevada were paying, I think, just 1 percent to depositors. That was actually in line with the whole country, so there was nothing wrong with what they were doing, but I was starting a small bank and we had only about $4 or $5 million in total footings and only a $75,000 loan limit, so I had to force things.

I had to argue this vigorously with my own directors, but I decided I was going to go after them on the deposit side.

I designed a pyramid ad and I remember I could hardly afford to run it in the papers. But I announced in the ad that we were jacking the interest up to 2.5 percent on depositors' savings. I put that number at the top of the triangle and then had "Insured by the FDIC" and showed the convenience of our branches and made the whole thing attractive. We really took them on in that ad, and it produced one helluva lot of business.

We had a good spread with loaning to the casino people, and after putting a pencil to it I just knew we could offer that higher interest and draw a lot of depositors. We picked up a considerable number of millions of dollars with that move, and then after we had the new savings account, we'd cross-sell and try to get their checking accounts. The other banks were very slow to follow our interest-rate increase and I remember them telling everybody that we were going to go broke. It was really nothing more than good management that helped our bank to grow as fast as it did.

Well, the *R-J* wrote an editorial, it might have been by John Cahlan, who was Herb Jones' brother-in-law and the editor of the paper, but in effect it said that there was a new boy on the street and he was breaking the conventional rules of banking. It mentioned that I'd raised depositor's interest up to 2.5 percent and said that maybe we should call this guy Crazy Parry. And the paper used that name on me several times after that, which was all right with me, just as long as they spelled my name right.

We started to do so well that there was not only a local newspaper war going on, but a banking war as well. I actually came to kind of like that nickname Crazy Parry. At least it showed they were paying attention.

CHAPTER TWO

# The Roaring '60s

## Parry Thomas

ONCE THE DESERT INN WAS UP AND GOING, IT BECAME THE SOCIAL hub of Las Vegas. The DI and the Sands were the two best places on the Strip in the late '50s and early '60s.

Through all the loans we did for them, I got to know Wilbur Clark and Moe Dalitz pretty well. When the ownership was finally settled, I think Wilbur had twenty-two percent and Moe's group of course had the bigger end of it. Moe had Morris Kleinman and Sam Tucker and the Rothkopf family in there with him, too.

I got very close to all of those Desert Inn people and hung out with them quite a bit. Allard Roen, who managed the place, was probably the one I was closest to.

The first financing I remember doing for the DI was when they had finished the golf course and they wanted to build a clubhouse for it. It was going to take about $270,000 to do it. Our bank couldn't do that much, but I got the bright idea of involving a guy named Brown Cannon, who was the head of Arden Meadow Gold Dairy, which was headquartered in Denver. I knew Brown from college. He would come to Las Vegas occasionally and we'd go out on Lake Mead. He was really a good guy. So I asked Brown if he'd put up the money to build the country club and participate with us. We put up some of the money, he put up the rest, and we agreed to get for him all the dairy product business at the Desert Inn. Brown agreed to do it and that's how the clubhouse was built.

But they had this tough little guy they'd brought in from back East who was one of the food and beverage managers. This guy evidently had a ball game going with one of the local dairies, because the next thing we knew we were hearing all these reports about how everything was going wrong with the products from Meadow Gold. It was just plain sabotage in my book, because suddenly the ice cream got sour and the milk went bad and there were nothing but complaints. They had no choice but to kick Meadow Gold out of there. So then I had to raise the money to pay off Brown Cannon and Arden for their participation because we needed to do right by them, but it all worked out in the end.

Of course, once the clubhouse was built, the Tournament of Champions became an even bigger social event each year in Las Vegas.

With Walter Winchell's involvement, and with its affiliation with the Damon Runyon Cancer Fund, the tournament brought in all the biggest celebrities. Hope and Crosby and Sinatra and Dean Martin and Jerry Lewis, and the movie studios' involvement generated terrific publicity, and from what I was told the golf tournament was all Moe Dalitz's idea. He had the foresight to see what that event could do for his resort. [*Dalitz has often been quoted as saying, upon completion of the Desert Inn Hotel, that "We have the steak, now we need the sizzle." The golf tournament and all the hoopla surrounding it provided that for him and his partners.*]

I have a good story about the Calcutta that they held in the early years of the tournament. [*A Calcutta is a betting pool for a competition or tournament, with odds of winning posted for each entrant. It functions much like pari-mutuel betting at a racetrack.*]

Jerry Mack and I would always go together and buy one player in the Calcutta. I'm not a golfer, but we would ask around and do a little research before we would make our choice. So in 1961 I was having lunch in Dallas with a fellow named Jimmy Ling, of Ling-Tempco-Vought, a big holding company out of Dallas. And his company owned Wilson Sporting Goods. I was down there going over some figures to look at buying a bank they owned, and the conversation turned to the upcoming Tournament of Champions in Las Vegas.

The president of Wilson was with us, and their number one golf star endorsing their products was Sam Snead. And it so happened that Snead had a terrible record at the Tournament of Champions, for the simple reason that he caroused too much when he was in Las Vegas, and he stayed up all night and gambled and fooled around and it adversely affected his golf game.

While we were talking, Jimmy Ling turned to this guy from Wilson and said, "You tell Sam Snead that if he doesn't win the Tournament of Champions this year, we're through with him. You be sure he behaves himself when he's in Vegas, whatever it takes."

So naturally I came back and talked to Jerry about it, and we decided to purchase Snead as a good bet in the Calcutta. I think we cut Irwin Molasky and Merv Adelson in for a little piece of the action. It cost us $17,000, I remember. And the way it worked, if your player came in sixth, you got your money back. There were only about twenty-five golfers in the field, because it was only for those who had won tournaments the previous year.

That particular Calcutta became probably the biggest in the history of golf. It was really big money. Even before the tournament started, Wilson Sporting Goods, sure enough, had guards placed outside Sam Snead's hotel room. He was forbidden from fooling around—no booze, no broads, no nothin'. And wouldn't you know, he won the tournament by six strokes. The payoff for us was right around $700,000. And this is nearly fifty years ago.

About one month after the tournament the PGA Tour announced that the Calcutta betting at the Tournament of Champions had to be done away with because it was getting too big and offered too much opportunity for corruption and interference. But that was quite a week for us because we got that good tip about Snead and cashed in on it. And that's the only time Sam Snead won the Tournament of Champions. He never won it again.

I've gotten a lot of mileage out of that story through the years because even though I don't play golf, I'm frequently at social events where people are talking about their golf games, and I can tease them and say I've won more money on golf than all you guys put together, and then I tell them how we won that Calcutta.

Once the Desert Inn was up and running the owners really didn't need too much financing because the place was so successful. The DI and the Sands were the only two places that never had any financial reorganization in the early history of the Las Vegas Strip. All the rest of them had troubles at one time or another. The loans we made to the DI were usually just commercial loans and something only for three or six months to carry them over the winter, for working capital loans.

Along the way Moe Dalitz was a great friend of Harry Helmsley in New York. And he had brought Harry out to Las Vegas to buy the land the DI was on. That's how I met Harry.

Moe and his partners bought the Desert Inn business and the lease hold, but then later on Howard Hughes' companies had to go back in and deal with Harry and buy the real estate. I sat in on that negotiation, but we weren't handling the money. The Hughes Tool Company handled that.

It's pretty well documented that the reason the Tournament of Champions moved from the Desert Inn in 1967 was because Howard Hughes didn't want all those crowds on his property after he bought the hotel.

The way Hughes' people put it to me, as I remember, was that the golf tournament had all those cherry-picking cranes [*from ABC Sports*] positioned along the fairways with cameras on them, and Howard was fearful that they would point the cameras at the windows on the ninth floor of the hotel, where he lived. Everybody was moaning and groaning when the decision was made to move the tournament because it had been such a popular event, both locally and nationally. So Moe and Merv and Irwin and Allard decided to move it to their new Stardust course, on Desert Inn Road between Maryland Parkway and Eastern Avenue, until they could complete their new resort at La Costa, outside San Diego. Once La Costa was finished, the tournament was moved there and had a very successful run for many years after that.

## Bob Maheu

I'LL GET TO PARRY THOMAS AND HIS INCREDIBLE IMPORTANCE TO LAS Vegas in a minute, but I first need to give some background on my relationship with Howard Hughes, and how I eventually got to Las Vegas. Some people think my relationship with Hughes began in 1966, when he moved to Las Vegas. Actually, I first spoke to Hughes twelve years before, in 1954, and three years after that I started working for him on a regular basis.

My company, Robert A. Maheu Associates, was a problem-solving entity. I had always been intrigued with assignments that were impossible. Most people who think they have problems—be it in business or otherwise—have trouble solving them because they do not clearly identify what the problem is. It remains in the realm of the unknown.

And nobody in the world is smart enough to solve the unknown. But I understood that as devastating as a problem may be, you have a shot at solving it if you come up with a good plan.

As a consequence, we had an investigative division in my company that we called a diagnostic division. So our reputation was as problem-solvers, and I'm sure that was part of the reason that Hughes hired me in the first place.

I was in the Bahamas in 1957 when my phone rang at three o'clock in the morning and his voice said, "Congratulations, Bob. I've chosen you to be my alter ego."

Now I doubted very much that Howard knew what "alter ego" actually meant, but much to my amazement, he *did* know. [*Dictionary definition: another side of oneself; a second self; a substitute or deputy.*] He explained to me that he wanted me to take on the assignment of coming up with a strategy whereby when I spoke, the world would know that Howard Hughes was speaking. Now strangely enough, at the time Hughes was not an important client of mine from a pecuniary point of view. My biggest clients then were Stavros Niarchos, World Tankers, Westinghouse, and United Steel Workers of America.

Howard explained to me that he did not want to ever make another public appearance, and that if anything happened with a regulatory body I would have to be the one who showed up on his behalf. Also, he said he would never go before a congressional committee again, and that if he ever was involved in a lawsuit, that people on the other side would have to be satisfied with dealing with me. I was just thirty-nine years old at the time, and while I was flattered by his offer, I also figured, what a helluva challenge this would be.

In 1957 my office was in Washington, D.C., and my home was in Virginia. My wife, Yvette, and I had four children. Hughes had me spending summers in Los Angeles from 1958 to 1961, and he eventually found that insufficient and so we moved there permanently in the fall of '61. He told me that L.A. was going to be our permanent residence for the rest of our lives.

Then in early 1966 Hughes told me he wanted to go to Boston, that I was to get two club cars ready at the train yards in Los Angeles for whenever he decided to go. There was an air strike going on at the time, and all the trains were overloaded. After doing my homework, I realized that I needed the cooperation of the presidents of the three major railroads to make this trip happen. Fortuitously, one of the presidents in Chicago was an old friend of mine from my FBI days. So I called Bill Quinn and explained the situation and how it had to be kept quiet, and before you know it he had me talking on a first-name basis with the other two railroad presidents.

Hughes wanted to go to Boston to get some medical attention, and some of the members of the Hughes Medical Foundation were there. But as usual, Howard would say he wanted to leave the next day, and we'd have everything set up, and then he'd tell us he couldn't leave. This happened more than once, but finally we got him going, and after four or five days and incredible security and intrigue we were able to sneak him into the Ritz Carlton in Boston, where we tied up the top floor.

The word had leaked out to some media that there was a mystery train traveling across the country, so we had to do a lot of maneuvering. And then as the train was pulling into the station in Boston we got the word that Hughes wanted a certain type of charcoal-grilled steaks prepared for his arrival. And we managed to do that. It was just one challenge after another getting him back there, rolling with all the punches and the unexpected requests. You had to be on your toes every second of the day, but we pulled it off.

Several months later, in the fall, Howard calls one day and says, "Put on your seat belt." Whenever he said that I knew a big one was coming. He says, "We're moving to Nevada."

Initially, the plan was for him to go to Lake Tahoe. He was going to stay at the Cal Neva Lodge on the North Shore. So we had to make a lot of plans from a security point of view to set that up. When I called Howard and told him everything was arranged, he said, "I've changed my mind. I want to go to Las Vegas."

There are a lot of stories that float around about why he came here, but this is the absolute truth. He told me he was sick of being a small fish in a big pond. He wanted to become the big fish in a small pond.

A principal reason was that he had just sold Trans World Airlines (TWA) for roughly $547 million, and in those days, that was big bucks. *Big* bucks. He said, "I want to buy a newspaper in Las Vegas. I want to buy the airport. I want to buy a TV station, and I want to buy all the land I can."

Okay, so once that decision was made, I needed the help of my three railroad presidents again. We managed to get Hughes out of the Boston Ritz Carlton through a decoy operation, even though the press got wind of it and was assembled there. Howard left Boston around November 20, and it was a four- or five-day trip and he arrived in Las Vegas on Thanksgiving Eve, 1966.

Along the way I get a call from Jack Hooper, who was running security for the trip, and he says that they have a problem, and that the train has to have some repairs. He tells me that rather than arriving about four in the morning when it is still dark, the train is delayed and will be arriving in broad daylight.

I asked Jack how much it would cost to get an engine and a caboose, whatever it took, and form another section of the train so we could get him here earlier, before the sun came up. Jack came up with a dollar figure and I approved it and told him to get it going. We finally managed to get Hughes off the train and into a long van and into the Desert Inn without getting any unwanted attention. It was in the wee hours of the morning.

Moe Dalitz knew that Howard Hughes was coming to the DI, but we'd promised Moe that his party would stay there for only ten days. And that period between Thanksgiving and Christmas was always a slow time for business in Las Vegas back then, so we were more than welcome. Most of the showrooms actually went dark during that period of time.

By the way, I should tell you it was a real challenge figuring out what I could do for the railroad presidents to show our appreciation for everything they'd done to help us. You can't just send these men a case of whiskey, or an autographed picture of Howard Hughes. Finally, it hit me. I had a contract with the people who put on the Academy Awards, and I was able at the last minute to get these gentlemen and their wives good seats for the Oscars. I told them they would be the guests of Howard Hughes, and we jetted them out and put them up at the Bel Air Hotel.

It's funny, Bill Quinn is still living and I talked to him recently and he reminded me that the limo we rode in to the awards pulled up in front of the Dorothy Chandler Pavilion right behind a car carrying the actor Gregory Peck, and how the crowd went wild when Peck got out. Then our limo pulled up and we got out, and nobody knew who we were. We had a laugh about that.

Anyway, the suites in the Desert Inn had just been remodeled, and they were ready for all the New Year's Eve high-rollers to come in after Christmas. And Hughes and his aides took every suite, the whole ninth floor. And we had the elevator changed so that the only way it would go to the ninth floor was by key, the way they do it today. We also had a security guard posted right by the entrance.

But it didn't take long for the word to spread that Howard Hughes was in Las Vegas.

## Brian Greenspun

MY FATHER WAS THE GUY WHO WAS RESPONSIBLE FOR HOWARD HUGHES moving to Las Vegas. The way I heard the story from my dad was that Hughes was in Boston in the hospital. He'd been in that plane crash and was really getting loony. He didn't want to stay in Boston, the press was hounding him, and he wanted a place where he could enjoy himself and be left alone. He used to be a habitué of Las Vegas. He loved it here in his earlier days, in the 1940s and early '50s, and Hank knew him them.

When I say Hughes wanted to move to Las Vegas, naturally, the communication was done through Bob Maheu or some other person, because it was rare that Hughes would pick up the phone and talk directly. I'm certain the way it worked was that my dad was called by Maheu, who said that Hughes was considering moving to Las Vegas and could we make it palatable for him here. Would he be hounded by the media, or would he be left alone? It was the constant attention and speculation that drove him out of Boston.

So my dad set it up at the Desert Inn for Hughes to stay on the top floor. And he gave Maheu his word that he wouldn't write about it or do anything until Hughes was safely in the hotel, so that no one could rush him or bother him.

Well, the day Hughes got to town, Thanksgiving eve or morning, he got into the hotel by daybreak. The *Las Vegas Sun* had an advertising company then, and the newspaper owned a big billboard on the corner of the Landmark, on Paradise Road. The billboard was revealed about an hour—or maybe only a couple minutes—after Hughes was safely in the Desert Inn. It read, in huge letters, "Welcome Home Howard." And Dad's "Where I Stand" column that morning also welcomed Howard to town. So Hank kept his word, but only by a matter of an hour.

## Parry Thomas

BOTH HANK GREENSPUN AND I KNEW RIGHT AWAY THAT HOWARD Hughes was in town. We heard it through our Washington attorney, Ed Morgan, who was a close friend and lawyer to both of us and who had done a lot of work for Hughes and Maheu as well. So we got involved in the whole affair right from the beginning.

Ed Morgan advised Bob Maheu and all the rest of them to do all their banking through me, that I could be trusted with their deepest secrets, which I really guarded all my life. They knew that I would never talk about their business, so that's how the banking relationship started. Then after Hughes had been here a while he started buying things, because he had just sold TWA for something like five or six hundred million and he had a lot of cash on hand that he had to put to work for the tax advantages.

Herb Nall was an associate of Hughes who did his real estate work, and so we created an office for him in our little bank building on Fourth Street, just south of Fremont. We had a couple of offices upstairs in the building and that's where we put Herb, so he could be close to me so that when Hughes wanted something, we could get right on it.

Herb didn't really know his way around Las Vegas or who to talk to at that time. We knew all the players and everything else, so when Hughes wanted to buy a property, I'd go out and buy it for him, and Herb would be at my side.

I did nearly everything through Bob Maheu because he was the boss. Although I'd met Hughes in the 1950s, as I explained, I never saw him during those four years he was at the Desert Inn, and neither did Maheu.

## Bob Maheu

WELL, THE TEN DAYS QUICKLY PASSED FROM THE TIME WE MOVED IN, and then another ten days, and Dalitz was getting increasingly itchy to get his Desert Inn suites back. I heard directly from Moe and Allard Roen that they wanted Hughes out of there. In the meantime they found out that we still had the suites at the Ritz Carlton in Boston, so they wanted us to go back there.

I'm telling them that Hughes wants to stay here, that he's going to help them build up Las Vegas, and that we're going to spend a lot of money buying land and all this stuff. I'm basically trying to hold them at bay. And it's important to understand that this was during a time when publicly held companies could not own gaming companies. And Moe Dalitz and other casino owners in Las Vegas were getting a lot of heat from the government.

Bobby Kennedy [*who was the attorney general under Lyndon Johnson at the time*] had Las Vegas in his crosshairs and he'd done a study on how to get rid of these shady elements in the gaming business. And the conclusion of this study was that about the only way you could get these owners out would be by new owners purchasing the hotels. And there's no disputing that the Desert Inn was on Kennedy's list of places he wanted to have different ownership.

A lot of these old gaming people in Las Vegas were getting on in years and they wanted to get their estates in order, but the buying end of the equation was not very big. Make no mistake: A lot of people wanted to be in the gaming business, but when they saw the application for a license they found it very intimidating. I mean, when the Gaming Control investigators want to see your first bank account that you opened up when you were in high school, and every important document in your life, it gives a person pause, even if you're clean as hell.

When people would ask me, as they often did, do you think I can get licensed? My answer was: You're the only one who knows.

So the days dragged on before Christmas of '66, and Moe Dalitz was getting more and more upset that Hughes wasn't moving out. I'm not sure what Parry's recollection is of this but mine is that Hughes never thought of buying the Desert Inn at that point. He just wanted to stay there. And I'd say to Howard, "But we made them a promise."

His answer would be, "I didn't make them any promise. You did."

This is just one example of how challenging my role as his alter ego was to become.

## Brian Greenspun

I DON'T KNOW THAT ONCE HUGHES WAS IN THE HOTEL ANYONE HAD even thought ahead to the New Year's weekend. I don't know if anyone thought ahead till the day after Thanksgiving. Their thought was, let's get Howard situated in the hotel and then we'll go from there.

Remember, the Hughes people around him were all Mormons, so they don't drink, they don't smoke, they don't gamble. They're probably the worst customers you can have in a hotel. They don't buy anything, and if they do, they don't tip. And Hughes never leaves the room, so you don't even get the star power of Howard Hughes walking around the place. There's no upside, other than his paying the rental on the rooms.

So as New Year's approaches, it's time to think about moving this guy out to make room for the high-rollers.

Moe Dalitz wants him to leave, but Hughes doesn't want to leave because he's got no place to go. So they call my dad. I'm sure it was Maheu who made the call.

First thing Dad does is arrange for an alternative suite of rooms for him at the Riviera. It was the penthouse suite, and the whole adjoining floor. But Hughes didn't want to move. He had his urine bottles all lined up the way he wanted them—I'm making this part up—but you know it was a mess in his room, and he didn't want to leave the Desert Inn.

So now the challenge was, how do we keep this guy in Las Vegas? My dad's plan from the beginning was that if we had the opportunity to bring Howard Hughes here, we had to keep him here because he would bring legitimacy to the city. This was at a time when Bobby Kennedy was going nuts against organized crime. They're raiding the Stardust Hotel lock-boxes, the IRS and the FBI are everywhere, they've got wiretaps galore on casino owners' phones, and it's a really ugly situation.

My dad's thinking was that it was not possible to get rid of these crooked hotel owners in the mid-1950s, but he knew we really needed to get rid of them eventually because they were bringing way too much heat down on the town. And then he hears that Hughes wants to come to town, and if he comes and invests, we can bring some legitimacy to Las Vegas and at the same time have him buy some of these places and remove the heat the government was putting on us. That was Hank's dream scenario from day one. And I believe it was just his. He was thinking twenty years out. I'm not sure anybody envisioned the same scenario that he did, but I'm admittedly biased about this.

### Parry Thomas

I RECALL THAT ALL THE BIG NEW SUITES HAD ALREADY BEEN PROMISED to the Desert Inn's biggest players, who would be flying in from all over the country during the Christmas-to-New Year's holidays. These were all gamblers with big credit lines who were expecting comped rooms, and Moe just had to have those rooms. The amount of money these big players could be expected to lose had a large impact on the property's bottom line. And Howard wasn't going to move. His people said he was too sick to move.

Morris Kleinman, one of the owners of the hotel and a very tough guy, said, "I don't give a goddamn what they want to do. I'm going up there and pull him out personally and I'm gonna take a couple of my strongest security guards with me, and nobody better get in my way."

And he meant it. Morris wasn't the kind of guy you wanted to mess around with.

So this was a pretty desperate situation with a lot at stake for everyone. The stakes were very high for Las Vegas as well.

Ed Morgan and Hank Greenspun came to me and we had a meeting. We just had to work this thing out. At the time Hank had a deal in place to sell his golf course, Paradise Valley, to the Hughes organization, and he couldn't wait to get rid of it. So of course if they kicked Hughes out of the hotel and he left for someplace else, Hank was going to lose his golf course deal. Ed Morgan also wanted Hughes to stay in Las Vegas, for a number of reasons, and Ed said to me, "You've gotta think of something, Parry. You've gotta help us keep Hughes here."

I thought about it for a little while and I said, "There's only one guy in the world who could ask Moe Dalitz to let Hughes stay in the hotel and that he'd listen to. And that's Jimmy Hoffa."

I understood all the relationships. Ed Morgan was regarded as one of the outstanding constitutional lawyers in America, and Jimmy Hoffa was under federal indictment for racketeering and his trial was going to be scheduled in about a month. I think it's well known that Bobby Kennedy and Hoffa hated each other. There's even famous footage of the two of them verbally sparring in the hearings.

I suggested that if Ed would agree to write constitutional briefs for Jimmy Hoffa's defense, then I was certain Hoffa would ask Dalitz to allow Hughes to stay there.

So we called Jimmy Hoffa, and Hank did the talking because Greenspun knew Hoffa even better than I did. Hank told Hoffa the plan and explained to him that I had thought it up, and asked if he'd call Moe and arrange this, to work it out so that Howard Hughes could stay in the hotel over the holidays.

And the damndest thing happened. By coincidence, two days later I'm meeting Allard Roen for lunch in the old Cactus Room at the DI, when Moe saunters in and sits down next to us. And the phone rings right at the hostess stand beside us, and the hostess hands the phone to Moe. We're no more than five feet from Moe when he takes the call, and it's from Jimmy Hoffa.

And I can see Moe's eyes grow wide, and he says, "No, Jimmy. No, Jimmy. We *have* to have those rooms! We've already booked them. It means a lot of money to the organization."

The voices were so loud by this time that I could hear Hoffa on the other end, and he says, "It's my freedom we're talking about here! You have no choice, Moe!"

Finally, Moe says, "Okay, Jimmy," and—bam!—he slams down the receiver. And he's right next to me and his eyes are flaming red, and the real Mob instinct comes out of him. Moe turns and looks at me and says, "You're the only guy in the world that could have figured that out! You figured that out!"

One thing I'd learned about guys like Moe is that you never lie or evade anything. I said, "Moe, you're absolutely right. I did figure it out for your best interests. I'm going to have Howard Hughes buy this hotel. You're trying to sell it and I'm going to get you a fair price."

Moe sat there for several long minutes without saying a word. He then stood up and turned around and pointed his finger in my chest and said. "You better!"

And he stormed off.

## Brian Greenspun

DAD KNEW WHERE TO GO WHEN IT CAME TO CRUNCH TIME FOR RESOLV-ing the Howard Hughes situation at the Desert Inn. He didn't go to Moe Dalitz, because they didn't get along real well. He went to Parry Thomas, because Parry's the banker and he's one smart son of a gun. Parry knew all the right buttons to push to make something positive happen.

I never remember hearing the stuff about Jimmy Hoffa getting in the middle of the deal. The only thing I heard then, and I was just twenty years old at the time, was that Moe decided to let Hughes stay. Now maybe that was my father's way of shielding me from all the shenanigans back in the early days, but I have no reason not to believe Parry when he says he brought Jimmy Hoffa into it. It makes a whole lot of sense, in hindsight.

I don't know what Parry says about first meeting Hoffa, but my memory tells me Hank introduced Hoffa to Parry when Parry was just getting started at the Bank of Las Vegas [1955]. My dad knew Jimmy Hoffa when he first started the *Las Vegas Sun* in 1950, and I think that connection happened when Hoffa was instrumental in helping get arms shipments to Israel as the head of the Teamsters local union in Detroit. The longshoremen in New York were dropping the crates of arms on the docks and breaking them open, exposing machine guns and other artillery so they could claim that they deserved to get hazardous-duty pay, or something like that.

Well, that wasn't a good thing because the feds were looking for this stuff. So my dad was given the task of finding someone who would talk to the longshoremen and get them to stop doing this.

Members of Detroit's Purple Gang [*which Moe Dalitz was connected to*] were contacted and all of a sudden the longshoremen saw the light and quit breaking open the crates. Well, if you go back another year or two from that, there was a big fight between the Purple Gang and Jimmy Hoffa's crowd over control of the local Teamsters Union in Detroit. Hoffa won that fight, and then they all got in bed together. So it made sense that my father called this guy in Reno who was connected to the Purple Gang, a guy named [*Mert*] Wertheimer [*who had helped launch Reno's Nevada Club*] and he put a call in to Jimmy Hoffa, who helped solve this problem of sabotaging the arms to Israel. So that's the origin of the whole Hoffa-Las Vegas connection, at least in my memory.

With all that's been written about Jimmy Hoffa, it shouldn't be forgotten that Hoffa had a great affinity for working men and women. Hoffa, like Frank Sinatra, had a soft spot for people who were downtrodden, oppressed, pounced upon. The Israeli story was a very compelling story. In the early days Israel was made up predominantly of Jews who made it through the Holocaust, mostly eastern European Jews. It was mostly Jews who came from socialist countries who believed in workers' unions, all that kind of stuff. So there was that union affinity. Hoffa was moved by unionists, number one, and people who were being oppressed, number two. And when you had fifty million Arabs and a million and a half Jews, there was a lot of room for oppression. It's my belief that Hoffa played a major role in the founding of the State of Israel. And so he became very friendly with my father, who was totally passionate about that cause.

## Steve Wynn

THERE'S SOME BACKGROUND HERE THAT'S IMPORTANT TO UNDERSTAND. Parry was the guy for all the casino owners, and about the only one who wasn't his guy was Moe Dalitz. And that's because Parry had befriended Hank Greenspun.

Hank was the world's worst businessman. He was always tottering on bankruptcy, and if he went bust, that meant he would lose that land he bought out in the desert. [*The land in Henderson that eventually was developed as Green Valley.*] Whatever bucks Hank had he was putting into that land, which was just a few thousand an acre then. And his newspaper was always busting him. It always lost money. You know Hank was a PR guy at the Desert Inn and Moe fired him.

Parry said about Hank that he could be your strongest friend or your worst enemy.

## Bob Maheu

ED MORGAN WAS AN EX-FBI AGENT, AND HE WAS ALSO MY ATTORNEY in Washington, D.C., at the time. Jimmy Hoffa also owed me a favor. And that came through Edward Bennett Williams, who was a year behind me in college and was on the debating team with me.

Williams was more famous than Ed Morgan ever was. He later owned the Baltimore Orioles and Washington Redskins.

It should be clear that Hoffa didn't *ask* Moe to let Hughes stay on at the Desert Inn. He *told* him to let him stay. It was a command, not a request.

The idea at that point was that Hughes would get out of the hotel after the holidays, but he didn't get out. The calendar moves along and some time in early March I got a call from Jack Donnelly, an attorney I knew well from San Diego. He was Moe's attorney.

I had never heard Jack even say "hell," and he was absolutely furious and spewing every swear word that I've ever known. When he finally took a breath, I said, "Jack, tell me what's the problem."

He said, "I'll tell you what the problem is. I have in my hand a letter addressed to 'Howard R. Hughes, Penthouse at the Desert Inn Hotel, Receipt Requested.' And it came back to me with the note, 'Not known at this address.'

"Now if the son of a bitch is not there, let us have our suites. And if he is there, in forty-eight hours we're going to have security drag him down the steps and put him out in the street."

Obviously, that directive was coming straight from Moe Dalitz. So I called Hughes and basically told him that time was up.

Howard said, "What do you suggest we do?"

"If you want a place to sleep two days from now, you better buy this place," I said. And that's when the negotiating seriously started.

I called Del Webb, who was a good friend, and for whom I'd solved some zoning problems in California. I'd also helped him with some political contributions.

"You cannot do any better than having Parry Thomas take the lead on this purchase," Del said. "I have implicit faith and confidence in him."

And I'll repeat: Hughes never expected to buy a hotel when he came to Las Vegas. That wasn't in his plans. He bought the DI out of necessity because he was going to get thrown out. That was his only reason for making on offer on it at the time, but things changed. A little while later, when Howard fully realized all the tax advantages he could get from putting this money from his TWA sale into play, he called me on the phone laughing and said, "How many of these toys are available?"

I said, "Howard, what is this all about? Are you saying you want more hotels?"

"Strangely enough," he said, "I've been talking with my tax people in Texas and Washington, and the gross revenue of the casino qualifies as active income."

Active income was just what he needed. When TWA was sold, naturally all of the money from that $547 million was put into accounts where Hughes would draw optimum interest. But that is earned income, and therefore taxable. His accountants had told him he needed a ratio of active income to passive income of about four or five to one. So the Desert Inn could provide him that active income. But the casinos back then were small places compared to what we have today in Las Vegas, so the DI alone wasn't going to do all that he needed tax-wise. He had to buy other properties.

Hughes was excited when he talked to me about this. I remember him saying, "This is going to solve my tax problem, which has been worrying me to death."

That's when we really got aggressive in our buying.

Dean Elson was the head of the FBI office in Las Vegas at that time, and we were cooperating with him in trying to make the right moves. Things were not very good here at the time. The economy was in a downturn, and we knew that Hughes' interest in the city was beneficial to everyone. I've said this before, and it's true. If you went to central casting and tried to find one person who could do what Howard Hughes eventually did, you'd be hard put. Here was a man who had name recognition all over the world, by virtue of his oil ventures, his aviation exploits, and his movies. There was nothing in his record that would preclude him from obtaining a gaming license, and he had the ability to pay. He did not have a board of directors from whom he had to seek approvals. If he made up his mind to buy something, he could go and make a handshake deal and get it done quickly. He was the perfect buyer at the perfect time. And the government and Bobby Kennedy couldn't have been happier to see Hughes buying out these old owners, whom they had so much concern about.

## Parry Thomas

THE ORIGINAL SALE PRICE THAT WAS AGREED UPON WAS SIX AND A half million dollars. The lawyers were getting into it and doing all the work, and then about a week later I get a call from Bob Maheu. He says, "We've got terrible problems. Hughes is going to back out of the deal."

I asked what happened and he said that they'd learned that the Stardust owed the Desert Inn $300,000 from a previous loan, and because the hotels had the same ownership, and because it was an intra-company loan, that they were gonna wash it. Hughes was upset about this and he was not going to budge. He wasn't going to move an inch on the price.

Also at this same time, Moe Dalitz was getting seller's remorse, so everything we'd worked so hard on was at an impasse.

I said, okay, let's go figure this thing out. So I brought the parties together in a conference room next to Allard Roen's office. I didn't want to talk to anyone from the Desert Inn but Allard, because Roen never lost his temper. He was always a cool customer and you could get through to him. So Maheu's and Hughes' lawyers are there, and Allard is there, and Ed Morgan is there and in walks the famous Mob attorney Sydney Korshak and the notorious Johnny Roselli. Those guys sit down and they want to hear what my plan is. I guess they were representing themselves and the guys back in Chicago, whoever.

I tried to ask them to leave but they just stared at me. They weren't leaving.

I knew better than to press it, so I just started talking and every time I'd say something, Roselli would butt in. Finally Korshak grabs him by the arm and says, "Shut up! You're not to say anything!" And that quieted Roselli, who was one of the toughest mobsters that ever hit the West Coast.

Suddenly, it got very quiet in the room. There was so much at stake in this negotiation, as you can imagine.

I finally asked Allard, "How much is the morgue at the Desert Inn?" [*Each year casinos total up all their outstanding gambling markers, move them off the balance sheet, and charge them off as tax deductions. That amount is called "the morgue."*]

I knew that historically about twenty percent of those bad markers would eventually come forward and pay, because if the gamblers didn't settle them, they would never be allowed to gamble again. The information came back that the morgue was over $15 million, closer to $16 million, and that at least $1 million to $2 million, maybe even $3 million, was going to be recovered. At the very least, three times the $300,000 loan that was holding up the deal.

The morgue had never been included in the sale price. The DI's owners were going to keep the morgue. So I convinced Moe Dalitz and Allard Roen that the morgue had to go with the sale.

We wrote it all out for Hughes, that he would get the value of the morgue, which would be twenty to thirty percent productive, in our opinion, and that he would gain over a million dollars over the $300,000 outstanding loan to the Stardust.

That was acceptable to him to let the deal go through, and he bought the plan. And that's how the deal was finally consummated on the Desert Inn, and that's how Howard Hughes stayed there.

In sum, that's exactly how the richest man in America was allowed to stay in a hotel owned by the biggest gamblers in America, by the most outstanding lawyer in Washington agreeing to write a brief for the most notorious labor leader in the country. Now there's a four-way parlay for you.

That deal got me off the hook with Moe Dalitz, who had told me that I better make it happen. It's amazing how fast you can think when a man like that points his finger at you.

⚭

While I'm thinking about Johnny Roselli, let me say a thing or two about him. He was the kind of guy who'd just come over and sit down with you and start in. He didn't care if it was a private luncheon or a business meeting, he'd just jump right into the conversation. I knew he was connected to the Mob, but I didn't know how connected. So one day I asked a guy who would know about it, exactly what Johnny did in Las Vegas. The guy told me he really didn't do anything, but he collected revenue from the valet parking concessions all over town. He said that at several of the hotels whenever you valet-parked your car and gave the guy a dollar, Johnny got fifty cents of that. That's the deal the boys cooked up for him so he could make a living here.

I knew both Roselli and Sydney Korshak were from Chicago and that's why they were close. Syd was actually his boss. Syd was the number three guy in the whole Chicago syndicate. Sam Giancana was number one, and I heard that Roselli one time got as high as number two, but then slipped out of that.

Another story at the time was that when the government reopened the hearings on the Kennedy assassination, and heard testimony on Cuba and the attempted assassination of Fidel Castro, that there was a connection between the two. And both Johnny Roselli and Sam Giancana were subpoenaed to testify. As I heard the story, Jack Kennedy's father, Joe, had made arrangements through the Chicago Outfit to put a contract on Castro, and Roselli and Giancana were the two guys to get the job done. Bob Maheu knows a lot more about that than I do.

Anyway, I remember like it was yesterday how Roselli butted in on that meeting to get the DI sold, and how quickly Korshak shut him up.

[*Johnny Roselli was born Filippo Sacco in Esperia, Italy, in 1905. He did a three-year stretch for racketeering in the mid-1940s, and by the mid-'50s had become the Chicago Mob's chief representative in Las Vegas. His job was to ensure that the Chicago and Los Angeles Mob bosses each received their fair share of burgeoning casino revenues. He actually was listed as a movie producer on several Hollywood films during that time. After testifying in front of U.S. Senate committees in the mid-1970s on both the President Kennedy assassination and the plot to kill Castro, Roselli was murdered. His decomposing body was found on August 9, 1976, in a 55-gallon fuel drum floating off Dumfounding Bay near Miami. It was theorized that he had provided too much information at these hearings, thereby violating the strict Mafia code of omerta (silence).*]

## Brian Greenspun

THE MASTER PLAN, AT LEAST IN MY DAD'S MIND, WENT SOMETHING like this: Let's use the Mob to build the town and then get rid of the Mob when the town is big enough to support itself. And with Howard Hughes coming here, we had a man who provided the instant credibility in terms of attracting Wall Street, and the instant ability to get rid of the Mob ahead of Bobby Kennedy's minions who were focusing on corruption in Las Vegas.

These guys were all chess players, figuratively speaking. My dad and Bob Maheu and Parry.

## Parry Thomas

I'M THE GUY THAT GOT THE MOB OUT OF LAS VEGAS, WITH GETTING the legislation passed to have corporate gaming and putting in the safeguards such as anybody with over five percent interest in the

133

place having to stand for licensing. It didn't say you had to be licensed, just that you had to stand for it and be investigated for it and so on. And the thing that got the Mob out quicker than anything else was passing that law, because before that the corporations couldn't come in. If I'm insistent about taking the credit for that, it's because I did it all by myself and it took years of hard work and negotiating with the Legislature to make it happen.

∞

There are two sides to the issue of the Mob's role in building Las Vegas. In my viewpoint, I don't think they were builders at all.

When I arrived in 1955, the Mob was in full force running every hotel on the Strip. I don't know about downtown. I know they had influence in the El Cortez—New Jersey did—but keep in mind the whole situation was under the hierarchy of the Mob, and the important people in the Mob could never get licensed, so they hid behind shields.

Every individual involved in gaming had to be licensed separately and so every place had what they called points. There was a hundred points in each place. The Mob had people get licensed that they would have a piece of. A shield would get licensed and appear to have ten points and in reality he might have only half a point. All the rest belonged to the Mob.

The whole thing came down to the counting room and cutting up the take in there and siphoning off all the dollars. You could just not build a future under that type of operation because there wasn't that much money to begin with back then. The real owners couldn't identify themselves. They had to hide all the time.

Like Jakey Friedman had twenty points in the Sands and Jack Entratter had twenty points and Carl Cohen had ten points and so on. Aaron Weisberg had twenty and he probably owned only half of it because he was Meyer Lansky's man. This went on everyplace.

I don't think there's any question that Hank Greenspun knew the intimacy of the hotels as well as, or even better than I did. He started out with Bugsy Siegel, and from there graduated to the Desert Inn with Moe Dalitz and Wilbur Clark and those guys. He was very intimate with them originally, but the fact is they didn't trust him. They actually hated him, Moe Dalitz in particular.

One time Moe pinned me down at his house. It was at a dinner party and he took me into the bedroom and sat me down and said, "I want you to stop loaning money to Hank Greenspun. He said, "We got him on the ropes and we gotta break him. He's attacking us and we can't have him in this town any longer." [*Nate Mack had told Parry early in his career in Las Vegas to make certain that Hank Greenspun's newspaper never went out of business, that he was a friend and that he was to be protected at all costs . . .*]

I just had to stand up to him. I said, "Moe, I never talk about banking business of one individual with another, and I'm not going to talk about yours with him or his with you, and that's where I stand on it."

Moe respected that, and that was the end of it.

Hank might have seen the evolution of Las Vegas all along, but the Mob had absolutely no idea of building big here. It was all about hidden interest. Their whole involvement was predicated on getting involved in gaming and skimming off the top. Period. Their whole interest in the city was getting tax-free money.

Having said that, there's no question that Moe Dalitz was very good for Las Vegas. He was a real cornerstone in advancing all the good causes. When I formed the United Fund, which became the United Way, I went to Moe and explained to him that the community chest was in dire need of social services, and that the gaming business was going to feel some repercussions if the social services weren't taken care of. I remember telling Moe at the time that he and his people were very generous, that they were giving a lot of money for charity, but that it was all going back to Cleveland or wherever they came from, that they weren't giving it in Las Vegas. And it was like a light switch went on.

"You're absolutely right," he said. "We have to do more here."

So he joined with me in the United Fund effort, and we became the two drive chairmen.

Moe was the most effective drive chairman I ever saw. He never asked anybody how much they were going to give; he told them. And it worked out just fine.

## Brian Greenspun

WHEN NATE MACK SAW THE EXTENT OF PARRY'S TALENTS IN RUNNING the Bank of Las Vegas, and that he and his son Jerry could be effective partners, I know Dad said he was willing to help them. Dad liked Nate and Jerry already, and he saw that Parry was the kind of guy that Las Vegas needed, and so Parry became Dad's banker.

Well, early on my dad never had any money. I remember many, many times when we needed to make payroll for the newspaper, which was more times than not, and we'd go down and I would have to sign personally on loans. This happened for my dad in the '50s and '60s and for me in the '70s and '80s. Parry would make sure that we had the money for payroll that week, and it certainly wasn't me that that he was counting on for repayment. In many cases it was my dad's word that he was counting on.

Parry, in effect, was my dad's banker as well as his financial consigliere. He was also one of his closest friends, and vice versa. Those two men would go to war for each other. They were both visionaries and they were two of the very few who saw the vast potential of Las Vegas right from the beginning.

In a documentary film on my dad, Parry says something very flattering and respectful of Dad when he talked about his fighting the

Mob. Parry said my dad was the only one with the guts to stand up to them. And by saying that, he meant that Hank had the guts and he didn't. And that's a hard thing to say. But he said it and he meant it.

They all had their own missions along the way. Parry's mission was to get the money to people to build this city. My dad's mission was to get 'em here, then get rid of 'em and move on to greater respectability, and Parry helped greatly with that with his work on softening legislation for casino licensing. All these men we're talking about had their missions.

If I were asked to rank Parry Thomas regarding his importance to modern Las Vegas, I would certainly put him in the top five, perhaps the top three for all time. I'm admittedly biased, but I'd put Hank Greenspun number one, mostly because he was the moral force. In terms of impact, I'd put Moe Dalitz up there. I'd also add Jack Entratter and Nate and Jerry Mack.

If you look back from 2008 and make a list, it would certainly have to include Steve Wynn and Kirk Kerkorian, the great builders. All those names would belong in the top ten, easily, but their order would shift depending on who you talked to.

## Steve Wynn

I VIVIDLY REMEMBER MY INTRODUCTION TO PARRY THOMAS. IT WAS through Maury Friedman, and it happened just before we moved here permanently in 1967. I was a slot manager and had three points in the Frontier and I was responsible for raising some more money for the Frontier, which gave me another three points. There were the real owners and then there were the squares who were out front. I was one of the squares. But I had a relationship with John McArthur, which made Maury nervous. McArthur was the landlord and he wanted me in the count room.

Anyway, the introduction was made but I was like the caboose in the room. Maury said to Parry, "These are some of our stockholders," and then he turned to us and said, "Gentleman, this is our banker, Parry Thomas. He's the most important guy in Nevada."

It was like being introduced to a celebrity. During those years, from the mid-1950s on into the 1960s and late '70s, Parry was the only real source of money. He WAS the money. And then later on Mike Milken kicked in.

But for about twenty-five years Parry Thomas was Eeny, Meeny, Miney, and there was no Mo. That is the absolute truth. If you wanted to build a building, you wanted to build another tower, if you wanted to buy a casino, or if you wanted to get a bankroll loan for working capital, he was the one guy. Literally, the other bankers wouldn't do it. He and Jerry Mack would get the money.

First National Bank jumped up and down when Howard Hughes showed up, but Parry lured him away from them. Because Hughes wasn't looking for money. He was looking for contacts. And Parry had all of them.

He was the overwhelming dominant guy. It wasn't any of the casino owners. Parry walked in the building and they all stood at attention. I mean, he was their link to survival. These guys only had two or three hundred rooms in their hotels back then. They never felt secure. They could careen from one precipitous moment to another. This was before the convention bureau got going and large groups would come into town.

Only the Sahara and Stardust had big towers and a bigger room base. Fourteen hundred at the Stardust and a thousand at the Sahara. Those were monster hotels at the time. The Riviera, the Tropicana, the Thunderbird, the Flamingo, the Desert Inn, the Frontier, the Sands and the Dunes were all two or three hundred rooms with twenty-five or thirty games and two or three hundred slot machines.

## Tom Thomas

DID MY FATHER AND JERRY MACK AND HANK GREENSPUN AND BOB Maheu sit around and discuss these big questions about where Las Vegas was going, and how it was going to get there? I suspect they did, whether it was at lunch at the Desert Inn or after a game of tennis or an afternoon on a boat out on Lake Mead.

These were men who cared deeply about this city. Their financial and personal fortunes and those of their children were tied irrevocably to this odd place in the desert, and they were in positions, each with their own individual strengths and areas of expertise, to greatly influence the directions Las Vegas would take.

Did they discuss the political ramifications of certain events happening, such as Howard Hughes coming to town and purchasing hotels, and thereby giving the city the image of a place where legitimate businessmen could come and make smart investments? I would say definitely they did.

## Peggy Thomas

PARRY'S ATTITUDE ABOUT THE PEOPLE HE MET IN THE GAMBLING INDUStry in those first years was that what they were doing in Las Vegas was legal. They may have learned the business someplace else where it wasn't legal, but they were engaged in a legal industry here. Many of them were experts in the business and very smart men. If Parry was going to be a good banker, he was certainly going to have to deal with those who ran this major industry.

So we got to know them all well. We'd have them to functions at our house, and we would meet them socially. The people that we met were nice, and they were good family people. I didn't have any reason not to like them. Actually, I was usually very impressed with them.

## Steve Wynn

THE GUYS WHO CAME OUT HERE WERE EX-BOOKMAKERS, GUYS WHO came out here with the Jews and their families to get peace and quiet and not have to worry about getting pinched anymore. These were men like Eddie Levinson, Jake Friedman, Aaron Weisberg at the Sands, and Ross Miller, whose son Bob was our governor and whose grandson Ross is our secretary of state. Carl Cohen was in a different category. He was a gambler who knew how to run games and knew how to run a casino. Jack Entratter was a club owner from New York, and nothing's bad if you're in with that kind of guy. He ran the Copacabana. Then there was the Dunes group with Charlie Richardson, Sid Wyman, and Major Riddle. They were guys who had committed victimless crimes all their lives, running crap games and taking bets on sports.

These were nice people, most of them Jewish, who wanted peace for their families and a little respectability. Dalitz was another one of those guys. He might have been a little tougher than the rest, but nobody was as tough as Benny Binion. Binion was the only real live shooter in the group. The other guys were bootleggers and they came here and ran casinos.

## Bob Maheu

PARRY MADE FRIENDS QUICKLY AND GAINED PEOPLE'S CONFIDENCE effortlessly. He wouldn't judge a person by their past or by rumor. I've met so many people who were so easily disposed at condemning the old-timers. Now, on two different occasions before congressional committees, when I was asked about so-called old-timers, I told them that as a category, I'd never met a nicer people. And Parry recognized that as well. I think Parry was partially responsible for my arriving at that appraisal.

The fact that I remember Syd Wyman and how he had been in an illegal crap game at age 15 does not make him a bad person when he's a good person in his sixties. You know? And all this crap about they all belong in jail is nonsense. They were nice people. They lived well. They had nice families, and they knew how to run gambling. Most importantly, if they gave you their word, you could live by it.

## Bill Boyd

I USED TO GO INTO THE BANK OF LAS VEGAS WITH MY DAD, SAM, WHEN I was a boy, because Dad owned some stock in the bank. My dad knew Nate Mack quite well. My dad borrowed money from Parry at the bank intermittently, and I also borrowed some money when we were building the Hotel Nevada downtown. It was a several-million-dollar loan, which was big in those days.

What impressed me about Parry was that he seemed to be much more interested in the character of the people he was loaning to than how much security they had for the loan. Parry and Kenny Sullivan also helped us when we were building the California Hotel downtown in the early 1970s.

I know before Parry got here, people in our industry were just not able to get loans from the two banks here. At the Thunderbird, where my dad worked for a while, it created quite a problem. The owner, Marion Hicks, ran out of money, and from all the stories I've heard, he had to go to Meyer Lansky, the top guy in the Mob, to get the money to finish the building. Same thing happened to Wilbur Clark at the Desert Inn, because the banks here wouldn't have anything to do with them. That all changed after Parry arrived in town, although those other banks still wouldn't make loans to gambling for many years.

When I moved here with my parents in 1941, the gaming industry was more important to Las Vegas overall than it is today, because we have so many other things here now. And yet, the banks' attitude was that we were second-class citizens in the gambling industry. Parry made us feel important, and that we were his partners, and that he would support us all the way.

I would say that the two most important people in the twentieth century for the future of our community were Parry Thomas and Howard Hughes.

Parry's importance was for opening up the marketplace. His belief in the gaming community in Las Vegas legitimized our industry. Then Howard Hughes comes along in the late 1960s, a man who at the time was considered the wealthiest man in the world, and he silenced all the doubters about Las Vegas. When he came in and invested the amount of money that he invested here, not only our country but the world said, wait a minute, if Howard Hughes is willing to invest there, then Las Vegas must be okay after all.

Those two men had the most profound effect on our city's image and ability to grow. You can put them one and two, in whatever order you prefer.

## Bob Maheu

SO AFTER HUGHES HAD BOUGHT THE DESERT INN—SO THAT HE COULD stay there and get the tax advantages—there were other problems to solve. If he was going to take advantage of the active income, he had to run the casino. Howard knew nothing about running a hotel, even less about the gaming.

I went to Parry Thomas and told him we were way above our heads with this. This was not my bag, and it wasn't Howard's bag. I asked his advice on what we were to do going forward, and he said, "Keep the people in place who are running it now. They're the best in the business."

The perception in Las Vegas was that with my background in the FBI, we would come in with bulldozers and get rid of everybody working in the hotel, but Parry wisely advised us against doing that.

I used Sid Wyman as an adviser. Cecil Simmons was helpful. Al Benedict was a terrific operator. Through those years we relied on the smartest people in the business. Carl Cohen was a great operator at the Sands, when we bought that hotel.

We got the accounting firm that had been handling things for Hughes in Texas, Haskins and Sells, to come into Las Vegas and set up accountability systems. They were foolproof.

Parry advised us that Haskins should come up with an accounting system that was completely divorced from the operation of the casino. I remember him asking me once, "Have you ever been in a casino cage?"

I told him, "No."

He said, "Good. Don't ever go in the cage. Don't ever handle the money."

That advice turned out to be very beneficial to me later on.

I must say I never felt competitive with Parry Thomas in any way. He helped me in countless ways, so I looked up to him. The others in the Hughes organization would have beaten my ass if it hadn't been for Parry. I mean I'm even wanting to plead guilty to not being a good businessman, and he was.

I don't know on how many occasions Howard would tell me he wished he had Parry working for him full time to solve problems. He just felt that Parry was the brightest guy on the block who could work his way through every situation. He trusted him implicitly. He even entrusted Parry with all of his personal housing problems in Las Vegas. It was Parry who got the houses for Howard's wife, Jean Peters, when she was planning on moving here.

## Parry Thomas

I GET A CALL FROM MAHEU ONE DAY AND HE SAYS THAT HOWARD HAS everyone all upset, that Jean Peters is planning to move to Las Vegas and she won't stay in a hotel. Howard had instructed Bob to buy her a house, and Maheu said he had found one on East Oakey by the Jewish Temple. I knew the house he was talking about and it wasn't a very good house. It was just a lot of tinsel, not the kind of house you'd think of when it came to Howard Hughes and his wife.

The first thing you've got to think about in that situation is security, and I don't think that had been given much thought. I was up in Reno when I got the call. We had started a new bank up there and officially changed the name statewide from Bank of Las Vegas to Valley Bank. Can you imagine with all the intrastate rivalry in Nevada how the people of Reno would have responded to a bank in their back yard called Bank of Las Vegas? We wouldn't have had a single account.

Anyway, Maheu wanted to send their plane up to Reno right then and bring me back down, but I told him I could get to the airport and fly commercial and get there faster. Everything had to be done immediately when you were working with Hughes.

I got back to Las Vegas and met with Maheu and told him about a house on Edgewood Street that had ten acres and very good security control to it. The house belonged to Major Riddle, the owner of the Dunes, and he and his wife were getting divorced and she was desperate to sell the house and move back to her home in Denver. Norma Riddle was really in bad shape emotionally at that time. One of her three sons had recently committed suicide, and she was splitting up from Major and her life was really in a shambles.

It was about six in the evening when Maheu and I looked at the house. I got the electricians and the plumbing guys and the air-conditioning guys to assess the house and give me their findings, and then I wrote up a detailed report about it for Hughes. He was really insistent that these reports be very complete and accurate.

Norma was a lovely lady and I really felt bad for her and her predicament. The son that she'd lost was named Charlie Riddle, and he'd gotten mixed up with some bad guys and some drugs, and his life just spiraled out of control.

The other house that Maheu and the others had looked at was owned by a guy named Rylie, and he'd recently moved back to San

Diego. It was the next thing to a whorehouse, with all these gaudy decorations. But the realtors had made up a pretty pamphlet and made it look much better than it was. But again, it had no land around it for security.

This was all happening in the summer of 1967, after Hughes had been here for about seven or eight months. I had Peg and the family down at our place in Newport, where we went every summer to get out of the heat. Jerry Mack had his family down there, too. During the week Jerry and I would take a two-bedroom suite in one of the Strip hotels in the summers because that made things much easier than staying in our own large homes. We'd go down to Newport with the families on the weekends. It was just easier staying in a hotel to get our laundry done and get our meals there. So we'd just close up the Las Vegas houses for the summer.

At this time I was staying on the eighth floor of the Desert Inn, on the floor right below Hughes, and by midnight of the same day that I'd been contacted by Maheu, I got all this information about the two houses to Howard. About an hour later, I got a call from Maheu. Hughes was so nocturnal that he'd call at all hours of the night. It seemed like he never slept.

Maheu says, "The boss says to buy both houses, and then we'll let Jean have her choice."

So then I tried to go back to sleep and about three hours later the phone rings again, and Maheu says, "Hughes has been thinking about this. If he owns those houses and everybody knows he owns those houses, people are going to stare at them and drive by them all the time. He says he wants you to buy them and lease them to him."

So here's another situation to be resolved. Jerry and I, as always, are partners in everything, so we buy these two houses and lease them to Hughes. We close them in our name.

The next morning we get another phone call from Maheu—check that, I got a written note from Hughes. I should have kept it but I didn't. I didn't keep anything written down on paper. To paraphrase the note, it said, "Thanks for everything, but now I want everybody out of those houses within twenty-four hours."

No one was in the Rylie house, but Norma was still living in the Riddle house. So I had the uncomfortable job of going to see Norma and telling her she had to move within twenty-four hours.

I'll never forget what she said: "You tell that rich son of a bitch that I couldn't even pack my sewing basket in twenty-four hours." Those were her very words.

I got thinking real fast, because I had to have her out of there and I felt very badly for her at the same time. Plus, her mother was living with her. My family was down at our Newport Beach house, and Norma had been over to our house on the corner of Alta and Rancho Road a few times and I knew she liked the house.

"Peggy's living at the beach this summer and I'm living at the Desert Inn, so why don't you just move into our house?" I said. "I promise you that we'll see that all the packing is done in perfect order and every box will be itemized and numbered, listing every item in it. And we'll do that for nothing and you won't have to worry about a thing."

She looked at me with tears in her eyes—here she'd lost a son and Major had run off and was divorcing her, and she had her mother to take care of and she was just as busted up as she could be.

"You're crazy," she said, "but I'm so down I have to take you up on it." She moved into our house that next day.

My next problem is that I'm now scared to call Peggy. I didn't have the guts to tell Peggy what I'd done, but I had no other choice. I was under orders from Hughes to make it happen immediately, and I followed those orders.

Rumors started to fly about what had happened, and reporters were trying to pick up on where Jerry and I had bought property and why. So I had to be careful where I went. I avoided bars and restaurants and either ate dinner at the home of Kenny Sullivan, who was the

COO of our bank who lived down the road from our house, or I'd eat at the hotel.

Kenny's barbecuing steaks for us at his house one night about two weeks after this, and I drive by our house on Alta and there's a big party going on. Cars are parked all over our lawn and up and down the street.

Norma Riddle's teenage son was having a birthday, so he asked his parents if he could invite a couple of friends over to the house for a small party. Norma told him he could invite a maximum of seven people and reminded him to be careful because it wasn't their house. Well, he invited seven and those seven invited seventy and seventy invited seven hundred, the way high school kids do.

When I went into our master bedroom, where Peggy had just bought a beautiful new bedspread from Portugal, there was a cigarette hole right in the middle of it. And of course neither of us smoked. The house was as thoroughly trashed as it could be. So now what was I to do?

I was pretty shook up about our house, but the more I thought about it, Peggy and I were never really satisfied with that house. It was on that busy corner and we were always worried about the kids and dogs running out into the street. It had been an old broken-down house when we bought it, and we'd done what we could to fix it up.

Rex Hardy was one of our officers at the bank at the time, and I knew there was one lot left at Rancho Circle, and he was the administrator of it. I quickly called him and asked if we still had that lot, he said, yes, and I said, good, because I just bought it, for whatever the price is. I was really scrambling to patch the tires that night, I remember that. So then I called Peggy and I lied a little bit and told her that I'd just bought the lot she liked over in Rancho Circle and that she could get a hold of her architect, Ron Molen, and her interior decorator, Jinny Snow, and go for broke because we were going to build a nice house on that lot.

I was at the bank about four days later and Peggy called and said she was talking to somebody and she understood that someone was living at our house.

So I lied again and said, "Well, as long as we're building a new house, I thought you wouldn't mind if I rented ours for a little while and got some income out of it."

She seemed okay with that, and then we talked it over some more and we decided that it might be a good experience for the children to go to school there in Newport for one year while we were building the new home. We had a nice big home in Newport, full of bedrooms, and Peggy and the kids loved it down there.

So that was going along okay, for about a month, until one day when George Larson, my tax attorney from Salt Lake, was in Las Vegas for a board meeting. I told him what we were doing and he said, "Oh no you're not. You get those kids back here in school in Las Vegas. If you don't, you're going to end up paying California taxes big time."

## Steve Wynn

LOST IN ALL THE STUFF ABOUT MOE DALITZ WAS WHAT A TWINKLING sense of humor he had. One year Elaine and I were at his place in LaCosta during the Tournament of Champions. He actually gave me my first German shepherd, a dog we named Killer.

Anyway, we were sitting around with some of the golfers, Arnold Palmer and Miller Barber and Doug Sanders were there, and when he introduced me to the guys he said, "Steve Wynn's a liquor distributor, the same business I was in."

"Yeah, but you had less overhead. You made money," I said.

I then asked him how fast his boats were that were on the Detroit River, running that booze.

He held his fingers about an inch apart and said, "Just this much faster than the government."

He said it wasn't like in the movies. That nobody got shot, nobody got killed. Everybody wanted a drink. Even the politicians. He said that everyone was sympathetic to the bootleggers, but then there was always someone in the hard-ass department who would enforce prohibition, but basically it was limp-wristed enforcement. It was fun. It was cops and robbers without any danger.

He said, "You know, Steve, it's not like the drugs dealers with all the violence. If you got caught with a boatload, you got arrested. But you didn't have to hide in shame. If you ran a casino, you paid off the D.A., and then if there was a change of administration and there was a crusader, you were screwed, but then the crusader'd get thrown out because he usually didn't know how to run the government.

"We ran the Beverly Club in Covington, Kentucky, for seventeen years," Moe said. "And we never missed one night. We had Sophie Tucker, Abbott and Costello, Frank Sinatra, Lena Horne, Martin and Lewis. Never missed a single night."

And then, after setting me up perfectly to give him the straight line he was looking for, I said, "Well, if you went seventeen years, why did you close?"

Moe looked at me with those blue-gray eyes, and said, "We found out it was against the law!"

He delivered that line with the perfection of Gregory Peck in an Academy Award-winning role. Arnold Palmer about fell down laughing, and so did the other Tour guys. I'll never forget it. I'm like in my late twenties at the time and here was Moe Dalitz holding court for Elaine and me and all these great golfers. He really had a great sense of humor.

## Parry Thomas

CONNECTED TO THE ARRIVAL OF HUGHES IN LAS VEGAS AND HIS ACQUIsition of hotels—which meant the removal from power of some of those colorful characters that were part of the old guard of casino operators—was the necessity of changing legislation on gaming licenses in Nevada to make it more palatable for corporate ownership.

One of my proudest accomplishments, and on a scale with anything I did in Las Vegas, was the fact that I almost single-handedly forced through new laws which paved the way for corporate gaming in Nevada. It was about a three-year-long process, and I stayed with it until I got it done.

I ran up against a brick wall when I first started. His name was Bill Harrah. In the 1960s Bill Harrah had all the power in the Nevada State Legislature, and I was about to get my first lesson in how it worked. But I learned and I learned fast.

In the banking laws of Nevada, as they were written then, it stated in the code of regulations that the state treasurer of Nevada was to keep all state demand deposits in Nevada banks. Then there's a clause after that, in smaller type, that said, "at Carson City." First National Bank therefore had all the state's deposits. Now this law had been crafted during the Great Depression, during which every bank in Nevada failed except First National. That stipulation had been written into the language of the law by an attorney in Reno named Bill Cashell, and it so happened he was First National's attorney and they had the only bank branch in Carson City.

I just thought that was the damnedest law when I learned about it, and how unfair it was for all the other banks all through Nevada, which could not get any deposits from the state. This was particularly true in Southern Nevada, because of the intrastate rivalry and the Northern-based power of the Legislature.

So I got a state representative from Elko who agreed that the law was unfair to introduce a bill into the Assembly that would delete the words "at Carson City." Well, the great day came and he got the bill introduced, and we were able to get it out of the committee and onto the voting schedule and guess what happened? I got one vote, and that was the guy who introduced it for me, and he never got elected again. So that was my introduction to politics in Nevada. I thought to myself, I better learn from this lesson and figure out how to get things done in this political process.

As I mentioned, Bill Harrah was the key to getting things done in that Northern Nevada-based Legislature.

Harold Smith, who had Harold's Club, had been the kingpin of gaming up north, but Bill Harrah came along and passed him up. Bill had come out of Stanford University, he was an extremely bright guy, and he worked hard at it and passed Harold up. He deserves all the credit for being an outstanding businessman.

[*Bill Harrah used his influence to create the original Nevada Gaming Board in 1955, an organization used to regulate gaming in Nevada. In 1959, Harrah helped create an even stronger Gaming Commission to regulate the casinos in Nevada with the intent of ridding them of corruption and crime.*]

Getting this legislation passed to allow corporate gaming in Nevada was a monumental feat. That may be the most far-reaching thing we ever accomplished because can you imagine the limits that would have been put on Las Vegas growth without publicly traded companies coming in here? But there were some big hills to climb in getting that legislation passed.

Bill Harrah's attitude initially was that he didn't want corporations coming in and invading his turf up north. He wanted to protect what he'd built up, because by the time we approached him he had the best properties in South Tahoe, and he ended up owning the best places on Virginia Street in Reno.

But an essential law of economics is that when you build a business up to its maximum potential or capacity, there comes a time to sell it.

My whole philosophy in economics, and particularly in Las Vegas—the thinking that guided me from the very beginning—were the simple lessons I learned in school in a class called Econ 1. And that is that there are three steps in operating a company: There's Phase

One, the pioneer phase, the start-up, usually it's a ma-and-pa shop or the small formation of a company by an individual or a group of individuals. If they are successful in that business, then they are entitled to go into a Phase Two, which is the expansion phase. The expansion phase makes them bigger, but that usually requires credit— help from a bank or lending institution. When they expand, if they are real good at their business, then comes further expansion. But there will come a time when that business gets really large and they enter Phase Three, which is corporate acquisition and merger. That's the way the economics in America are structured. And those three steps, those principles, never left my mind from the first day I studied economics. It was ingrained in my mind that when I got into the banking business, those principles of Econ 1 would guide my thinking.

When I moved to Las Vegas and started running the Bank of Las Vegas, I was attracted by the fact that the city was already in the pioneering phase. We came in and were willing to loan money to the gaming industry, so we were providing capital for Phase Two, the expansion phase. And when we did loan expansion money, if the loans ever got in trouble, we'd expand them even more—make the hotels even bigger—because there's big leverage in gaming.

But the question in Nevada became, how, with the cockeyed intrusive licensing process, do we get to the third phase of corporate takeovers and acquisitions?

It was very helpful that at that time I was on the Nevada State Board of Finance, and Jerry Mack was on the state's insurance board, so we were able to use our political connections in that regard.

I knew that I had to somehow force the state Legislature to approve corporate gaming. I started in about 1963 or '64 working with the governor, Grant Sawyer, and certain legislators. I started hammering on them about the importance of this, and I explained to them my theories about corporate licensing and how it should be formed and administered. I explained how the clause of full disclosure under SEC rules would be a major tool in the control of gaming.

I had learned as I handled company bank accounts and personal accounts, particularly for all the major owners of the casinos, that the law was that every individual in gaming had to be licensed and approved. And I saw two things happening. One was that as I went around the country gathering up money for these expansion loans, one of the questions from lending institutions that continually popped up was, how can we loan money to an organization where if the top operators die or quit or get removed, there's no succession of the management? What happens then?

I couldn't adequately answer the question. The only thing I'd say was that somebody would have to come in and buy the property or take over, and then those individuals would have to be licensed as well.

Well, that was very cumbersome and unsure, there was nothing positive about it, and that was disquieting to money lenders.

The second thing that bothered me even more was that when some of my older friends and operators passed away, whether they owned two points or five points or ten points, whatever they owned would have to be sold either to existing management—people already licensed—or if outsiders were brought in, they'd have to wait and go through the licensing process, whether it be six or nine months, for suitability to be determined. That was also awkward and cumbersome, and the value of the points in the property would plummet in the meantime and it wasn't fair, it wasn't right. I could imagine my own estate being caught up in such a mess.

Plus I knew inwardly back in the '60s that it was just a matter of some years before the influence of the Mob in the casinos would inevitably have to falter and go by the road. It just couldn't keep going on and going on.

I recognized that if we could get to Phase Three, the next business level, that we could be successful in bringing in public corporations who would report to the SEC on their full disclosure forms, and this would lead to a diminishing influence of the Mob. It might take time, but it would work.

So I started with Grant Sawyer, and then Paul Laxalt defeated him for governor in November of 1966, and so I worked with Paul once he was in office.

☙

We were eventually able to get Bill Harrah's attorney, Mead Dixon, who was also the executor of his estate, to understand the problems Bill was going to have after he was gone. There was no logical heir to take over the operation, and without corporations becoming players in the gambling industry he would be limited in what he could do.

I tried to talk to Bill several times about it, recognizing that he had a political office up north and basically controlled most of the votes in the Legislature, but I could never get through to him. I was finally able to get through to Mead Dixon, who was a very bright fellow and who understood very well the implications for Bill Harrah's estate if this didn't go through.

I said to him, "When Bill dies, you've got a helluva problem. Who are you gonna sell the company to? And what are you gonna get for it when you do try to sell it?

Mead finally said, "You're absolutely right."

I told Mead that we had to create a marketplace for Bill, that he had to go public and that he would be the biggest beneficiary of the introduction of corporate gaming. I said to Mead that he needed to explain to Harrah that he would make the most money for his properties if he would listen to our reasoning. Finally, I had a meeting with Mead and Bill together, and Bill agreed, with certain limitations, to allow us to go ahead and introduce the legislation. We got Laxalt to call a special meeting of the state Legislature in July of 1967.

## Michael Milken

THE RELATIONSHIP I WAS TO HAVE WITH PARRY THOMAS IS ACTUALLY linked to Bill Harrah. In the mid-1970s I had a chance to meet Bill Harrah, who had a relationship with Parry. Bill was just a prince of a human being, but my own firm [*Drexel Burnham Lambert*] would not let me raise capital for him.

When I moved to California from New York, shortly after my arrival there an event was scheduled to honor Harvey Silbert. I believe it was the Scopus Award at Hebrew University. I bought a table for the event at the Beverly Hilton. So I get a note from one of the crack due diligence groups in New York telling me they're not sure I should go to this event, because did I know that Harvey Silbert was involved with Frank Sinatra and a lot of the gambling crowd in Las Vegas. And the note said that he was friends with Parry Thomas and Jerry Mack and others, and that this was perhaps a relationship that I should not be associated with.

I told them that I had never met finer individuals than Parry Thomas or Harvey Silbert, and that they should go back and figure out their analysis more carefully, that they didn't know what they were doing.

I went the night they honored Harvey and after that I invited him as the very first outside board member of the Milken Family Foundation. I will never forget that night, and it led to my determination that among the best human beings our country had produced were associated with gaming.

I knew that Parry Thomas was instrumental in allowing the control of casinos to pass to corporations and entities and away from individuals in the late 1960s. What a monumental accomplishment that was. It just strikes me, as I think back about those days, how far the public perception was from reality about these people in gaming. Eventually Steve Wynn was the first person that our firm allowed us to bring capital to. Before then we could trade the security but not raise the capital.

I'd put Parry Thomas in the top five in his importance to Las Vegas. It took someone who was willing to commit and put their reputation on the line for capital to build that city. He not only put his own reputation on the line, he put the financial success of his financial institution on the line to help build a city he loved and was committed to.

In baseball terminology, he not only took Las Vegas from A-ball up to double-A or triple-A, he brought it to the major leagues and the World Series and the Olympics.

## Parry Thomas

ONCE PAUL LAXALT KNEW THAT BILL HARRAH HAD GIVEN THE GREEN light, he was very much in favor of doing it. He understood the long-term value of this, and I made a point of explaining that he could be known as the governor who fathered in this legislation. He liked the political stature of that.

I well remember a couple of sweaty afternoons up in Carson City. It was really hotter than heck and I made a couple of speeches to the Legislature while there was no air-conditioning.

We outlined the legislation and explained that anybody who owned five percent or more of a corporation had to stand for licensing. Also, the board of directors would have to be licensed, as would anyone that the Control Board and Gaming Commission designated as key people in the operation of the corporation. Those were the basic principles of the law. During the process of trying to get this on, Barron Hilton came to me and said he wanted to buy the International Hotel from Kirk Kerkorian. Kirk wanted to sell to Hilton, but Barron knew he couldn't get Hilton licensed.

Barron came to me and explained the situation and I told him we'd take a shot at it. So right in the middle of arguing with the Legislature and everyone else at that time, I brought Barron Hilton to Carson City and met with Governor Laxalt. As it happened Barron was the first guy that was able to take advantage of the new corporate gaming laws when he completed the purchase of the International in 1970.

When Bill Harrah finally went public, he was able to get over a couple hundred million dollars in value for his stock. But for one reason or another, his estate was a real mess when he died in 1978.

Bill never liked me too much. He did all his banking business with First National. Harrah once made the statement to Mead Dixon that he didn't do banking with me because I knew too much and had made quite a bit of money and that I was too wealthy for him to do business with. He wanted somebody to control and he knew he couldn't control me.

So going back to Hank Greenspun's idea about the Mob's importance here, I would differ in my opinion. They came here because Nevada was the only one of the fifty states where casino gambling was legal. I was on the board of the Del Webb company and one day Del quoted Bugsy Siegel to me. Bugsy had told him, "Guys like us would walk through a river of cowshit up to our ears to have gambling legal everywhere."

I'll never forget that expression.

It's been interesting to see what happened with the Harrah estate after Bill's death. Holiday Inn, run by Phil Satre, came in and took it over and made a big success of it. Then they bought Caesars' properties, and now it's the biggest gaming company in the world, with something like fifty different places. None of that would have occurred without that legislation allowing corporations to come into Nevada. It was that legislation also that set the stage for Steve Wynn and others to come in and have public financing. It opened up all the work that Michael Milken later did for Steve and other Strip properties. Without those laws being passed, nobody could move. They were on dead center.

Before that, I was running around like a fireman trying to find money, even the Teamsters' money, and making endless trips to Dallas and Galveston and New Orleans and all over, trying to find money to participate in these bank loans. It was really just a Mickey Mouse arrangement when you looked at it from the overall financing standpoint, although I'm very proud of what we were able to accomplish.

Prior to corporate gaming being allowed, there was no protection for the estates of people who had created their life's work in the gambling business. And that bothered me to no end. We had to get more sophisticated in Nevada and we had to stay ahead of economic events as they presented themselves.

Of course it would be a few years before the Mob was totally cleared out of Las Vegas. The funny business carried on even into the late '70s, when they started playing games with the Stardust and Tony Spilotro and Frank Rosenthal got in there and it became a real mess.

∞

Getting back to Howard Hughes, it was a shame what happened to him as the years went by. The split with Bob Maheu was unfortunate. I like Bob very much and think he did great work for Hughes in Las Vegas, but what happened to him with Hughes and the guys they called the Mormon Mafia was partly brought on by Bob himself. As the months and years went by, and he was the top guy representing Hughes in all these major acquisitions, he started living like Howard Hughes himself should have been living. He had them build a big house for him on the Desert Inn golf course, and he traveled well and lived in style. I believe resentment set in from those others around Hughes.

I could tell from the other fellows that there was an edge there. Bob had a boat he was using and he was flying all around and I think an outright jealousy emerged from the internal structure around Hughes, and I think Bill Gay was involved in it. And Bill was a good friend of mine.

I put Bill Gay on the board of the University of Utah when I was on it, and that was very important because the school became a beneficiary of the Hughes Medical Foundation money for grants.

The only guy I didn't care for was one of the prominent attorneys for Hughes, who I know worked hard behind the scenes to oust Bob Maheu from the Hughes organization. I just had an inherent reaction to be on guard and watch my back and be extra careful what I said around him, and I'm sure that Maheu had the same problem with him.

As I said, I never saw Hughes in person during the '60s. The last time I'd talked with him in person was with Jakey Friedman at the Sands Hotel in the late '50s. There are important people who say they saw Hughes in the '60s, but I would be suspicious of some of those stories. I mean if Maheu never saw him, how could these other people get meetings with him?

In hindsight, the impact of Howard Hughes moving here when he did was just enormous. I think more than anyone else who was here at the time, I realized the depths of the financial depression this city was in just before Hughes came here. We were having real troubles in Las Vegas, corporate influence hadn't yet set in, and we were scrambling at the bank to keep things on an even keel.

There's so much ballyhoo about Hughes and so many different stories. Some of the purchases that were made I didn't agree with. There has been a lot written about Hughes and Kirk Kerkorian, and the competition between them. When Kerkorian announced that he was going to build the International [*now the Las Vegas Hilton*], I was asked by the Hughes people to study the Landmark, which was across the street. I went through that study from top to bottom and all over, and I wrote about an eight-page yellow-sheet report on it. With Hughes, you wrote only one report and that was it. He got it, you didn't keep any copies, and that was the rule. In that report I told him it was a terrible situation, that the place was built upside down. The casino was located on top of the building then, and that didn't make any sense to me. You could never make it economically there because there weren't enough rooms and you couldn't haul in enough customers or food or anything. You couldn't make a go of a three-shift business there. The floor plan would only afford so many tables, particularly crap tables because of their size.

The owner, who as I recall was connected to the Mob, was asking $8 million for the Landmark at the time and I just absolutely slammed the hell out of it in that report. The next thing I knew, about a half year later and unknown to me, they sent Maheu or whoever in there and ended paying some god-awful price like $18 million for it. I have to think it was connected to ego, and the fact that Kerkorian was building the International across the street and Hughes wanted to own a taller building than Kirk's. I had absolutely nothing to do with that sale. Sure enough they eventually had to tear the damn thing down. It was impossible economically. It was a helluva good piece of land, though. I wrote in the report that if they could buy the land cheap enough, it had some land value.

There weren't a lot of buyers out there for these Strip properties. Carl Cohen and I had been to Dallas to meet people we thought might buy the Sands, but we found the market was flat.

Then Hughes comes here with all the publicity surrounding that, and the charisma and aura of this man, with all his wealth and fame, just lit a fire under everything. If you took all the wealthy guys in Las Vegas together, the sum total of their wealth wouldn't have equaled that of Howard Hughes at that time. His presence and involvement gave us the Good Housekeeping seal of approval. Las Vegas was no longer just a place for old gambling guys with shaky backgrounds.

As we started buying properties for him—and I spent over $300 million of his money—we instantaneously had eighty or ninety millionaires running around town. It was unbelievable how the wealth trickled down. You just couldn't make a bad loan in that kind of atmosphere.

*(Top row, l to r) Olive Etta Parry (mother) and Julia Parry (grandmother); (bottom row l to r) E. Parry Thomas, and his older sisters Myrene and Marian, 1924.*

*Thomas Edward Thomas and son Parry, age four, 1925.*

*Parry Thomas, age 7, in a goat cart in Ogden.*

*Thomas Edward Thomas, age 16.*

*Thomas Edward Thomas
and Olive Etta Parry, E.
Parry Thomas' parents,
early 1920s.*

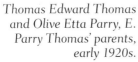

Mona Chatterton Young, Peggy's mother.
Peggy Chatterton at age six, 1932.

Jack Chatterton, Peggy Thomas' biological father.

Parry Thomas as an Air Force Cadet, 1942, age 21.

(left) Las Vegas Sun Editor/owner/publisher Hank Greenspun, a good friend of Parry Thomas' who joined with him in making many important decisions shaping Las Vegas through the 1950s and beyond. (lower left) A Las Vegas bank publicity shot of Parry upon his arrival 1955. (lower right) Parry as the president of the Bank of Las Vegas, 1969.

Parry Thomas and Nevada's U.S. Senator Howard Cannon. *"I learned to work well with politicians on both sides of the aisle,"* Thomas says.

Nate Mack, in 1981. The father of Jerry Mack first recognized the business talents and leadership skills of Parry Thomas in Las Vegas, and partnered Thomas with his son Jerry Mack, an outstanding real estate executive. The Thomas and Mack partnership was to become arguably the most successful business partnership in Las Vegas history.

(above) Dr. Jerry Vallen, chairman of UNLV's acclaimed Hotel Department, and Larry Ruvo choose a bottle of wine for UNLVino, a long-standing fundraising event for the university, in 1974. (below) Bill Boyd, shown with his father Sam Boyd at an event at the Stardust Hotel and Casino in 1987. Bill says that he and his father received important business loans from Bank of Las Vegas and Valley Bank, and without Parry's support their careers in gaming would have been far more difficult.

*Parry Thomas receiving the Distinguished Nevadan Award from UNLV President Donald Baepler for "significant contributions to the advancement of our state and nation, and for exceptional service to the well-being of mankind," at commencement ceremonies in May, 1975.*

(l. to r.) Irwin Molasky, Kirk Douglas, Susan Molasky, former Nevada Gov. Mike O'Callaghan, and Parry Thomas at a reception following Parry's receiving the Prime Minister's Medal from the state of Israel, Dec. 1977.

Cover of Town & Country magazine, January, 1977. Parry and Roger with "The Last Farewell" by Edward Fraughton, part of the Valley Bank Western Art Collection assembled by Roger.

Courtesy of the Thomas Family

(above) Long-time partners, (l. to r.) Jerry Mack, Parry Thomas with attorney Harvey Silbert, who was their partner in several business ventures. (below left) Moe Dalitz, civic leader and one-time owner of the Desert Inn, who reluctantly took Parry's advice in negotiating the sale of the DI to Howard Hughes. (below right) Horseshoe owner Benny Binion, thought by many to be the most savvy gambling man ever in Las Vegas. Benny called Parry Thomas "Wall Street."

Courtesy of the Las Vegas Review-Journal

Courtesy of the Las Vegas Review-Journal

(above) Parry Thomas, Wayne Newton, and Frank Fahrenkopf, at a gaming board licensing hearing. (below) UNLV President Robert Maxson with Runnin' Rebel coach Jerry Tarkanian, in 1987. These two men would be embroiled in a struggle that would see both of them leave the school by 1994, but they have moved on and today are cordial with each other.

The Thomas kids, mid 1980s: (l. to r.) Tom, Roger, Jane, Peter, and Steve.

(l. to r.) Parry Thomas, Doré and George Eccles, and Steve Wynn, circa 1970.
George Eccles was a Utah banker who with his brother Marriner founded First
Securities Corp., one of the largest banks in the inter-mountain West.

(above) Horseshoe owner and director of the World Series of Poker, Jack Binion, seen with 1995 WSOP winner Dan Harrington. The event founded by Jack and Benny Binion and Doyle Brunson has evolved into one of the most watched televised sporting events in the country. (below) Las Vegas Sun publisher Brian Greenspun, son of Parry's good friend Hank.

Courtesy of the Las Vegas Review-Journal

(above) Michael Gaughan, in 1996. Gaughan currently owns and operates the South Point Hotel and Casino. He got many of his early construction loans from Parry Thomas and Valley Bank. (below) Parry Thomas, Joyce Mack, Jerry Mack, and Peggy Thomas.

Courtesy of the Thomas Family

(above) Parry Thomas and Steve Wynn, upon Parry's receiving a Lifetime Achievement Award from the American Gaming Summit in 1996. (below) Barbara Walters at Caesars Palace in 2004. Parry Thomas introduced Barbara to Adnan Khashoggi, and she later scored an exclusive interview with the arms dealer for her show 20/20.

*Debbie McDonald and Brentina, World Cup winners in 2000.*

*Peggy Thomas, equestrian champion Debbie McDonald, and Parry Thomas at World Equestrian games in Spain, 2004.*

*(l. to r.) Peggy Thomas, Gillian Wynn (Steve and Elaine Wynn's younger daughter), and Parry Thomas, circa 2000.*

Courtesy of the Las Vegas Review-Journal, K.M. Cannon

(above) Herb Jones, a lifelong friend of Parry's, who wrote the original charter for the Bank of Las Vegas in 1954. (Below) California Governor Arnold Schwarzenegger and Michael Milken at the Milken Institute Global Conference in 2007. Parry Thomas gave Milken a silk necktie at the Mirage opening in 1989, a tie that Milken still wears today for special occasions.

Courtesy of the Milken Institute

(right) Steve Wynn, in a portrait by famed photographer Timothy Greenfield-Sanders in 2008. (below) Steve and Elaine Wynn with their good friend Michael Milken. (bottom) This sculpture, by the artist Stephan Weiss, the late husband of designer Donna Karan, was a gift from Steve and Elaine Wynn to the Thomas family, and welcomes guests to River Grove Farm in Hailey, Idaho. One of the other two sculptures from this cast sits in front of the Wynn Resort in Las Vegas.

*Parry Thomas in a reflective pose, at the Thomas & Mack Company offices in Las Vegas.*

It's important to understand the interconnection between the political power in Nevada and what was taking place on the Strip after Hughes came to Las Vegas. Paul Laxalt had just been elected governor a matter of weeks before Hughes arrived in 1966, and he immediately got behind everything Hughes did. Laxalt knew that what Hughes was doing when he started buying hotels was in keeping with what everyone wanted to see happen: it was cleaning up the ownership of the Strip and it was infusing energy into the economy. I can't underscore enough that we were in a horrible economic slump when Hughes came to town.

In my first twelve years here in Nevada, we went through at least three depressions locally in Las Vegas. Things got really tough and it was very hard to keep some of these places going. It got down to where your belly button touches your backbone supporting these places to keep them open.

As I've said, there were only two hotels on the Strip by the mid-'60s that didn't have to go through some financial restructuring, and they were the Desert Inn and the Sands. Laxalt was a lawyer by education and he had represented some of the Las Vegas hotels in reorganization. He knew their economic problems and that weighed on his mind very heavily. He also wanted to get rid of the Mob influence in these casinos, which was breaking them, because those guys were taking all the money off the top and leaving no working capital.

So Paul Laxalt became very important in Hughes' acquisition of hotels. The Gaming Commission and the Control Board and the Nevada Legislature recognized that no one person should own too many casinos. When we started buying hotels for Hughes, it got down to that issue of monopoly and that became a very hot issue. In order for him to acquire several casinos, it took the full weight of the governor to pave the road with those bodies to get him licenses, particularly when nobody had ever seen him.

Laxalt basically supported everything Hughes did. My role was just buying the hotels for him. I was just a mechanical human being in there getting the job done. Mainly because I knew all the hotel owners really well, and I knew their strengths and weaknesses and I could deal with them. I also knew the ones that should be sold and whatnot, so that helped. But Laxalt was tremendously beneficial, you bet.

Basically, everything was for sale on the Strip because of our economic posture at that particular time, including the Desert Inn and the Sands, because those were the two most successful, and therefore commanded higher prices.

During that same period that Hughes was buying hotels, for some reason he initially shied away from saying he wanted to buy the Sands. And so I took Carl Cohen with me to Dallas and introduced him to Troy Post, who at that time was a very influential financier. He controlled the Great American Insurance Company. Troy was a cordial man who had founded Great American from selling insurance door to door. His wife was the head of the Democratic Party in Texas and they owned a huge mansion. On the property they had an original log cabin from the Daniel Boone era that had been restored, and I stayed there on several occasions.

Troy was interested in purchasing the Sands, but he had a hard time convincing his people to go with him. While Troy was considering it, I let Maheu know what was going on. My interest was in marketing the Sands to get it sold. The guys operating it were getting old and they wanted to retire and get out. Once Hughes knew that there was another interested buyer, that triggered him to buy it. I remember on that Dallas trip with Carl we were convinced we were being tailed by two FBI agents. That sort of thing wasn't unusual when you were doing work for Howard Hughes.

I agree with Bob Maheu when he says that Hughes wasn't initially interested in buying hotels when he first got to Las Vegas. Early on, I was instructed through Maheu to start buying for him properties around both airports, McCarran and the North Las Vegas Airport. We also bought some other properties for him, but nothing to do with gambling initially. I think the airport properties appealed to him because of his love for aviation.

The unfortunate part of it was that Jerry Mack and I owned most of the property around McCarran, and we did have some difficulty arranging the sale to Hughes there because we really liked the property we owned there and were reluctant to let it go. In hindsight, we made a helluva mistake in selling it, too.

We had bought the property for $260 an acre, and we sold it for like $20,000 an acre, and although that looks on its face like a great deal, the property was worth way more than that later on. We should have held on to it, but we felt obligated to sell it to Hughes because we were kind of in the middle of everything with him.

Before I ever met Bob Maheu, my attorney friend Ed Morgan, who worked for Hughes and Maheu, told me the biggest reason for Hughes coming here was that he was told by his doctors that he had inoperable brain tumors, probably from that plane wreck he was in. Morgan had advised Hughes that he needed to prepare his estate because he had to recognize that he wasn't going to live forever, and that Nevada was one of three places that didn't have inheritance taxes. Hughes had always had an affinity for Nevada, and he'd once had a home here, so Las Vegas became a logical place for him to go.

# UNLV: Building a University

## Parry Thomas

JERRY MACK AND I ALWAYS STAYED INTERESTED IN EDUCATION, AND particularly higher education. We had both stayed closely connected with our alma maters. I was on what they call the National Board of Advisors at the University of Utah, and Jerry at the same time was on the Board of Trustees at UCLA.

Every quarter we'd spend time with our respective universities, and the administrators would show us what they were doing, so we stayed fairly current with university-level requirements and buildings that were going up and how the schools were faring academically.

As Las Vegas was growing in the early '60s we were quite aggressive in branching operating centers for our bank. I wanted to put a branch and a large computer center on the UNLV campus, or close to it, because I had a vision of the university really growing. At the time the school had fewer than a thousand students, but we knew it would grow exponentially as the city grew.

I asked for a property map of the university to see where the best location might be for an operating center. Ideally, we wanted to be on Maryland Parkway someplace between University Street and Tropicana Avenue. The traffic patterns made that an advantageous location.

Jerry and I were floored when we learned from the map that the university had only fifty-five acres. We knew from our experience working on the boards at our alma maters that no one, except for the U.S. Army, needed land more urgently than a university. And we knew that having a strong university was essential for the greater good of the community growing up around it.

We said to ourselves, this isn't going to work, and so we formed the Southern Nevada University Land Foundation [*later changed to the UNLV Foundation*]. Fortunately, this was during a recession in Las Vegas, when land values were down. So we set a goal of buying up all the land around the university that we could, and paying ten thousand dollars or less an acre for it. And we were going to have to fund it.

We tried to get the other bank, First National, to come and work with our bank on the joint loan. They wouldn't do it, nor would any of the other banks. So we had the Land Foundation issue $2 million worth of secure bonds, and we had our bank buy all those bonds, the whole $2 million. I had to explain to the Federal Reserve Board about our financing, and they weren't too happy about it because that was a pretty steep number in proportion to the size of our bank at the time. So Jerry and I personally guaranteed the loans, basically put up the money ourselves. Because we had good credit, it was ruled to be okay.

Jerry Mack just did an incredible job on that land project. In our partnership, he handled anything that had to do with real estate or land or buildings. That was his end of the business and he was super at it. He gathered up most of the four hundred acres around the university for future expansion. I got some of the bigger pieces.

Irwin Molasky and his partner, Merv Adelson, had a big parcel that we needed, and yet I knew they were very community minded. They wanted to keep that parcel and develop it, which is of course why they had purchased it, but after I met with Irwin they could see the value to the university, so they went along.

It's interesting to note that after we bought all the land for the university, we decided not to put our computer center next to the campus. About three weeks before we started the groundbreaking on it, the students at UC Santa Barbara staged a big campus riot and some buildings were destroyed, and that gave us pause. So while we did put a bank branch on campus, we moved the site of the computer center to East Charleston.

## Irwin Molasky

PARRY AND JERRY'S NUMBER ONE LEGACY COULD WELL BE THEIR VISION for UNLV and what they were able to accomplish for the school.

Parry called me one day—and this was when the school was still called Nevada Southern University, I believe—and he said that they were putting together a land bank so that the university could grow into a great school. I was partners on forty-five acres on Flamingo and

Swenson with Merv Adelson, who was the former vice chairman of the board of Time Warner and who later on married Barbara Walters.

Parry said, "You and Merv have those prime acres on Flamingo and Swenson, and I want you to give them to the university."

"Are you out of your (bleepin') mind?" I said. "Just give it away?"

We had paid something like $10,000 or $12,000 an acre for the land in those days, so it was like a half-million dollars. I didn't have that kind of money.

"I can't afford to just give the land," I told him. "It's worth a lot of money." And he said, "I know, but I need it. So I'll help you give it."

I told Parry we still owed something like $200,000 or $250,000 on it. He said not to worry, that he'd handle that, but that we should give the university the rest. So he talked me into giving much more than we could afford in those days. That land is now the location for the athletic fields, the baseball stadium, the tennis courts, on into the Thomas and Mack Center.

There's nobody else in the world who could have talked me into doing that. Nobody. But I knew with his foresight it was the right thing to do. At the end of the day I could not say no to Parry Thomas, and I don't remember his ever saying no to me in anything I needed or did.

## Parry Thomas

I KNEW I COULD COUNT ON IRWIN TO DO THE RIGHT THING FOR THE community. He's always been far-sighted and community oriented. An outstanding fellow.

There was just one group that showed resistance, and they owned a sizable parcel on the corner of Flamingo and Paradise. I had to get a little persuasive with them, and I told them it was very important that we finish our project and that we needed that parcel. I explained that the state of Nevada gave us the right of condemnation if need be, so we could threaten people with the taking of property for university use. But eventually we paid them a good price and they were satisfied with it.

In purchasing those four hundred acres, we used up the whole $2 million in bonds. So then we had to figure out how in the hell we were going to get paid back.

There were challenges in doing that. The reason the university didn't have the land in the first place was because the Nevada Legislature could afford only so much money for higher education, and they were pouring all the money into the University of Nevada at Reno. The political power in the Legislature was all up north, and the loyalties were to the older state university there. The politicians just didn't have it in their vision to support two state universities, particularly with all the intrastate rivalry that existed between the North and the South. So Nevada Southern University was getting very little money, and no money at all for land, which is why they had only fifty-five acres.

In Jerry's and my view, it was just horrendous if Las Vegas didn't have a university of size here, and one with the capacity to grow, because we had complete faith that Las Vegas was going to experience big growth. Not everybody here could afford to send children away to school, and Jerry and I just felt that we had to do something.

With the limitations that existed with those fifty-five acres, it meant one of two things for the future of the school. Either we were going to have a high-rise university, which was going to be very limited because of its location close to the airport, or we were going to have a split campus. And from my way of thinking, neither one was desirable.

About a year into this process of getting the necessary land, we could see that it was going to be a long road before we ever got paid back on the loans we'd guaranteed. So we had to get a little ingenious. We got hold of Jay Sarno [*the developer who conceived and built Caesars Palace and Circus Circus*], who was working on a new project. Jay was a heckuva guy, maybe not the best businessman but an incredibly far-sighted and talented designer. He was a creative genius, without a doubt.

It turns out the seventeen acres we bought on the corner of Flamingo and Paradise we ended up selling to Jay Sarno for $1.7 million. He was going to build another big hotel on that property. [*The projected 6,000-room Grandissimo, Sarno's dream project, was never built. He died in 1984, but held out hope to the end that his dream would be fulfilled.*]

Jay had some partners with good credit. We financed some of that purchase, but the bottom line was that the university ended up getting approximately four hundred acres for three hundred thousand dollars, the difference between the $2 million we had to spend to get it and the amount we got for the Flamingo and Paradise parcel.

We were fortunate in the sense that Las Vegas has had a history of ups and downs in the real estate market, and land values have followed those ups and downs. At the time we were acquiring these parcels, land values were in the trough and we knew it. So we had to strike fast and get these purchases on quickly while the values were down. We eventually averaged less than ten thousand dollars an acre for that land, and some of the parcels we got for considerably less than that.

We arranged it so the state of Nevada got a helluva windfall. It was some of the most valuable real estate in Las Vegas at the time it was purchased, and UNLV has grown just like we hoped it would. It's now a respected state university that just gets better and better every year and which has educated tens of thousands of children of the people who've helped Las Vegas grow.

Jerry and I were both very proud of what we were able to do in acquiring that land for the university. It's one of the finer things we accomplished. In 2008, UNLV is basically using all of those four hundred acres. Oh, there are some spaces between buildings, but the land has been put to pretty full use. They could use two thousand acres for the future. You have to think big on these matters.

∞

Later on, we came up with the idea for the UNLV Foundation, which was designed to provide money for the university president, and to allow the college to take on projects for which it couldn't otherwise get funding.

Jerry and I again had seen from our involvement at Utah and UCLA how important a foundation like this was for a college. No matter how modest it was going to be in the beginning, at least it would be a starting point for UNLV. I asked Irwin Molasky to be the first president of the Foundation Board.

## Irwin Molasky

YEARS LATER, IN THE 1970S, AFTER THE FOUR HUNDRED ACRES WAS purchased for Nevada Southern and the school was now called UNLV, Parry came to me and explained how every great university has a foundation to help the president raise money for pet projects that could go on the books. This meant special projects that the university couldn't get funding for.

He told me that I first had to learn about how these foundations work. So I took trips to Michigan and to Arizona and saw how they worked at these large universities, and I came back and had lunch with Parry again to report on what I'd learned. He then asked me to be the first chairman of the foundation.

The first thing I did was to form a committee of the most influential and brainiest people in Las Vegas. We had Tom Wiesner and Claudine Williams, Marjorie Barrick, Jim Cashman Jr., Michael Gaughan, Louie Wiener, Kenny Sullivan, Jerry Herbst, and of course Parry and Jerry Mack.

I chaired the foundation for the first couple of years and that allowed me to sit with the Board of Regents as counsel to them, and help further the goals of the university.

One of our first goals was to find out exactly what the university needed. We started to raise money for the president to live properly and to augment his or her income. We also gave parties that would bring in money, and we hired people to go out and start getting donations. We also hired tax planners who would reach out to people who had built up some estate money, and who could show them how to donate lifetime gifts upon their death, and things like that.

## Elaine Wynn

PARRY THOMAS UNDERSTOOD WHERE LAS VEGAS WAS GOING BEFORE all of us did. He understood about the diversification and then the consolidation and he saw it coming in advance and he talked to us about it.

The role that Howard Hughes played and all of the other moving parts kind of were serendipitous, but nevertheless Parry saw that this was going to be an attractive place, that there was something going on here beyond just the Bugsy Siegel moment.

And he was exactly the same way with the community and the real estate. That's why Parry and Jerry Mack were such a good team, because they knew how things were going to unfold, and strategically where they should be in terms of their family commitments, both professionally and in every other way.

So when Parry talked about the university and the land and having the foresight to see that that place was soon going to be landlocked, and that if they didn't acquire everything they could get their hands on at that moment, that it was going to be too late, well, everyone listened. Thank goodness they did see that and acted on it, or else the UNLV campus would be in Summerlin or some other outlying area. It would have been spread all over the place.

Of course Parry had had the history at the University of Utah, and Jerry had the history with UCLA, so they brought their own personal involvement and experience with those two institutions to bear on this young university. And he would share this experience with me over and over again. So when I became chair of the UNLV Foundation, I could see that with the athletic boosters and the academic supporters we needed to have some structure to it. We used to have to worry about paying the bills and so Irwin Molasky had the foundation office in his building. We had to move on campus.

Parry was always there to help me as I was putting form to the foundation. And I think the greatest period of growth at UNLV happened when Bob Maxson came to town as the new university president. I was running the foundation then and we started to get all these buildings constructed. We've never had anything like it since. Bob was a round peg in a round hole, and the support that Parry and Jerry gave Bob was invaluable. Bob and Parry and I were a triumvirate, you know. We just watched and oversaw all that growth, and if it hadn't been for Parry, I wouldn't have known exactly what to do. He was there at every turn to help.

### Parry Thomas

WHEN I WAS ON THE BOARD AT THE UNIVERSITY OF UTAH WE HAD A super president, David Gardner, who later became chancellor of all the California state universities put together, one of the biggest jobs in education. But before that he got an offer from the University of Southern California to leave Utah and go there, and we wanted to hold onto him. So about five of us got together and created what we called the President's Chair, and we funded it so that it gave him an annuity every year.

I wanted the same thing for UNLV, so I had the foundation form a President's Chair here and a bunch of us put in $25,000 each and we raised $400,000. We then used that money as an endowment, and the earnings went to supplement the president's salary.

When you think about it, when you take into consideration all their land and their buildings and several thousand employees, a university is comparable to a large national corporation. And yet the head of a university is traditionally paid a miserable salary. Back then it was maybe $150,000 or $200,000 a year, while a corporation president would have been paid in the seven figures. And so it was hard to attract really good people into becoming president of a university. Because the president is the real cornerstone of any university, and that president is the one who would attract the best professors, we felt this President's Chair was critical to the future growth of UNLV.

When I was in the foundation I also started a president's slush fund, where we would give the president $100,000 a year in expense money with no questions asked. He was to use that money as he saw fit for the benefit of the university, because in academics, as in any business, you have to be free to make deals. For instance, if a president wants to recruit a top professor from some other university—and that's what they do at the top schools—he has to do it in a clandestine manner. He has to have the capacity to buy an airplane ticket and have that guy come in, he has to put him up in a nice hotel and buy his meals, and this and that. And he can't be put in a position where he has to go to the Board of Regents and request money for that because the confidentiality would be gone.

That idea ran into some trouble because some of the do-gooders started wanting to have an accounting of every nickel that was in that slush fund. It's small-minded thinking. I remember one foundation meeting where I got pretty upset because they were all going to gang up on Bob Maxson. I could see it coming. So I gave a little talk and told them of the value of having an anonymous fund and some confidentiality because of the importance and value of attracting the top professors and the top coaches or whatever else we needed, and it took a vehicle like this slush fund to finance it.

Anyway, the bean counters and the accountants in there wanted to have Maxson put in a report on all the money spent. I said that was ridiculous, that we didn't need that and we didn't even want to know about it. The less we knew about it, the better off it would be for the university. But I couldn't get many of them to see my viewpoint on that.

## Robert Maxson

I'M NOT CERTAIN WHAT ROLE PARRY THOMAS PLAYED IN MY RECRUIT-
ment to UNLV. I do know that he let the university regents know at the time that if they hired someone he considered to be the right person for the job, Parry would do whatever he could to support not just the university, but a trust fund for the president. And he made it clear that what UNLV did not need, in the mid-1980s, was a short-term president. He believed that continuity was important.

Shortly after I was hired I went on the board of Parry's Valley Bank, and he was instrumental in setting up a fund that I don't think had been done before and hasn't been done since, that would accrue to me if I stayed for X number of years.

Parry's motive was always right. He wanted strong leadership for UNLV, and leadership that would be there for a while.

I remember being smitten by Parry immediately when I first met him, just like everyone else has been. How can you not be when you meet this charismatic, quiet, gentle man, who is arguably one of the two or three most important figures in all of Las Vegas?

It took me a while to learn how his fingerprints and footprints were all over the city, because he would never tell you himself. When I first came to Las Vegas, the city was in its adolescence. We're used to cities, especially back East and in the South, that are hundreds of years old, and here was this upstart city in the desert that just overnight appeared like an island emerging from an ocean. Almost in the blink of an eye, Las Vegas has become one of America's great cities. And if you look at the development of the city from its infancy through its adolescence and then now into its young adulthood, I think you can argue that no one played a greater role in that than Parry Thomas.

I came to learn all of these things about him almost by accident, because not only did Parry not tell you about what he'd accomplished, but other than the large events center on campus, he didn't allow his name on a lot of things. He was this soft-spoken, humble man whose focus was never on drawing attention to himself, but on planning ways to make the city a better place to live and to raise children.

I discovered that with his quiet manner he was truly a behind-the-scenes man, who contributed immeasurably to the financial status of so many people in that city. And that if he did lend his name or his expertise to something, it was money in the bank; it was going to be successful, no question about it.

### Irwin Molasky

THE LAND ACQUISITION THAT PARRY AND JERRY MACK SPEARHEADED and the foundation that was started with their influence, my gosh, what a legacy that has been for Las Vegas. That probably ranks in importance right up there with everything they did to fund hotel-casino projects downtown and along the Strip. What is UNLV up to today, nearly thirty thousand students? The school would never be what it is today without their efforts.

### Robert Maxson

WITH PARRY GETTING IRWIN MOLASKY INVOLVED IN THE UNIVERSITY, and so many others like him, you've got to remember that he did these things without considering any monetary gain to himself. Let's face it, he was hugely successful financially as a businessman . . . hugely successful . . . and I think that is because people trusted Parry Thomas.

Trust is the single most important quality of a leader. We could all probably get on a blackboard and name twenty or thirty of the most important qualities of a leader. But the single most important quality is personal integrity. If people don't trust you, they won't follow you.

Parry believed that by definition it was impossible to be a great city if you didn't have a good university. He would ask you to name any important city in America that wasn't home to a good university, and you couldn't name any. He realized, and got other community leaders to realize, that the university provided the intellectual product for the city, and that it was the intellectual base for the city. Parry understood this completely, and he went about spreading that message without a selfish bone in his body. Sure, he went to a few basketball games and a few football games, but he understood that the university's most basic function is about the life of the mind.

When he went about fundraising for UNLV, no one questioned his motives. They knew he wasn't doing it out of any self-interest. He had already accumulated a nice fortune by all his smart business decisions early on in helping those people early in the casino business. He was always far-sighted. I mean Parry Thomas in the '50s and '60s helped people and entrepreneurs that Wall Street wouldn't touch with a ten-foot pole. He built his bank, and at the same time he built his city. Without Parry Thomas, I'm not saying Las Vegas wouldn't have happened the way it has, but it would be years behind where it is right now.

One other thing that has to be mentioned: Parry Thomas in ten years never once made a call to my office asking for anything. Every call he made—and we talked a lot through the years—was to say, "How can I help?"

I don't recall ever once hearing him ask for a favor to get someone into school, or for a few extra tickets to a game or an event. Every time I picked up a call from Parry, he was calling to see what he could do to help. That's something you notice as a college president, and you certainly appreciate it.

## Larry Ruvo

THERE WERE PEOPLE IN LAS VEGAS IN THE 1950S AND '60S WHO MADE millions of dollars, but Parry Thomas was different in that he had this master plan that wasn't just about himself and his children, but it was about the future of the city. He knew that he couldn't stay in Las Vegas and bring up his family if there weren't restrictions on what could go on in this town. There had to be limitations and there had to be solvency and there had to be a commitment from others in the city and state to make Las Vegas a great city and a great place to live.

Las Vegas was extremely lucky the day that Parry Thomas moved here. He saw to it that we would become a respectable neighborhood. He made people accountable and responsible for paying back some of the successes they had reaped from living in Las Vegas. He became a role model for involved citizens. If he asked you to do something, he had already done it. That manifested itself in everything he did for the university, and for the many charitable causes he either started or joined through the years.

## Parry Thomas

IN THE MIDDLE '80S, WHEN WE BROUGHT IN BOB MAXSON, WHO WAS a terrific catch as the new president of UNLV, that really showed what the UNLV Foundation could do. We brought him in and we wanted to keep him here. He did a terrific job with fundraising and increasing the school's awareness in the community.

After watching Bob for about four or five months on the job, I realized that he was the first real professional university president we had ever had at UNLV. We'd had Pat Goodall, who was a gifted professor and a really fine man filling in, but the professionalism of administration and overseeing the university and getting out in the community to create good will and raise the endowment level just hadn't existed before Maxson came here. When I saw what he could do, I was so impressed that I finally asked him to sit on our board at Valley Bank. I really got behind him and worked with him, and then all of that ridiculous stuff happened between the academic side of things and the basketball program and it was just a shame. [*The UNLV basketball scandals of 1991, which led to the basketball team being put on NCAA probation for two years.*] It was just not called for.

I liked Bob Maxson very much and I also liked Jerry Tarkanian. I don't place the blame squarely on either of them for what happened. I do think a lot of people got over-involved in athletics and they became very vocal. The balance between the academic role of a university and the athletic side of things got out of balance, and all the basketball enthusiasts kind of raised hell, and that was the trouble. It was just a shame that had to happen, but we've moved on from that and the progress of the university in the last three decades has just been overwhelming. I'm more than pleased at what has happened.

Pat Goodall was the interim president of the university when the whole idea of naming a building after Jerry and me came up. He expressed to us that he appreciated that our acquisition of the land was the biggest thing ever done for the university. He realized the value of that more than some of the others. He asked us one day in his office if we wanted something named after us for creating the campus. And we said we'd think about it.

We didn't know at that time that they were in the earliest stages of planning to build a large sports pavilion on campus. But as that progressed, Goodall told us they would like to name the biggest building on campus after us, and we agreed. Jerry and I put up sufficient money to cover all the architectural expenses and off-site improvements for the new pavilion. It wasn't too much, somewhere between $300,000 and $350,000 to do that.

I think the final cost of the building was around $36 million. The same structure today would cost about $200 million. [*In 2006-07, the Thomas and Mack Center was ranked as the second highest revenue-producing all-purpose facility in the United States, behind only Madison Square Garden.*]

## Joyce Mack

WHEN THEY WERE BUILDING THE THOMAS AND MACK CENTER, OUR daughter Karen wanted that sign to be big, you know. She wanted a BIG sign. She'd even measured the letters to make certain that it was a big sign.

Jerry once told me, "You know what? After all the stuff we've done for this town, guess what people are going to remember us for? A basketball stadium."

## Parry Thomas

OPENING NIGHT FOR THE NEW BUILDING WAS REALLY SOMETHING. They had the Rat Pack open the place, with Frank and Dean and all of them performing together again. That was a big thrill for Jerry and me and our families. We were all puffed up over that.

Funny story, one time shortly after it opened, Jerry and I were in a cab coming back from the airport and as we drove by the Thomas and Mack I asked our cab driver who it was named for.

"Oh, everybody knows it's named for two of our Runnin' Rebel basketball stars," was his answer.

We got a big kick out of that. Goes to show you'll rarely get an "I don't know" when you ask a cabbie a question.

CHAPTER THREE

# Steve Wynn: The Fifth Son

## Parry Thomas

I FIRST MET STEVE WYNN WHEN HE WAS ABOUT TWENTY-FOUR YEARS old, maybe even younger. His father, Mike, who I never met, had already passed away by then.

I learned that even as a young boy, Steve had an ambition to get away from the East Coast and relocate to Las Vegas. I think he always sensed the possibilities here.

Early on we had helped a man named Maury Friedman with some financing at the New Frontier Hotel. It was previously called the Last Frontier but after those early troubles it was renamed the New Frontier. Maury was as sharp as they come, a really bright guy, and he was a loyal friend of mine.

[*The Last Frontier was the second hotel built on the Las Vegas Strip, after the El Rancho Vegas. It was opened in 1941 by R.E. Griffith and his nephew William J. Moore. In 1951 Moore sold the Last Frontier to Jake Kozloff and Beldon Katleman. They refurbished it and in 1955 reopened it, calling it the New Frontier. Soon after, they sold the hotel to Maury Friedman, T.W. Richardson, and Warren "Doc" Bailey, who owned the Hacienda. The Banker's Life Insurance Company acquired the property in 1964 after Bailey's death, tore down the original buildings, and began construction on a new 500-room hotel. Maury Friedman had brought in Steve Wynn as a minority owner and had him run the slot operation. Just four months after the hotel had reopened in July 1967, Howard Hughes bought the New Frontier along with an adjacent casino and nightclub, the Silver Slipper. Parry Thomas helped negotiate the sale to Hughes.]*

I think next to Jake Friedman [*no relation to Maury*] at the Sands, there was no one who helped me develop my career more in those early days in Las Vegas than Maury Friedman. Somehow Maury got connected with Steve Wynn, through John MacArthur I believe, and Steve purchased three points in the New Frontier. So I believe it was Steve's second day in town when Maury brought him down to the bank and introduced him to me, and told me about his background as an outstanding student at the University of Pennsylvania. That was our first meeting and the beginning of a wonderful friendship. Steve was in and out of the bank quite a bit in those first few months. Within a couple of weeks, we got to meet his wife, Elaine.

Perhaps because of the connection from their Jewish faith, Jerry Mack and Joyce sort of took Steve and Elaine under their wings and invited them to dinner on occasion and helped them feel comfortable in their new home of Las Vegas. So we saw a lot of Steve and Elaine early on, usually in the company of Jerry and Joyce.

When you talk about Steve Wynn, you have to mention how wonderful the woman he married is. Elaine Wynn is an outstanding person. She just sparkles and has an exceptional intellect.

### Elaine Wynn

I CAN'T PINPOINT THE EXACT MOMENT THAT I MET PARRY THOMAS. I think that Parry began for me as an illusion. Steve had talked about him when he was working on the Frontier deal, before we had moved to Las Vegas, that he was the banker who was instrumental in assisting with that deal. And so I'd heard a lot about Parry before I met him.

I came to Las Vegas in July of '67, because our daughter Kevyn had been born in September '66, and I know she was just ten months old. I remember getting off the plane on July Fourth, at night, and they opened the gang plank and oh, it was hot!

I felt the first thing I should do was meet the local people, and that I better join the Jewish temple. There was only one in those days—Temple Beth Sholom. It was actually Jerry Mack's dad, Nate, who was the founder of that temple with Jack Entratter. And so I joined the temple and I remember that the Macks invited us to have dinner at their home for the Jewish holidays. It was September, either Rosh Hashanah or Yom Kipper. It was just the most wonderful gesture because Steve and I were brand new and didn't know anybody, really. And the Mack girls were there and I remember thinking, oh, I hope I can raise children to be this sweet and this wholesome and this smart. They were pre-teens and teens. They were young and all in school. I just thought they were the most perfect family. And that evening augured well for me because I had such question marks about living in Las Vegas and having just moved here. I was questioning whether it was possible to have some kind of a traditional life.

## Marilyn Mack

I REMEMBER IT WAS DURING THE JEWISH HOLIDAYS AND DAD SAID THAT he wanted to invite this new young couple over to the house for dinner because they didn't know anybody. I was like twelve or thirteen years old. They were this gorgeous couple. Oh my God. And they were so nice. And I remember they were so beautiful. She was blond and beautiful and so nice, and he was so handsome and nice. Then later I would see them in temple with their two little daughters. They were like the perfect family. Of course I had no idea as a young girl how they would one day change Las Vegas.

## Elaine Wynn

I THINK I HAD BEEN TO LAS VEGAS TWICE BEFORE WE MOVED HERE. I was here once at the Sands and saw the Rat Pack and then I came again in June of '67 to find a house. It all happened very quickly. We rented a house on the Desert Inn golf course.

This story has some irony to it. We sublet a house that was owned by the cantor of the temple. He had leased it to a guy who was doing a show from one of the hotels. So the show went bust and this guy wanted to get out of his lease. He decided to sublet his lease to us without informing the cantor that that was what he was doing. So we took over his lease and moved into the house and one day the cantor and his wife showed up, obviously surprised to see us there. But they turned out to be lovely people.

Fast forward to today. We now own the property the Desert Inn was on, and our daughter Kevyn was married to the cantor of the temple. We've really come full circle.

But as I said, the Macks were for the Wynns the gateway to Las Vegas. Then of course we met Peggy and Parry but I can't tell you the exact moment. It was just like a warm spring fountain that came into our lives, and especially so in Steve's case.

Parry became the father that Steve never had in his business life, and although Steve had a wonderful dad, the history is well known. His father died in open heart surgery during Steve's senior year of college. So there were a couple of years—formative years when he really could have used the advice and love of a father—when his whole plan in life just changed. He was going to law school and all that went kaflooey because we had mouths to feed and obligations. And so by coming to Las Vegas and finding a man like Parry Thomas . . . well, I think everybody in their life needs to have that significant other, and it could well be a family member. But it's that guiding hand, that mentor, that unselfish person who reaches out and gives that extra bit of direction and selfless guidance that helps you sort through the trials and tribulations of your life.

They come to you at different times of your life, but for Steve to have somebody like that man enter our lives at that time, well, to me it's always been divine intervention.

## Steve Wynn

I SECOND THAT. IT *was* DIVINE INTERVENTION. MY FATHER, MIKE WYNN, died on March 29, 1963, two months before my graduation from Penn, at age forty-seven. Parry Thomas took over in my life four years later. Parry was just five years younger than my dad. In effect, he adopted me. What are the chances of coming to this growing young city of Las Vegas, a young Jewish kid from Utica, New York, in the bingo business, and being adopted by the most powerful man in town?

Over those first years I asked Parry the question many times: Why did you take me in like that? And the answer he gave was: Walter Cosgriff.

Walter was responsible for Parry's first big career break when he got out of the Army. Cosgriff put Parry in business at his bank and gave him an executive position, made him a management trainee and promoted him rapidly. He did it because Parry was smarter than the others, and he dressed sharper and was better looking. He had success written all over him.

You need to understand that when he was younger, Parry wasn't just good looking. He was like Cary Grant. He was movie-star handsome. And you combine that with great intelligence and a wonderful, self-effacing demeanor, and you have a powerful combination.

Parry had asked Walter Cosgriff years later, after he'd become successful in Las Vegas, why he had given him so much help, and Walter said that he always wanted to help a deserving young man get started. And so Parry paid it forward. He saw that it was the right thing to do for a lot of reasons. And he determined to do the same thing himself. He'd tell me, "I'm keeping my contract with Walter Cosgriff."

## Parry Thomas

OF COURSE, JUST ABOUT THE TIME STEVE GOT TO LAS VEGAS THE GOVernment task force had been pressuring the owners of the New Frontier to sell out because of their connections to the Detroit Mob, so after Howard Hughes had decided to put his money into Las Vegas hotels, he bought the New Frontier in 1967 and that sat well with everybody.

## Elaine Wynn

STEVE AND I WERE MARRIED IN 1963. STEVE HAD JUST GRADUATED AND I was at the end of my junior year.

We were just plodding along. Steve had a mother and a kid brother and a new wife, and the only viable thing we had was this bingo business in Maryland that he'd taken over after his dad died. The business was not doing all that well in his dad's last year because his dad was sick and wasn't focused. But the bingo parlor allowed us a way to pay the bills, pay our tuition, and have a roof over our head. And in those days we didn't have the great luxury of saying, what do we want to be when we grow up?

Steve was on a career path in law school. I think he always wanted to become a businessman and yet there was no business opportunity that was obvious to him, so guys in those days were told to go to law school and get some experience as a lawyer so that when the business opportunities emerged, they'd have some legal background. But I think in hindsight his undergraduate studies in the liberal arts have served him so much better.

Anyway, and Steve can talk about this, but once he had met John MacArthur and Maury Friedman and that opportunity at the Frontier in Las Vegas came up, we decided if we were going to be in the

184

gaming-entertainment-amusement business, why not go to where it really exists in a much greater capacity? We hired a manager for the bingo business, and we used the proceeds from some of the good fortune we had at the bingo [*parlor*] as an investment—as our initial investment—in the Frontier.

In those days when you invested, they had investor points and worker-bee points, and the worker points were discounted so that you could get a share of the ownership at a discounted price from a regular percentage point. So Steve brought in a group of people who were investors, and then he came in as an employee. He started as the slot manager at the Frontier. And we brought in as investors some people from New York who had manufactured our bingo cards. It was all very glamorous because everybody wants to be in the gambling business.

Steve was just twenty-four when he first got a gaming license, which I think at the time made him the youngest licensee on record in the history of Nevada.

For me in those early days, as we all know, there was no such thing as women's lib. You married the guy and if you thought he was your trip to the moon, then you hitched your wagon to him. Of course Steve was a very compelling young man, not much different from the way he is now. And I trusted that our goals were the same. We both were ambitious. And I trusted that he would make good judgments for our future.

So off we came to Las Vegas. And initially I did feel very out of place because I still was in most respects a very traditional middle-class Jewish girl who had some core values, and life here seemed pretty fast. But I had grown up in Miami Beach, and it was a similar environment to Las Vegas minus the gaming. There were a lot of hotels in Miami, and a lot of the same people who wound up in Las Vegas, like Morris Landsberg, Jerry Gordon, and Jerry Zarowitz. And then the added element of the gaming and the ex-bookmakers and the showgirls and the entertainment, so Las Vegas was a very grown-up place. And I was intimidated.

I had a complicated first year, in that we had moved into this house on a golf course with a swimming pool, and I had come from a teeny tiny three-bedroom apartment in Landover, Maryland, between D.C. and Upper Marlborough, where our bingo parlor was located. We commuted. I would drop Steve off at law school at Georgetown and I'd go on to George Washington University, where I was finishing up. And then when we went to work, we were about half an hour from our business, so it was a central location.

And then into the first year in Las Vegas came Parry Thomas. And you know Parry was just perfection. He still ranks as number one on my all-time list of extraordinary, unforgettable men. And he only got better through the years.

You know how sometimes you'll meet somebody and they give a great first impression, and then as you live your years and go through it all, you see some of their mortality and their fatal flaws. Well, there's no question that like all human beings Parry had those as well. But his persona was so overwhelmingly dominant in his influence on Steve's life separate from mine, and on my life separate from Steve's, and on our joint life together as a couple, and even on our children's lives. There's never been a person I could point to that I could say impacted us from the tip of our head to the tip of our toes in every respect in terms of his integrity, his personal taste and style, his intellect, his business acumen, and his foresight, like Parry.

Mike Milken is also one of those characters who I think is off the charts. The difference between the two is the quality of humility that Parry had then and still has to this day, and the extraordinary background where he was brought up in this conservative Mormon environment, how he became a rounder but never lost his basic values either, and how he came full circle in his life.

The staying power that I had living here is grounded on the example that Parry Thomas set for me. That you can be true to yourself, veer off and experiment in your life and be challenged and be tempted and indulge your temptations and be human and have a wild side, but in the end, when you've lived your full rich life, you come back to the bedrock of who you are and what you are. And it gives you such supreme confidence.

## Steve Wynn

I'LL JUMP AHEAD A LITTLE TO CARRY ON THE POINT ABOUT HELPING young people. After our Golden Nugget in Atlantic City was opened, we started the Golden Nugget Scholarship Foundation to put deserving kids through four-year colleges.

We'd have dinners every spring in New Jersey, and one time in Las Vegas, for the new kids who were winning the scholarships and those already in college. We'd have speakers like the remarkable [*scientist and historian*] Stephen Jay Gould, and Shelly Glashow, who won the Nobel Prize for discovering a sub-atomic particle [*called a "quark"*].

On the fourth year of this program, I invited Dave Edwards, my English teacher from Manlius Pebble Hill military school, who was also the faculty adviser when I was editor of the school newspaper. I went there from the eighth to the twelfth grade. I was the battalion adjutant, which was the second-ranking kid there, and Dave Edwards was my favorite teacher. We invited him to the dinner that night, at a time when he was dying of cancer. And that evening we were honoring our first graduating class—these wonderful young people who were graduating from Princeton and Yale and Dartmouth and Harvard and MIT—and they decided to present to Elaine and me a thank-you gift. It was a Steuben glass piece that Elaine still has in her office.

Parry and Peggy Thomas were in the room with us.

When I spoke, I told this group of young people and their families that I wanted to share a story. I said that when my father died we were broke and we were in trouble and we made our way for a time in the family bingo business in Maryland. And then we went off to Las Vegas. As a young couple with a baby and very little money—only a few thousand dollars—we were invited to stay and become extended members of the Thomas family. And I said that everything that had happened to me, the existence of the hotel we were in that evening in New Jersey and the Golden Nugget of Las Vegas, was due to the fact that I had been adopted and patronized and sponsored and guided by a man who had become my second father. And that this man had taught me a lesson he had learned from a man named Walter Cosgriff, who had given him a head start in the banking business. And that Parry Thomas had told me that if I wanted to thank him, that I should remember what Walter Cosgriff had told him.

So what I told those young people that night is that if they were as good as we thought they were, when they got to be in their mid-forties and their careers started to mature, I was passing on to them the mandate of Walter Cosgriff and Parry Thomas and Steve Wynn, and that was to go help other young people get their start in life.

I remember looking out at Parry Thomas and my teacher Dave Edwards and it was very emotional. There were tears in that room. That was one of the sweetest moments of my life.

[*At that point in the interview, Steve took out his cell phone and played a saved message from Garrett Reisman, who attended the University of Pennsylvania on a Golden Nugget scholarship. Reisman went on to receive both a master's and doctorate degree in mechanical engineering from Cal Tech. The cell-phone message was coming from outer space, where Reisman was serving as a NASA long-term mission astronaut on the International Space Station.*]

Garrett had said on his application for the Golden Nugget scholarship that he wanted to be an astronaut, and there he is on my phone saying hi and thanking me from outer space. How about that?

We keep track of all the kids who were awarded those scholarships, and it's always a thrill to hear about their accomplishments.

## Parry Thomas

SHORTLY AFTER I MET STEVE AND ELAINE, I INTRODUCED THEM TO Sun Valley, Idaho, and snow skiing. We went skiing there a couple of times, and they eventually bought a home there. Steve actually lived at Sun Valley for about six months in the early '70s and he got in with the Sun Valley Company and became a ski instructor. We had several conversations about what direction his career should go at that time, after he had sold out of his deal at the Frontier.

## Steve Wynn

WE COMPLETED THE SALE OF THE FRONTIER TO HOWARD HUGHES IN November of 1967, and Parry told me to stay in Las Vegas. He said that the city needed a young guy like me. He said to me several times, "Stay in Vegas. You'll own the place." I had a few hundred thousand dollars was all, and he gave me that advice. He said that he and Jerry Mack would find something for me.

I had been snow skiing since I was a boy. I actually competed on a ski team in high school. And Parry invited me to go for a week to Sun Valley where he went every winter. Elaine couldn't go so it was just me, and also there was Bud James, who was the Del Webb guy at the Sahara, and the Macks, the Greenspuns, and Herb Jones and all their kids.

I was in my mid-twenties, just barely older than some of the kids that were there. But I had been introduced to the others not as a kid, but as a friend of Parry's. That put me on the right side of Hank Greenspun right away. If I was a friend of Parry's, then I was okay with Hank. And from that point on I was Parry's boy, like the sixth child in that family. Neither of my daughters ever got to know their grandfathers. They both died before their time. So Parry became the grandfather they didn't have. He showed total paternal indulgence to me.

The relationship that Parry had with me was the most profound that a young man could have. I did not have the kind of confidence that you get from real achievement, or from a long life of solving problems. There's a certain amount of confidence you get that you earn, that I have now at age sixty-six. When you're just twenty-six, what you have isn't earned confidence, it's bravado. It ain't common sense, it's wishful thinking.

Every young guy who acts confident will admit, in spite of all the bravado, that underneath he's thinking, "Oh, shit."

As a young man I derived my confidence from the fact that Parry had confidence in me. I would tell myself, if Parry thinks this, then I must be okay, even if I'm scared shitless. If Parry thinks I'm okay, he wouldn't be wrong. It's possible that *I* could be wrong, but *he* wouldn't be. So my source of self-confidence in my late twenties was based on his opinion of me. Especially when I was most at risk.

I shouldn't have been in the Frontier deal. Face it, I was lucky it lasted for only three months. Parry said that if that deal had gone on any longer, I would have been stigmatized by those guys. But he said it turned out great because the wiretaps showed that the guys from Detroit hated me, because I was screwing them all by helping sell the joint to Parry Thomas and Howard Hughes. So in hindsight I got out to Las Vegas in the wrong deal, but when I got out of it Parry told me that we'd figure it out because the town needed good young people. He said some day I would own the place, and I thought, what a ridiculous thing for him to say. But he wasn't laughing when he said it.

And shortly after that he found the liquor business for me.

## Elaine Wynn

SUBSEQUENT TO STEVE GETTING HIS GAMING LICENSE IT WAS SHOWN that we had partners in the Frontier who we were totally unaware of, who were not the partners we thought we had. A little background on the Frontier will tell you that Maury Friedman had brought in some people from Detroit, and they were fronted by the owners of record. So there was a whole investigation subsequent to our sale of the hotel. There was even a wiretap with an audio recording of these guys saying that Steve Wynn was green and that he didn't know any of these guys. Thank goodness for that wiretap, or it would have been a short happy career. That would have been the end for us in Las Vegas.

## Parry Thomas

IN THOSE DAYS IN OUR BANKING BUSINESS, THE BIGGEST LIQUOR DIS-tributor in town was DeLuca Liquor and Wine. Bob Keyser was the manager of that operation and he was also a director of our main banking competitor, First National Bank.

For whatever reason, Bob never had good things to say about Valley Bank or about me. He was always sticking pins in us, and it kind of galled me that here we were financing all of the hotels, and Bob had all the liquor business in town, mainly coming from the hotels that we were financing. We felt he should be more appreciative of what we were doing to assist his biggest customers. That stuck in my craw that Keyser would continue knocking the hell out of us.

So I told Steve that we needed another big liquor distributor in Las Vegas, a person who banked with us, and that Jerry Mack and I could help him get some good accounts. Jerry and I knew everyone in town, and we just knew we could get something going for him.

## Steve Wynn

BOB KEYSER WAS ON THE BOARD AT FIRST NATIONAL, AND THE PEOPLE at his bank were afraid of Parry because his bank was coming up, growing every year, and Parry had a death grip on the gaming industry. The only gaming account First National had was with Moe Dalitz, because Moe was pissed off at Parry due to his support for Hank Greenspun.

Parry and Jerry were mad at Keyser. Why should that guy get all his business from joints that they were controlling or helping to grow? And so Parry promptly ensconced me in that shitty business, so that I could give it a go.

## Parry Thomas

I ASKED JAKE GOTTLIEB, WHO OWNED THE REAL ESTATE FOR THE DUNES Hotel, if he knew Meshulam Riklis, who owned Schenley Liquor. Riklis was at his office in New York at the time, and Jake sure enough knew him well. They were good friends. So Jake introduced me to Riklis and I had long talks with him about this brilliant young man that I thought so highly of, and I told him that if we put Steve Wynn in the liquor business in Las Vegas, with everyone's help he could have a very successful business here.

I got Steve together with Riklis back in New York, at his office at 711 Fifth Avenue. Isidore Becker was the president of Schenley and he was Meshulem's right-hand guy and he was in on the negotiating.

Steve and they worked out a deal for Steve to become the exclusive distributor of Schenley's products, and with it their premier brand, Dewar's Scotch. Steve was very bright in his whole approach to it, and on his own he worked out some good wine contacts. We didn't help him at all on that aspect. So he formed the Wynn Distributing Company, and Jerry and I did everything we possibly could to get him in business with all the hotels.

## Steve Wynn

JAKE GOTTLIEB KISSED PARRY'S RING IN THOSE DAYS. HE UNDERSTOOD that Parry was the link to the real money. So Riklis hears from Gottlieb that Parry needs this favor, and he wants Parry on his side. So Gottlieb takes Parry to dinner and Parry has me in tow. This was really big for me, but it was small potatoes for Riklis.

Parry says, "Let us have the liquor deal in Las Vegas. You'll get all the business."

Riklis's response when he was told about it was like, "Anything you say, Jake. Why not?"

Best Brands was losing money. Riklis asked who was gonna buy it. Gottlieb told him Steve Wynn. Next thing you know, Riklis issues an order to the president of Schenley, Izzy Becker, to sell the wholesale house in Nevada to this kid Steve Wynn. [*Wynn snaps his fingers.*] It was done just like that, a non-event sale of an asset. For $65,000.

## Parry Thomas

IN THOSE DAYS IT WAS JUST DESERT OUT THERE WHERE STEVE BUILT his warehouse. There was no street, no nothing, and he had to have a street to get into his office and so he called it Wynn Road. That north-south street that runs near the Strip still has that name.

There were just the two distributors in town. DeLuca had Coors beer and all the Seagram wine, and Steve started to get a big share of the market. In a short time he became very successful in the liquor distribution business. The trouble was that it grew so fast that the volume of his business outran the capital accounts of both Steve individually and the bank to carry all the receivables and all the inventory.

Steve wisely renegotiated with Schenley to take over directly and they put one of their larger distributors from Florida into that deal. And that's when Larry Ruvo came into the picture.

## Steve Wynn

I RAN THE LIQUOR BUSINESS FROM 1968 TO '72 AND IT WAS INVALUABLE training. It taught me everything about the whole back-of-the-house routine, the purchasing aspect and the ethical framework of how that operated in Nevada. I learned who was honest, who was dishonest, how frequently kickbacks occurred. I was actually surprised to learn there was less than I would have thought. The actual exchange of money for business was rare. If there were twelve hotels, maybe one paid kickbacks, and it was usually at the boss level. Purchasing agents were afraid of doing it because they knew they'd lose their jobs.

What was rampant, and is even today, is that relationships, not price, very often determine the deal. It was all about how you courted the purchasing agent and flattered his ego and attended to him. It wasn't a question of how big the gift was; rather, it was the fact that you remembered the important birthdays, remembered Christmas, showed up at their kid's bar mitzvah or christening, or went to a wedding.

Of course I was willing to do that, because I understood to what extent personal relationships could influence the judgment of a buyer. And that's very important to me even today in understanding my own business. I've just gotta make sure that my relationship with my purchasing agents is better than anybody else's relationship with them.

If I wasn't maintaining those relationships properly, then I was turning them loose at the mercy of other very smart businessmen who were competitors.

### Larry Ruvo

I MET PARRY IN THE LATE '60S. STEVE WYNN WAS BUYING BEST BRANDS wholesale liquor company [*and changing the name to Wynn Distributing*], and Parry was very instrumental in that acquisition. I was still in Los Angeles, working as general manager of the Playboy Club. I subsequently left that job to come back and work with Steve at the liquor company.

In 1969 I was working with Steve at Wynn Distributing, and even then Steve had these illusions of grandeur of making it bigger and better and capitalizing on a market that he thought one day would come, and that market was people drinking wine. There just wasn't a lot of wine consumption in Las Vegas back then.

I sat in on many meetings with Parry and from time to time he would give us some direction, some guidance, or some help. Steve even then and still today looks at Parry as a father figure. I knew that Parry was an investor in some Las Vegas properties at the time. He certainly knew all the major players, and through my relationship with Steve I developed a friendship with him.

I was running the sales for the liquor company when I came back from L.A. I had known Steve from when we were both working at the Frontier, and you knew even then he was going to become hugely successful in Las Vegas. Parry was just terrific in talking to us about how to branch out, how to further develop our business. He had set an example of how to grow through all of the personal relationships he had developed, and there was just a great business sense that he was able to instill in us.

When Steve left to get involved in the Golden Nugget in about 1972, the name of the company went back from Wynn Distributing to its original name, Best Brands. I was then twenty-six years old, and the company needed more lines of liquor, particularly a major brand.

I was fortunately able to get a major liquor line, W.A. Taylor, which would bring me some great business, but I needed financing to buy the company. I put together all these business plans, and I made an appointment to meet with Parry Thomas downtown at his bank office.

I remember clearly how nervous I was. I recall walking into Parry's office and he had this big executive chair, with this black-and-white hound's-tooth pattern. And he sat there looking so regal with his white hair against this black-and-white print chair. I remember when the conversation started he didn't ask anything about my business plan. He just had a way of talking about neutral subjects and putting you at ease. You almost felt like a member of the family.

I had prepared for that appointment with all these sales projections and charts, to show him what I wanted to do with the company. I believe the amount of the loan I was seeking was $700,000, which was just a huge amount of money back then.

I talked a little about my business plan and as I was reaching into my briefcase to pull all this information out, Parry looked at me and said, "I don't need to see the numbers. I just want you to tell me what you're going to do with this money, how we're going to help you, and what you can do to make this a success."

For the next ten minutes I just spoke from the heart and told him exactly what I thought I could do, and what I was confident I could do. When I had finished, he looked at me and said, "Okay, you got it."

You could have knocked me over when he said that.

This was about a banker who believed in people, who wanted to help the little guy. Parry Thomas certainly helped this little guy, and he certainly changed my life and our company's life, but to him it wasn't just about business and the almighty dollar. It was about giving a kid a break.

I remember looking at him after he said he'd give me the money, and I said, "I promise I'll do everything I can to make you proud and pay this money back . . . on time or ahead of schedule."

"I knew that before I agreed to loan you the money," he replied.

Well, I got the line of cordials and liqueurs from W.A. Taylor, and although that line has since been dissolved, at the time that brand really put our company on the map. We didn't have any really major international brands, other than Dewar's and some of the Schenley products, so that really catapulted us to the next level.

## Parry Thomas

LARRY RUVO IS A VERY CAPABLE MAN AND HELLUVA GUY, AND SO AT the time Steve moved on, he was very fortunate to have Larry there.

Larry took over that business and he's made a brilliant success of it. I'm so proud of Larry.

## Steve Wynn

I DIDN'T PARTICULARLY CARE FOR THE LIQUOR BUSINESS, BECAUSE when I was involved there was no margin. The buyers had too much power. There was no large community here. There were just a couple hundred thousand people in Las Vegas, so you were at the mercy of your customers. Eighty percent of the liquor business then was in the hands of maybe twelve or fifteen people. They told you; you didn't tell them. And I had to work too hard, kissing the ass of bar managers. I'm not cut out for that. It's not my skill set. I'm a designer.

With the tremendous growth of Las Vegas and his own considerable talents, Larry Ruvo changed that balance of power. He now controls the liquor industry in this state the old-fashioned way. Larry has outworked his competition and he's got all those important liquor brands because he could outsell everybody else. He never said no to any hotel president's charity. He never said no to any request for help. He always remembers everyone's birthday. He shops incessantly for lovely, appropriate gifts that fall below the level of bribery, but certainly fall into the level of coercion . . . legitimate coercion. Ruvo's a master at that. And he controls this market for all the right reasons. Then he went and got the law changed with price controls and the distillers couldn't take the brands away.

## Parry Thomas

WHENEVER I COULD IN THE BANKING BUSINESS WHERE I THOUGHT young people had the ability and the work ethic, I did everything I could to try and always help them.

I certainly took that approach with Steve Wynn, who in my opinion was far and away the brightest, quickest learner of any young man I'd ever met in my life. Steve liked to learn. He would study situations.

He wanted to know everything he could about a subject. He never asked silly questions. A lot of the young men would ask silly questions. Steve would always ask the right questions. He was thinking all the time. So anyway, when Steve left the liquor business he had a little bit of money and was looking for something to do.

Things kind of came together at that point. There was this little strip of property between Caesars Palace and the intersection of Flamingo Road and the Strip that was about 160 feet wide and 1,500 feet deep. That property was owned by Jake Gottlieb. What had happened was that we had merged Jake's company, Western Transportation, into a company we owned called Continental Connector. But even after the merger, Jake ran that company as though he owned it by himself. And Jake was a horse-player. He loved the race track and he loved to bet big. That was his preferred way of gambling. But he got behind and he owed Western Transportation a lot of money.

Bill Schindler, who was his right-hand guy, came to me and said, "What are we gonna do about Jake? He keeps pulling money out of the company and it's a public company and we have disclosure issues and all these other problems."

So I sat Jake down and said, "You've gotta sell this property, but don't worry about it. I'll have Howard Hughes buy it."

So Jake sold that strip of land to Hughes. I think the price was about four or five hundred thousand, which was a pretty good price back then. But it was a bastard property because it had all these Nevada Power cables going over the top of it, which put serious limitations on what you could do with it.

Before Hughes bought the property, I had informed Caesars Palace of the sale first, just out of a matter of responsibility, because it was the property next to them and I figured they should definitely own it to protect themselves. The Perlman brothers owned Caesars at the time, and they said they just didn't want any part of it, so I went to Hughes. The Perlmans passed on the deal, which was a big mistake, because even with the limitations of the power lines, an owner could always make money on that property because of its location right on that major intersection.

Steve and I talked about the possibilities there and he got very interested in that property right away. He spoke with Herb Nall, who was our guy doing all the real estate work for Hughes. Steve worked a deal with Nall, who went to Bob Maheu and subsequently Hughes agreed to sell that parcel to Steve and his partner and long-time friend Abe Rosenberg.

I think they paid about a million dollars for the property, maybe a little more, so it wasn't a bad deal for Hughes. He'd doubled his money in a short time.

## Steve Wynn

I WAS PAYING ATTENTION TO THE LIQUOR BUSINESS JUST AFTER HOWARD Hughes had left Las Vegas when something happened.

You know during the late '60s Hughes continued buying stuff. He bought Shelby Williams and Sam Diamond out of the Silver Slipper. And those guys . . . a lot of these old bookmakers and gamblers that owned little joints now had some real money, and they were too young to go away. They were still in their sixties, and they weren't done yet. They'd each made about a million-five on the deal, Shelby maybe two million.

So they were all sitting around at the Las Vegas Country Club playing cards and bored to death. They had *schpilkes* [*Yiddish for "ants in their pants."*]

My family had outlived our house on the Tropicana golf course, and Parry told me about a house for sale near him on Rancho Circle.

It had been owned by a guy named Fox, who had been brought to Las Vegas to run the airport Hughes owned [*now the North Las Vegas Airport*], and the house was on the market. When I went to look at it, I could see it was not right for our purposes. Our second daughter,

Gilly, had just been born here, and the house wouldn't work for us. It was more of a tear-down.

The realtor who showed me the house was Hughes' long-time real estate guy, Herb Nall, and we had a good conversation that day. And in that conversation I said to Herb, "Why don't you sell me that corner next to the Dunes? What are you going to do with that? It's just a skinny piece of property."

I knew that Shelby and Claudine Williams and Sam Diamond were sitting around with nothing to do, and I knew they would be interested in building a little joint on that corner and I thought I could do a thing like John MacArthur had done at the Frontier and become a landlord. I could make something like twenty grand a month, which to me was end-of-the-world money and instant security for my family. I mean, here I was, 29 years old with two young daughters and I could make a real score.

So I said to Herb, "I'll give you a million dollars for that property." "Yeah?" he said. "Listen, son, if you've got a million dollars, I advise you to spend it somewhere else. I've worked for this guy [*Hughes*] for twenty-one years. He doesn't sell. He buys."

I asked him how much they'd paid for it, and he said he wasn't free to tell me.

He then said, "I had nothing to do with buying that. That was the other group." [*Nall's reference was to Bob Maheu and the previous group of Hughes Nevada operators, who had been replaced by Bill Gay and his group when Hughes suddenly left Las Vegas in November 1970.*]

Then Herb Nall added something very important. He said, "I don't know why the hell we bought it. I think it's a lousy piece of real estate."

The revealing thing to me was that Nall expressed disdain and displeasure. He distanced himself from the transaction. That was important because it stood out in my mind. He was telling me that they didn't want this stepchild. Maybe that transaction represented a kinky story. Maybe somebody got paid off for buying this sliver, you know, for taking it off somebody's hands. But he wouldn't tell me how much they'd paid.

A day or two later I went down to the bank and talked to Parry about it. And I explained what had happened, and I told him I also knew that the Hughes organization was making a $10,000-a-month lease payment to Cliff Jones for a piece of land west of the Landmark. And the lease for $10,000 a month had an option to purchase for $1 million. So in effect they were paying twelve percent on their money, a hundred and twenty thousand a year for a million-dollar thing. It didn't make sense in those days of six or seven percent money. But as usual in a big corporation like the Hughes company, which was a headless monster, one hand often didn't know what the other was doing.

Parry then explained that Cliff Jones had gone into bankruptcy and to do Cliff a favor his bank had taken the Landmark property off his hands and written it off. So the Bank of Las Vegas owned it.

Suddenly, it wasn't a casual conversation anymore. Parry realized that Hughes could sell the Caesars property and use the money to buy the Landmark property and not have to pay that twelve percent each month. And I told him I could put another little Silver Slipper-type place on that corner and Shelby Williams and his partners could build a little joint and pay me rent.

Parry said, "You think you could do that?"

"Absolutely," I said.

You could see the wheels turning in Parry's head. He picked up the phone and told his secretary, Belle James, "Belle, get me Bill Gay, will you?"

Parry said to Gay, who was now running the Hughes Nevada operation because Maheu and the others had been de-fanged, "Hey, listen, Bill, I think it's time we got rid of that odd, strange piece of property next to Caesars, with the heavy wire going over it. . . . No, I had nothing to do with buying it, either . . . Maheu did it. That's not one of the pieces I bought. . . . Yeah, I think I've got a buyer, and we could use the money to buy off that parking lot lease that we're paying ten thousand a month for at the Landmark . . . uh, huh . . . get back to me, will you?"

Parry hung up and pointed a finger at me and said. "Now listen to me. Do not repeat this conversation. These are very strange people."

He then told me that Hughes was in the Bahamas and he had to send a telemessage, or a fax, whatever it was in those days. And that it would be handled through the Hughes secretaries, Roy Crawford, Howard Eckersley, and that crew.

A couple of days go by and it's now Sunday morning. My home phone rings. I'm at the pool with Elaine and Kevyn and Gillian, who is just a baby. I run into the den and I pick up the phone, and it's, "Hello, Steve, this is Herb Nall. I hope I'm not calling at a bad time. I got your number from Parry."

I tell him it's fine. I'm in a bathing suit and standing on a travertine floor. The moment is as fresh to me as if it happened an hour ago.

He says, "You still interested in that property next to Caesars?"

"Yes."

"Well, I'm now going to tell you what we paid for it. We paid a million and twenty thousand dollars for it, and I want a profit."

Now there was a critically important event that had happened between my first conversation with Herb Nall and this phone call, and that was that Kirk Kerkorian had announced just a day or two before that he was going to build a huge property on the southeast corner of Flamingo and the Strip, right across from the sliver of land next to Caesars. So I figured the land I wanted would have doubled in price overnight with this news.

But Nall says, "I want a million one for it."

[*Wynn whispers this next part.*] I still don't think he trusted the offer I'd made. But now my heart is beating faster. He wants only eighty thousand dollars profit! I can hardly believe my ears.

[*Back to a normal tone.*] I said, "Yes, that's good."

He said, "Let me read something to you, and please pay attention to this. It's very important, Mr. Wynn."

And I'll paraphrase what he said, but it was like this: "You may offer the property to Mr. Stephen Wynn, liquor distributor. But you are to stress that we want no publicity whatsoever. In order to ensure that, there will be no escrow. Simply a sale on the spot and at some appropriate moment. And if there's any publicity prior to that, you will not conclude the transaction. This is quite important that we not start the rumor mill that we are exiting Las Vegas, considering that this will be the first sale we've ever made, although it's an inconsequential transaction."

And it was signed "H R H," Howard Robard Hughes.

It turns out the corner was owned by the old man himself. There was no other entity involved. It was owned by Howard R. Hughes Jr.

I remember putting the phone down and, like Steve McQueen in *The Thomas Crown Affair*, I danced around on my bare feet on the travertine floor because I knew on the spot that I had just made my first big deal. I knew that this was the biggest score in my family's history . . . including my father and my mother and my grandparents from Europe. I had just made serious money.

[*In a long aside, Wynn then explained how as a way of attaining the cash for the transaction, he included his friend Abe Rosenberg in the deal. He further explained how he treated him more than fairly when the land was flipped back to Caesars, and how that gesture would pay dividends of good will later on.*]

## Parry Thomas

THE QUESTION NOW WAS HOW WAS STEVE GOING TO MOTIVATE CAESARS to buy the property from him, as they were the only logical buyer. He knew that they'd turned it down when I had initially offered it to them. So Steve had some plans drawn up to build a small gaming joint and a small hotel and he saw to it that the guys at Caesars got those plans.

Some people thought it was just a decoy to get Caesars' interest, because they certainly wouldn't want a small place competing next to theirs and occupying that prominent corner. But in truth Steve was serious when he drew up the plans. If Caesars didn't buy it from him, he was going to go ahead with building a place. And he would have done it and done damn well with it.

Caesars ended up buying the property from him for, I believe, $2.2 or $2.3 million, so that was a big score for Steve and Abe Rosenberg.

Around this same time, we were trying to buy the Golden Nugget for our Continental Connector company. But the SEC came in and accused the Siedman and Siedman auditors at the Dunes, which was part of Continental Connector, of an improper audit just two days before the deal was going to close. So that blew the deal for us.

I talked to Steve a lot about that deal, but I didn't pressure him to make a play for the Golden Nugget. He thought of it himself. I told him why I liked the property and how with good management it could be very successful. Although there wasn't a hotel there yet—it was just a casino—it was located on the number one corner of downtown, with the Horseshoe and the Fremont and the Four Queens on the other corners, and there was quite a bit of adjacent property that the Golden Nugget owned that could be developed for expansion.

Believe it or not, although corporate gaming was just coming into practice in Nevada, the Golden Nugget had been grandfathered in. It was a public corporation owned by stockholders that were spread all over the place. And the management of the Nugget didn't own very much stock. I knew that.

The biggest block of stock was owned by a guy named Jerry Zarowitz, who was a Mob-connected guy and one of the casino managers at Caesars Palace. The Nevada Black Book of excluded persons was about to include Zarowitz, and he was on the verge of being kicked out of the state.

Zarowitz owned about ninety or a hundred thousand shares of Golden Nugget stock, and Steve got Jerry to sell him that whole block. Then through brokers and whatnot, Steve quite rapidly starting buying up all the stock he could. We had a series of loans with him through the years on that property. There was a lot of work to be done on the Nugget. The first thing he had to do was straighten out the layout of the casino. It was built on a slope, on a hill. Everything goes so far and then you have to step down. He had to straighten that out so that it was a level floor all the way through.

Within a short time Steve owned about a third of the company in stock. He then presented his position to Buck Blaine, who was the president and general manager of the Nugget.

Buck was an awfully nice fellow. He had quite a background. Long before getting into the casino business he'd been a high-scaler on the Boulder Dam. He'd done that with Cliff Jones in the 1930s. Dangerous stuff. But in my opinion Buck was in over his head in running the Golden Nugget. Plus he was getting robbed blind by nearly every employee in the joint. Everybody down there was in business for himself, which is why I wanted to buy the Golden Nugget in the first place. I knew with good management we could get an influx in earnings in a hurry to Continental Connector. We had plans to expand the property and had high hopes for it until the government stepped in.

Anyway, once Steve explained his position to the board at the Nugget, he was able to take over. He treated Buck Blaine very fairly and gave him a nice retirement offer and was able keep his friendship and his good will, which was important.

Steve then had to come in and fire more than half the staff, literally clean house, so there was quite a bit of turmoil in the beginning. But within about four or five months, he had cleaned the place up and things were turning around.

Then he was able to buy the adjacent land from Art Ham Jr. so that he could really stretch his casino out. I think he paid him a million bucks for it. And after that was finished he wanted to build the rooms, and we financed the rooms. And then he built the second tower, which really enhanced the entire downtown area and made all the other owners take stock of their properties. Our son Roger did most of the design work on those later rooms, and that's where he really started to establish his reputation as a talented designer.

Steve's dad, Mike, had been in the bingo business and Steve had worked at the Frontier, so he had a good feel for the gambling business. But to think he had gone from running a successful liquor distribution company to operating a casino like that, and he was just thirty or thirty-one years old, is impressive.

With the possible exception of Michael Milken, Steve is the quickest learner of any man I've ever met. The two of them were really twins in intelligence.

When Steve was running the slot department at the Frontier, he was learning about other aspects of the business as well. He was really double-timing to understand how everything worked there. And when he was in the liquor business he learned a helluva lot about how hotels were operated and their purchasing and warehousing and all the details.

### Elaine Wynn

AFTER THE FRONTIER GOT FLIPPED SO QUICKLY, STEVE WAS PONDERING, well, what do we do next? The question was, do we stay here? Or do we go back East? He had made a nice enough score, and I think his appetite had been whetted. But we hadn't been here very long, maybe three years. Not even.

At that point, Parry was extremely persuasive, and he said to Steve, "Your business is up and running in Maryland, and we need young people like you to stay in Las Vegas."

Now what had happened is that they got a law passed that allowed Steve to maintain some ownership in our bingo business, because in those days Gaming Control had a foreign ownership rule that if you owned an interest in a gambling venture outside of Nevada, you had to divest yourself. So we advocated that a law be passed that could make some exceptions for people like us in this case, where it wasn't conventional casino gambling [*something that would be considered competitive to Nevada's interests*], but rather a bingo business. And then it got changed anyway because of New Jersey and everything else that was happening in the gaming world.

Parry made a case for Las Vegas being a young community that needed to have people of vision and energy, and that the city needed clean, college-educated, respectable people with families who were willing to settle here and become the next generation for this growing community with so much potential.

I'm not sure that Steve was the only person who Parry ever gave that speech to . . . probably not . . . but he was in a position to be persuasive at a moment when Steve might have toyed with the idea of leaving.

Parry's argument made sense to Steve, but he asked Parry, "Well, what do you think that I would do next?" And Parry said something to the effect of, "Don't worry, leave it up to me. Just trust me. There will be plenty of ventures, plenty of opportunity here." So Steve said okay.

Then the liquor company idea was presented to Steve. And Parry knew the guys who had the Schenley brand, and he thought that might be a good fit.

And this is where Parry showed himself to be the great chess player, always knowing how to move the pieces around so that it would make sense and so that Las Vegas would be the big winner in the end.

He stashed Steve at the liquor company for as long as Steve could stand it, until he got the whole thing torqued. What that business really did for Steve was it gave him an understanding of the business from the purveyor side of things. So by no means was it a lost exercise. What eventually tipped it for him was that the more successful he got, the more inventory he had to lay in. He could see it wasn't the type of business that was going to give him the kind of score that he wanted. He saw the liquor business as lucrative, but the more hotels he was servicing, the more inventory he had to lay in and pay for until the product got purchased. It was almost like arbitrage, and it lost its glamour once he prevailed, once he made it into the wine behemoth that Larry Ruvo then capitalized on.

I think it was a great exercise for Steve, because it did show him the shenanigans that go on in the back of the house, so if the liquor purveyors were fooling around with deals and stuff, he could imagine what was happening with food. When he went back into the business in the front of the house [at the Golden Nugget], he could understand what was going on in purchasing.

When we sold the liquor company, we went up to Sun Valley for the winter and Steve became a ski instructor. He had asked Parry to keep his eyes open to find him his next business in Las Vegas, and Parry said, "Don't worry. You take the season off and go skiing and I'll find something."

We built our house in Sun Valley and moved in around November of that year. By that March we were up on the ski slopes and looking at each other with nobody else around, and Steve said, "Okay, I'm bored. It's time to go home."

And shortly after that the Golden Nugget situation came along.

## Steve Wynn

THAT PURCHASE FROM HOWARD HUGHES STILL RANKS AS THE MOST thrilling business deal of my life. That's number one and it's a long way down to number two. I remember just going "Wow! Wow!" when Herb Nall told me they would sell it. I ran outside and told Elaine and started jumping up and down. I yelled that I'd just bought the corner next to Caesars Palace for a million dollars. Fuck! I couldn't believe it. I didn't immediately know where I was going to get the money, but I knew it would be easy.

So I got a third of it from Abe Rosenberg, who understood it as a real estate deal. I then began designing this little place, called The Godfather, that would look like the Golden Nugget. I was even going to get a loan from the plumbers' union or the pipe-fitters' union through Morris Shenker [*who was running the Dunes for Continental Connector*]. I let that news leak to Caesars and I even made an announcement about the drawings for the place when I appeared before the planning board.

Abe Rosenberg called me up after that news was out and said, "Look, Steve, I'm vice chairman of Liggett & Myers, a public company, and I don't want a casino license. If you're not going to sell the property or lease it, take it yourself. Parry Thomas will let you have the money to build this.

"You know I went into this as a real estate deal with you," he said, "not a gaming deal, so I wish you the best, but I'd appreciate it if you'd just take me off the loan. You keep the other third."

I said, "Abe, Kirk Kerkorian's just announced that he's building across the street. That means our property's worth two million dollars."

He said, "Steve, it may be worth two million some day, but you have to go find money, you have to build. . . . I don't need a profit."

I told him his three-hundred-some-thousand-dollar loan was worth at least seven hundred thousand and that what he was saying was ridiculous, that it was bothering my conscience.

He said, "I'll tell you what I'll do. You're being very sweet about it. You get me off the note and you give me a promissory note for a hundred thousand dollars with interest payable at prime rate at Manufacturer's Hanover. Interest only, for as long as you want. And when you get around to it and you think you've got the money, you can pay back the loan."

I sent Abe a quit claim deed and he signed off. Since I didn't own the liquor company anymore, Parry Thomas lent me the money. He just issued a new note and there was no more Abe Rosenberg, and I owned the land myself.

After I'd filed my plans for building The Godfather with the board, Billy Weinberger at Caesars called me up. He said, "Listen to me. We give your liquor company a lot of business and I have protected you around here."

That was true. He had.

He then said, "Cliff Perlman is ripping my ass off. He said that we needed that corner and that he had made that deal with Maheu and Bob gave him his word of honor that if ever Hughes was going to sell it, we would have the first right of refusal. And they sold it out from underneath us."

I told Billy that I had bought it from the other group [*the one headed by Bill Gay.*]

Billy told me that he understood that, but that Perlman didn't care about that. He said that Cliff called him an asshole, and that he'd never been bitched out like that in his life, and that I had to sell them the property. Cliff told him to do whatever he had to do to get the property back.

So I went down to the bank to talk to Parry. He was on the board at Caesars, so I told him the situation there and that I may have caused a problem.

Parry said, "I take very good care of Cliff. Don't get excited. I'm glad you're worried about me, but you don't have to be. This is about you. But this raises a good point. You have ten or fifteen thousand shares of Golden Nugget that I had you buy when we were merging it with the Dunes. I spoke at the stockholders' meeting in favor of it. It was a family affair. You still have those shares?"

I said yes.

"And I know you have this dream of taking control of the Nugget."

Parry took a long pause, then continued. "Now Steve, building a hotel on the Strip is a helluva thing. I've financed nearly every one of them. I've never seen one of them that was built that didn't need to be changed somewhat afterwards. And that's okay. But what bothers me about this narrow piece of land is whether you have room to change it down the road. Can you make any adjustments after it's built? It seems so prohibitively arranged that if you don't get it just right, it'll be hard to fix later."

He added, "I'm not telling you what to do."

And Parry never does. He just presents information to you in a logical way so you can make the right decision yourself.

"What I'm asking you to do is think about two things," he said. "Those guys that are in the Nugget are very worried . . . very stitched in politically in Las Vegas. They think of you as an outsider, someone they'd like to not have to deal with. And you don't have enough money or the position to deal with a hotel on the Strip *and* the Golden Nugget. You really ought to decide, and I'll be glad to help you. What do you prefer, buying the Nugget or building the little casino on the corner? Why don't you take some time and think about it. And if you want to concentrate on the Nugget, then I'll talk to Perlman. You don't have to do that. But if you don't, then sell the stock in the Nugget. Think about it, son? Okay?"

Parry gave no preference whatsoever in his presentation to me. He put it right on my ass.

I went home that weekend and sat around thinking about it. And I decided that being a pioneer on the Strip wasn't going to be so easy. I went back down to the bank on Monday and told Parry I'd thought it over and that the Golden Nugget was a much safer place for someone my age, that building on the Strip might not be the right time. [*Wynn was just thirty years old.*]

"Is that your decision?" he said.

"Yes," I said.

"How much do you want for the property?" he asked.

"I want two and a quarter million," I said. "But I don't want any of it in Caesars stock."

That was double what I'd paid for it.

"I think that's a wise decision," Parry said. "Let me see what I can do. And Steve, don't tell anybody what you decided, or even that you talked to me about it. Let me explore this. Let's just see what happens here."

That conversation took place on a Monday. The following day, Tuesday, Parry calls me and says come down to the bank. He hands me a legal sheet of paper. Escrow. Purchase price, $2.25 million. Proceeds to pay off loan, $1.25 million. Escrow fee to Bank of Las Vegas, $60,000, blah, blah, blah. Total, $1.23 million. Balance, $1.02 million.

He says, "It's also a quit-claim deed. Sign it."

"If I sign this, do they own it?"

"Yup," he says. "I've got a check here for a million two."

"Is this a final enforceable document?

"Yup. Congratulations, son. You just made a million dollars. I never made a million when I was thirty years old."

I said, "Let me understand this. This is an irrevocable document?"

"Yes."

"They overpaid," I say.

"Don't ever say that again," Parry says. "Don't make fun of someone you just sold something to. You promise me you'll never repeat that statement."

"Of course. . . . Is Cliff Perlman angry?"

"No, he's thrilled. Thinks I did him a favor."

"He's not angry that you helped me get it?"

"No, why should he be? I was taking care of you. I take care of him, too."

I said, "Can I make one change? Not in the price or anything."

"What are you talking about?"

"Well, you know, Parry, Abe went into this deal as a real estate deal, and when it started to be an operating thing with the gaming, because of his vice chairmanship at Liggett & Myers, he said he wanted out and you know, I got that silly $100,000 note. You know, if it wasn't for him, I couldn't have done this. And since it's only an escrow instruction, could we rewrite it and make it $677,000 for me, $333,000 for Abe Rosenberg?"

"But he sold it to you, Steve."

"I never changed the deed. It's at the courthouse . . . Stephen A. Wynn and Abraham Rosenberg doing business as a partnership. I just gave Abe the note and he gave me the quit-claim deed and I never recorded it. No one knows whether it's two-thirds, one-third, or what, and it would be such a kick."

He said, "You want to give him $333,000, even though you bought the property from him?"

"Well, when he went into this it was a real estate deal, and it turned out to be a real estate deal, a pretty neat one at that."

Parry called in Belle James and had her redo the checks, and I forged Abe Rosenberg's signature on his as his attorney-in-fact. Parry sat there quietly, and so did I. My heart was going a hundred miles an hour. I then gave Abe's address to Belle and I wrote on a piece of paper: "Dear Abe, Attached is an escrow instruction. It reflects the transaction, but at the last minute there was a change of plans . . . turned out to be a real estate deal after all. I'll send you a complete accounting in a few weeks. Meantime, congratulations. It worked out the way we thought. Warmest, Steve."

I folded up the thing in three pieces, folded the legal paper up, put a paper clip in with the check, put it in the envelope, licked it and asked Belle to mail it.

Parry Thomas was sitting there watching all this. He says, "I'm proud of you."

It was a happy day.

In the meantime, Shelby Williams had made a deal with Harrah's to build a Holiday Inn on the Strip with a casino in front of it, so he was out of the picture. But when I didn't need the drawings for The Godfather anymore, I gave them to Michael Gaughan, and he used them as inspiration for the Barbary Coast.

∞

I had to buy Jerry Zarowitz's stock at the Golden Nugget before the licensing hearing. Phil Hannifin, who was the chairman of the Gaming Commission, said, "I need you to clear this company if you're going to go forward with it."

I said, "Yeah, but you told me I couldn't put the bingo stock in Maryland up as collateral."

He said, "I don't care what you do, just get rid of Zarowitz."

So I said, "All right, you're saying I don't have to sell the bingo and I can put the bingo stock up?"

He said, "Yeah."

I went to Parry and told him what Phil said. Parry told me that Hannifin was right, that I didn't want Zarowitz in the deal now with my being in there. He said he would loan me another hundred G's. It was a $600,000 buyout and I used my money from the Caesars deal to increase my position to ten percent of the Nugget. It was all my money, but I was still short.

I called Abe Rosenberg on the phone and told him I was going to pursue a change of control at the Golden Nugget and that I was going to be making this tender offer for the purchase. The stock was six dollars a share and I was fifty thousand shares short of Zarowitz's position. I told Abe I needed some help, and asked him if he could buy $300,000 of stock.

He asked if he was going to be part of a group and subject to a gaming license. I told him no, that he wouldn't have five percent of the stock [*which would require the buyer to go through licensing*], but just two percent.

He asked again if he would be part of my group, and I told him I just needed the money to have someone hold the stock so that this guy Zarowitz wouldn't own it.

The stock was selling cheap and I told Abe I needed the favor, and that I was sure he would do well with it, that the stock couldn't do worse than its current price.

He said, "Okay, I'll split it between myself and my brother. Have your guys call me and we'll get it done."

Abe took the fifty thousand shares.

Anyway, when that sale was finished, we took out Zarowitz and I got licensed at the meeting in June 1973.

I believe I was the youngest to get a gaming license at the Frontier when I was twenty-four, and at age thirty-one at the Nugget was the first time anybody with foreign [*out-of-state*] gaming ever got licensed. It was me and Gary Primm, who had a piece of his father's card room in California.

So Abe Rosenberg got his fifty thousand shares of common stock at six bucks a share. As it turned out, the stock compounded at 24.9 percent a year for twenty-seven years, which was the third-best performance in American business history. Microsoft compounded at 51 percent, Berkshire Hathaway was at 31, and I was at 25, which was double Disney, Coca Cola, and the SNP 500 between 1973 and 2000. That's how we got to be the second-most-admired company in the country on the cover of *Fortune* magazine.

We had this tremendous record of growth, and Abe Rosenberg made something like $70 million off his $300,000 purchase in 1973. He complained to me [*laughing*] that I was screwing up his estate planning.

I guess that's a pretty good payback for the favor Abe had done for me when he put up money so I could buy the sliver of land from Hughes.

## Parry Thomas

ALTHOUGH THERE'S ALWAYS BEEN THIS STEREOTYPE THAT YOU CAN'T make a lot of money in downtown Las Vegas, I disagree with that. In my judgment downtown had its place and the Strip had its place. If they were properly managed, casinos would do well in either location.

Benny Binion did help change a lot downtown, no question about that. And when we loaned the Del Webb Company the money to build the Mint, that helped a lot to add all those rooms downtown. Rooms mean people and people mean good gambling. Rooms are the key to gaming in Las Vegas.

That's why you always see the ads that say, "More rooms, bigger rooms, better rooms."

The hidden interest in gaming is all those rooms, because in Las Vegas it's a three-shift business. In the day shift you have people wandering around, visitors coming in and out. On the swing shift you have entertainment bringing in crowds for the nightlife and gaming, and then graveyard complements the other two shifts.

I quickly understood this about gaming after moving to Las Vegas: Gaming is no different than commercial banking or investment banking. It's the exchange of money for a percentage of profit. The difference between gaming and ordinary financing and banking and investment is that banks and investment houses work on changing the money for a percentage on a per-annum basis. Gaming works for a percentage of profit on a second-to-second basis or a minute-to-minute basis. That's just the way I looked at it.

Gaming is a three-shift business while banking is a one-shift business, so your opportunity for profit is greater in gaming if you run your operation properly. And they are both money-handling businesses, so a lot of caution has to be taken there.

In those years in the late '60s and all through the '70s, I was trying to help Steve Wynn in every way I could. We had a very close relationship both in business and personally. He has such a wonderful family. I enjoyed watching his daughters Gillian and Kevyn come along, and Gillian loved Sun Valley and training with our horses when she was younger. To this day his daughters still call me Uncle Parry. It's just a wonderful family relationship. I'm just kind of a senior member now.

## Steve Wynn

THERE'S A STORY INVOLVING PARRY AND HE PROBABLY KNOWS JUST parts of this story. It's rather long-winded, but it tells of the one time in my career where I made the mistake of questioning him, if only for a brief moment. The point of it all is that Parry never, ever had a sense of his own power. Never did anyone ever see him wearing the power that he wielded. He was always the most humble man, and he never ever told anybody what to do.

Every June back in the 1970s I would go up to the Binion family ranch in Montana and help Benny gather cattle. I liked to ride, and it was such a peaceful time, separating the calves and the moms from the steers and the bulls. The mothers can nurse their calves and the bulls go separately. It's not mating season. It's a lot of hours in the saddle, but it's quiet work. The TJ Ranch, named after Benny's wife, Teddy Jane, had 250,000 acres and it's magnificent country up there.

So one day I get a phone call and my secretary says that Shannon Bybee is trying to get a hold of me. He was head of the Gaming Control Board, and he was Mr. Mormon, the straightest arrow you could find. I call him back, and he says, "Are you running a training school for the Mafia at the Golden Nugget?"

"What do you mean by that?" I responded. Of course I was offended by the remark.

I was sitting in the living room of Benny's little house up there, and Benny was on a Barcalounger with his feet up, listening to the conversation.

Shannon says, "Do you know who worked at your place yesterday?"

I told him no, that I'd been at the Binion ranch for the last nine days.

"Well, we get copies of all the work permits," he says, "and two nights ago John Spilotro started working for you. He's the brother of Tony Spilotro. John Spilotro is a break-in baccarat dealer at the Nugget."

"Who's John Spilotro? Who's Tony Spilotro?" I say. I had never heard of either of them.

"Tony Spilotro is one of the worst primitive gangsters that's ever been around here," Bybee says. "We almost took away Circus Circus's license because he had a gift shop there. He's a murderous, subnormal, primitive guy from Chicago who has found his way to Las Vegas and set up shop. And he's twisted up with some people in town at the Stardust. And we are highly embarrassed by his presence here. The Feds are on this guy, Steve. Everybody is on this guy."

"So who's John Spilotro?" I say.

"He's Tony's younger brother. He just turned twenty-one."

"Is he a gangster, too?" I say.

"No," Bybee says, "he's just the younger brother of Tony. I don't think he's ever been arrested or accused of any crime. But Steve, do you have any idea what it would look like with the Golden Nugget being a public company and you have the younger brother of this notorious guy working at one of your casinos? You would be tainted. It would look terrible if this were written up in the *Wall Street Journal*. You just got licensed and the Nugget's always had a reputation of being clean. Understand, I cannot tell you not to have this guy working at your place, and the Nevada Gaming Control Board has no authority to tell you to terminate this kid, but I think you can see this could be a big problem."

"You're absolutely right," I say. "He's not going to work a second shift."

The way Spilotro got hired is that Ed and Fred Doumani were two of my shareholders, and they loved Joey Cusamano. Joey was a blackjack foreman for me, and Joey is a charming guy and he wanted to be a wiseguy in the worst way. And he charmed Freddy Doumani, and Freddy recommended him to me and we hired him and he worked his way up to a blackjack foreman. A sixty-dollar-a-day job.

When we put in a single baccarat table, Joey went to school for baccarat and we made him the baccarat floor man. We operated only one shift of baccarat at night, and it was a low-limit game.

Anyway, I found out from my casino manager, Murray Ehrenberg, that Joey Cusamano had hired John Spilotro, so I had an animated conversation with Murray and told him to fire both Spilotro and Cusamano. He said he didn't think that was fair, that John Spilotro hadn't done anything wrong. I explained in volatile language that he had put me in an awkward situation with this hire, without running it by me first. I further told Murray that if something like this ever happened again, I was going to lose confidence in *him*.

Benny was sitting there quietly listening in on this. Now Benny was one of those guys you didn't try and make conversation with. He didn't like that. To him that was a sign of weakness.

After I got off the phone Benny looked over at me and said, "You fired him?"

"Sure did," I said. "Cusamano, too."

"Why?"

"John Spilotro's brother is a bad guy. That's what Bybee said."

"What Bybee told you is true," Benny said. "Not only a bad guy, but he *likes* being a bad guy."

Benny then kind of cocked his head and gave a little laugh. I didn't know quite what to take from that.

Jack Binion told me years later that shortly after that incident Tony Spilotro was in the Horseshoe and he started saying in a loud voice,

"Fuckin' Steve Wynn! Who the hell does he think he is? I'm gonna kick his ass!"

And Benny came over and pointed his finger at Spilotro and said. "Don't say that. Hear? You understand?"

And Spilotro backed off and said, "Oh, I didn't mean it."

Benny jumped right on him in my defense.

This little vignette continued to play out over the next weeks. I got a call from [*long-time gaming executive*] Yale Cohen, whose son Gil is still a dear friend of mine. And Yale questioned my firing of John Spilotro, and said he didn't think it was fair because John Spilotro had never done anything wrong,

Next I heard from Davey Goldstein at the Dunes who says the rumor he heard was that the Gaming Control Board was going to close down the Golden Nugget unless I fired Spilotro. So I had to explain to him that that wasn't true and the reason for the firing was the negative publicity that would come down if the news were leaked to a newspaper about having a Spilotro on the payroll.

After a long conversation Davey realized he was out of line and he started to apologize, and I told him if he was so upset about it, he could hire John Spilotro at the Dunes.

Again he apologized and I told him he was the second person to call me about this situation.

"Well, everyone's been talking about it at the Las Vegas Country Club," Davey says.

Now I get a third call, about a week later, from Parry Thomas, and Parry says, "Steve, what do you know about some kid named Spalatrone?"

Parry wasn't even sure of the name. Now this isn't Yale Cohen or Davey Goldstein on the phone. This is The Man himself.

"His name's Spilotro," I said. "John Spilotro."

"Yeah, that's it," Parry says.

"He's the brother of Tony Spilotro, who's a real hot potato," I say.

I explained the phone call from Shannon Bybee and the whole background of it, and how the hiring of John Spilotro could bring horrible publicity down on the Golden Nugget and that I wasn't going to subject our company to that."

And then I said to Parry, with an edge in my voice, because this was the third call I'd received on this matter, "Why are you asking me?"

"I got a call from Alan Dorfman," Parry says. "Alan called up and said the state of Nevada was acting like the Gestapo, citing guilt by association, hanging the guy without a trial, the sins of the brother being visited on the innocent, and that this kid went to work for Steve Wynn downtown and the state of Nevada had thrown him out of the casino without hello, goodbye, or kiss my ass.

"Dorfman said, 'Parry, it's terrible! Do you know Steve Wynn? The word is that you are his banker.'"

"I told him, 'Yes, I know him,' Parry said. 'He's like a son to me.'"

"Well, can you say something to him, Parry?" Dorfman said. "This seems so goddamn unfair.'"

I interrupted at that point and said, "What did you say to Alan Dorfman, Parry?"

I had a tone in my voice because I was a little fed up with these phone calls. I wasn't totally out of line, but I had uncertainty in my voice. That was a big mistake on my part.

Parry said, "What did you think I would say to him?"

Then there was a long pause, because Parry's got the longest fuse in the world. He's so comfortable in his own skin that you can't get him angry.

Finally, after a long time, Parry said, "I told him that under no circumstances, Alan, would I ever call a customer and give him any advice on the operation of his business. It is strictly a policy of the bank not to do that. And Steve Wynn is no different. And more so because of my personal relationship with him. If he made a decision, and I'm sure he had a good reason for doing so, under no circumstances should you think that I would make that phone call to him."

Parry then said to me, "And now that you've told me the facts, you did exactly the right thing. And that's why I called you. I was curious about the other side of the story."

The essence of the story was that I had for a brief moment questioned Parry Thomas, and that triggered a gentle but very distinct reprimand. It's the only time I believe I ever came close to hurting his feelings.

## Elaine Wynn

EVERY TIME I SAW PARRY, BACK THEN AND EVEN TODAY, HIS EYES WOULD light up. Now I know that he was charming with everyone, but I know, however, that I had a special place in his heart. I also would bet that every woman could probably say that about Parry, but Parry was the first person who I respected and admired who made me believe that I had worth separate and apart from Steve, and that my influence on Steve and the impact I had on Steve was very important and very critical to his success. And this is before I had a formal role in the business. I was just Steve's wife and the mother of his kids in those first couple years.

And Parry continued to give me that confidence going forward, as we evolved. And he got more verbal about it and more articulate as the years passed and my role did morph. And then of course for me, as I became more involved as a civic individual and took a greater interest and a more proprietary role in community building, he was my role model for that as well. So that when we talked about United Way—Parry was the one that brought United Way to Las Vegas—he explained to me why it was a good idea, and why we needed to get involved. He explained to me why doing good works paid its own dividends and was good for business.

He demonstrated to me, not just with his words but with his actions, the importance of the university. You know, he was my mentor in so many ways. When I got involved at UNLV, he was right there, at every meeting, telling us and guiding us and shaping for us the path. He was the pathfinder.

I think with Steve early on, Steve was like the hunting dog. What do you call them, pointers? He was a pointer.

The benefit of Parry's agreeing to do this oral history is that he has the best perspective of anyone on the big picture of Las Vegas. He has the benefit of having the scope of all that's taken place here, and he can put the moving parts in context. I don't think there's anybody else in Las Vegas in this modern period of evolution, which is *the* critical time, who has the capacity to put everything into place the way Parry can. Absolutely. He's the master storyteller.

Steve has this theory that you can go right or left at certain critical junctures in your life, but you must understand the contingencies that must be weighed. Parry Thomas was the kind of man who could work with contingencies. If things were going *this* way, he could help it along *that* path. If they needed to go *another* way, he could help it along *that* path. Now would he nudge and push and pull a bit to get it back to a course that he preferred? Yes, of course. But his brilliance was that he could work the system and get the situation running on track, and he'd do it with perfect smoothness.

I've been asked many times to compare these two men, Steve Wynn and Parry Thomas, who have been so vital to the growth of modern Las Vegas. Both have great integrity. That is number one. In Steve's darkest moments I've never heard him try to cut a corner or do the wrong thing or do an unethical thing. I'm not talking about little stuff. I'm talking about when it comes to the major stuff.

Both of them have incredible recall. They seem to remember everything they've ever done, said, learned, or read. They're total sponges. Parry has incredible recall, and when you sit with Steve, it's the same thing. You just want to kill them both out of envy, you know, to have memories like that.

They also have the ability to synthesize information. It's not enough to just know it and be aware of it. They can collect information and come up with original theses, which I think does set them apart from others who are gifted that way.

Parry had the vision to understand a business environment, the macro environment in Las Vegas that involved all businesses.

Steve was more self-indulgent. Las Vegas for Steve was an experiment in an art form. Steve is always coloring. For him, Las Vegas has been a canvas, knowing full well that he would get rewarded as he painted on it. He never thought in terms of building a city. Whatever it was he was doing was because it stimulated some kind of creative process that he was indulging himself in. But the byproduct from both men was the same: a city that became what it's become.

Very often Steve will kid with me when people are complaining about the traffic and all the infrastructure that's needed when he calculates all the jobs that were created from Mirage Resorts, and the families that were brought to town for the peripheral businesses. Many of these problems were created because of what we created here. And he's concerned about these things. And he does have the capacity to expand his impact beyond just the selfish projects that were done.

Regarding the issue of humility, well, Parry is the most humble man you've ever met. Steve, on the other hand, is not a humble person. And I don't think it's anything they have control over. I think you either are or you're not.

Both are extraordinarily generous with their energy and their enthusiasm and their willingness to pay it forward. You know, Parry created such a wonderful role model for Steve, that Steve will very often give people time and energy and guidance. They both are humanitarians. People don't appreciate that as much with Steve because they don't see it at the same level as I do. They may see it as a donation of some kind, but they don't hear him talk about Bodhisattva and people who live their lives unselfishly to better other people's lives. [*In Mahayan Buddhism, the Bodhisattvas take vows stating that they will strive to liberate all perceptive people from samsara (suffering), and deliver them to nirvana (enlightenment)*].

While it's true that Steve has not found a young, talented person to nurture in the same way as Parry did him, it's not that he hasn't been looking. But we're living in a different time. Because, as we look at the next generation, these are not kids who had parents from the old country or parents who struggled through a depression or a world war. You know, we're dealing with generations of kids who are sort of entitled. And they knew they were going to college and they had all these choices, and sometimes we give our kids so many choices that they're confused by the choices. If they had to go get a job just to get a paycheck, life would be simpler, and they would be hungrier. When you're a little desperate, you don't worry about the stuff you don't have, you worry about the stuff you need.

## Parry Thomas

WHEN HE WAS IN HIS EARLY THIRTIES, I COINED A PHRASE THAT I thought Steve Wynn was a combination of the famous Jewish financier Bernard Baruch and the showman Flo Ziegfield. I could see that he had talents in the gaming and hospitality industry that were enormous, far better than anybody else in that industry.

I know Steve had a lot of respect for Jay Sarno, and he gives Jay a lot of credit for being the guy who started the notion of themed casinos in Las Vegas [*with his creation of Caesars Palace and Circus Circus*]. Steve really admired Sarno for his brains and inventive instincts and how he could turn an idea into a commercial success.

What Steve did in Atlantic City was just another example of his own creative genius. I remember when Steve first considered Atlantic

City for the Golden Nugget. I went back with him before he ever started building just to look at the place. We spent about a week going through everything, looking at Resorts International and different hotels, and Steve said, "I'll tell you why I want to be in Atlantic City. You see that pier out there? When I was a kid my dad used to bring me here and they had a tower and they used to have a horse go up on that tower and it would dive into the ocean. I've never forgotten that. The people came from all over to see that horse jump in the ocean."

That's where the Ziegfeld influence comes in: understanding, as he proved later on, that a big attraction and public spectacle like the exploding volcano in front of The Mirage or the dancing fountains at Bellagio would draw people in.

Now Atlantic City was a damn miserable place to be in business. I had bitter experiences in Atlantic City, so I don't have a lot of objectivity about it. But let me back up.

At least two of the most prominent banks in New Jersey came to us at Valley Bank sometime after 1976, when the gaming referendum was passed legalizing gambling in Atlantic City, and said they were getting into gaming. They admitted that they didn't know anything about gaming loans or how to handle them, and they asked me if we could teach their people about them. They even went so far as to ask us to help manage their loans and even participate in the loans with them. We agreed to be helpful to them, because in part we thought maybe we'd have an entry into Atlantic City later on. But the state regulations were that they were going to require the top operators, especially me, to stand for licensing.

This was before Steve built the Golden Nugget back there. So I went back and was there for over a week being interviewed for the licensing process, and they treated me like a criminal. At least that was my perception.

My view was that their gaming control people all had aspirations of going on to bigger political success. It seemed as though every question they asked me was guided by the idea that they were preparing themselves for political office, and that they didn't want to take chances that they might license someone and it would come back and hurt them politically later on. The feeling I got was that they were all a bunch of bureaucratic politicians.

Coincidentally, it was right about that time that Sydney Korshak was working as a labor attorney for Barron Hilton, and primarily because of that, they denied Hilton a license in Atlantic City. And Hilton never did get a license. Can you imagine them turning down Barron Hilton? He's as pure as the driven snow.

Korshak was at the time probably the world's best labor attorney, but he didn't negotiate or sell anything. He just dictated to the unions. But it was also thought that he was the number three guy in the Chicago Mob, and that he could do any damn thing he wanted.

So the Atlantic City gaming board asked me if I knew Syd Korshak. I said yes, that I had met him and I knew him a little but that I'd never done any business with him. And then I told them something that had happened two weeks before.

Peggy and I were at a horse show in Burbank, and while there we drove over to Beverly Hills to buy some flatware for our Sun Valley house. As I was going in the front door of Tiffany's, I heard some guy yelling my name from down the street, and here was Syd Korshak walking towards us.

I remember telling Peggy, "Jeez, that's the last guy I want to see right now."

I knew he had been tagged by the regulators in Atlantic City, and here I was about to go up for licensing. I also knew that in an inquisition like that, the interrogators already know the answer before they ask the question. You always had to work on that presumption because that's how they trip you up for perjury. So of course I answered truthfully and told them I'd seen Korshak recently.

And one of the people on the panel said, "Well, we're going to have to investigate this relationship."

By that time, I'd had enough of the circus, so I told them. "No, you don't have to investigate it, because I'm withdrawing my application. I don't want any part of you guys." And I walked out of the hearing.

That ended it right there.

## Steve Wynn

SYDNEY KORSHAK AND JOHNNY ROSELLI BOTH HUNG OUT AT THE DESERT Inn in the '60s. I never met Korshak until much later in his life at the Hillcrest Country Club. One day I was having lunch with Mickey Rudin [*Frank Sinatra's longtime lawyer*] and this old, tired gray-complected man walked up.

Mickey said, "Hello, Sydney."

He said, "Hello, Mickey."

"So Sydney, say hello to Steve Wynn."

"Hello, Steve Wynn."

"Hello, Mr. Korshak."

That was my one introduction to him.

He was a legendary figure, and a hot potato. Korshak was the reason that Hilton had licensing problems in Atlantic City. He was the reason they didn't get a license.

Korshak was considered the best labor lawyer of his time. He represented the unions in the big labor disputes and he could get it handled. He was friends with the union guys, and people always accused him of being connected. No one ever proved a fuckin' thing, and he was a prominent citizen of Beverly Hills. If anybody said anything about him, it was from an unsubstantiated, raw report that sometimes got in the papers. But nobody ever, ever accused Sydney Korshak of anything while he was breathing. I mean, Korshak was all rumor. There was never anything concrete on him.

Understand, there were a lot of stories where people in a proper way asked Parry Thomas to talk to someone who was improper, so to speak, so that he would have a tangential relationship with that individual. The Teamsters . . . because Parry was a banker for so many hotels . . . when the Teamsters fronted a loan, they fronted it through Valley Bank. So a guy like numb-nuts, Alan Dorfman, would know Parry, and big fees were paid to hold the money and be the dispersing agent for the Teamsters Pension Fund. Dorfman, for example, would be a guy who paid big fees to Parry. And because Parry was a guy that could keep a secret, Dorfman would be proud to say he knew Parry Thomas. Dorfman would step into Parry's world. Parry wouldn't step into Dorfman's world.

Yeah, Dorfman would tell everybody, "I know Parry Thomas. He's the man."

And Parry *was* the man, but for all the right reasons. Traffic moved in one direction. Parry dispensed favors, he never got any. Not in the sense that he ever got his hands dirty. But certainly he did hold all the Teamster money.

## Michael Gaughan

IT'S HARD TO BELIEVE THAT PARRY HAD A PROBLEM WITH LICENSE suitability in Atlantic City. The commission back there even caused Peter Thomas grief. When I did the Coast Casinos merger with Boyd Gaming. Peter was on our board of directors. Peter had a tough time because of his dad. How can you say anything bad about Peter?

My dad also got turned down by the gaming board in Atlantic City, and the commission overruled them the first time. Dad was working on the Showboat with the Houssels, back in 1987, when it happened. Dad was a bookmaker in Omaha before moving to Las Vegas and they brought that up, and they also gave him a tough time about his friendship with Benny Binion.

## Parry Thomas

THE ATLANTIC CITY GOLDEN NUGGET DID WELL RIGHT AWAY, AND MADE Steve a celebrity back on the East Coast. His hotel and Resorts International were the ones that made the biggest splash when everything got going back there. And that's something that really irked me about the commission in New Jersey. They licensed Resorts, and yet that company was notorious for its Mob affiliations in the Bahamas. They were some of the worst, and that just made no sense to me. And at the same time Resorts got a license, they were giving a bunch of grief to Barron Hilton and Jackie Gaughan and me.

Unlike some others in Atlantic City, the building and all the physical facilities at the Golden Nugget were built correctly. It was a bright, beautiful place, and Steve brought in first-rate entertainment and the whole thing just came together because he knew what he was doing and he was professional about it.

He had Frank Sinatra back there and Diana Ross and Dolly Parton, and he ran all those cute ads back there that he also ran in Las Vegas, where he would play the part of the room attendant bringing towels to the celebrities. Those helped to make him a likable person in that market.

Of course, after a few years Steve got tired of the Atlantic City marketplace. I think there were two reasons he sold out to Bally's and left. One was that he got tired of the New Jersey environment and their commission there, because they were such a pain in the ass. And two, Bally's gave him an offer that he couldn't say no to. The sale of the property gave him a big score, just as the Caesars deal had done many years before. The sale of the Atlantic City Golden Nugget gave Steve the money to show what he could really do, and that was to build a spectacular hotel-casino on the Las Vegas Strip.

After a long negotiation, Steve was finally able to buy that fantastic piece of property that everyone wanted to buy, and that was the eighty acres on the Strip from Spring Mountain Road south almost to Caesars Palace. It was just a big vacant piece of property then, with those small casinos, the Silver Slipper and the Castaways, located on them. We had tried to buy that land a couple of times, but the owners [*Most of the property was owned by the Howard Hughes estate, and there were smaller parcels with different owners.*] wouldn't sell it. Once Steve acquired that land, history took over. With his building of The Mirage, Steve wrote the book from there on.

There were three phases in the financial success of Las Vegas. As I've explained, there are three major steps in any business: pioneering, expansion, and the corporate acquisitions and mergers. I came along in the first two phases. I was successful during the transition from the pioneering phase into the expansion phase. Most of my financing was not starting new hotels, it was expanding existing hotels. I had to do it to make them safer investments, too, because I was convinced the only thing that really made gaming was more rooms, more rooms, and more rooms. It was a three-shift business and when I studied it, I realized that was what you had to do.

Then over the years we got onto the corporate game track, and getting that law passed through the Legislature that made gaming palatable for corporations was probably the most important thing I ever did for the state of Nevada. It was tough, and I want to be clear that I didn't have help from anybody other than the politicians who helped me push through the legislation.

Where Mike Milken fits into the picture and is enormously important is when Steve decided to buy the eighty acres where he built The Mirage and Treasure Island.

Steve's vision for that was so big, so much bigger than anything we'd ever seen in Las Vegas, certainly bigger than anything I'd seen, and I'd seen it all. And that project was going to take a different type of sophistication and financing. No longer could we just syndicate a bunch of banks and insurance companies, which is what I'd been doing for the previous thirty years to build these hotels and build this economy. We had to get beyond that. We had to get into the markets, we had to get into securities, and we had to get into the upper echelon of financing.

With the financing of the Golden Nugget, we loaned the money for the tower and all the expansion. We brought in First Security of Utah and American National Insurance and a couple of other ones, but it wasn't that much money. We could handle most of it ourselves. But The Mirage was a far bigger deal.

So with that Steve contacted Mike Milken. He had gotten to know him well when Mike helped Steve with the financing of the Atlantic City Golden Nugget. Then Mike got behind Steve and financed the majority of the money for The Mirage. We put up some of it, but virtually all of it was handled through so-called junk bonds that Mike was handling then. So that opened a whole new set of standards for Las Vegas.

When Steve and I first talked about the idea of The Mirage, I asked him a lot of questions about the sheer size of the place. Three thousand rooms, casino floor space of a hundred thousand square feet, and so on. And it was clear that it was going to absorb a lot of money. I asked him, "Do you really think you can, under the economics of Las Vegas, make this work?"

He looked me right in the eye and said, "Las Vegas has gotten to a point where bigger is better."

232

The Mirage was the beginning of the new modern Las Vegas, no question about it. And then Bellagio really anchored it.

## Michael Milken

IT'S IMPOSSIBLE TO OVERESTIMATE PARRY THOMAS'S IMPACT ON LAS Vegas from the mid-1950s, when he first arrived, to the late '70s. First, he was a person who you could trust. The term that was used then was a "stand-up guy." If he said he was going to do something, he was gonna do it.

When I first began looking at these gaming companies in 1968, long before we could invest in them, there was this perception by the investment community and the insurance companies in Hartford and in many of the more established countries that they could not invest in any company involved in the gaming industry.

I would say that the turning point was the success of Atlantic City in the late 1970s, and then the permission to allow us to finance the expansion of the Golden Nugget and then the Circus Circus and many others.

During this earlier time, the perception was that you had an industry controlled by individuals that you would not want to associate with. Parry separated them from one another, and individually they dealt with him with an element of trust, and in turn he dealt with them with an element of trust.

He understood early on that this industry was a good investment. I consider the hotel-casino industry to be a job machine. There's maybe no other business in the world where every time you build a building, you create thousands and thousands of jobs, both inside and outside. During the '50s and '60s, Parry understood the value of the commitment he was making to an individual, and the value of the commitment his bank would make to them. And it was really up until the end of the '70s, through a series of conferences we held [*with the investment firm Drexel Burnham Lambert*] that introduced people to the gaming industry and allowed them to understand the industry better, that it became institutionalized.

If I had to analogize it to myself, the non-investment-grade [*junk-bond*] companies created all the jobs, or ninety-nine percent of the jobs, in the gaming industry. This was an industry shunned by regulation—internal regulation, not external—whether it was Travelers or Connecticut General or whoever in Hartford. Most of the large companies in the investment world banned investing in gaming companies. So Parry was that unusual individual who had come to town and through a mutual trust that he built up, served as a bridge from 1955 to the late '70s in helping entrepreneurial people in Las Vegas have access to capital.

Parry represented a single financial institution, and there was a limit to how much money he could loan to any company or individual. With the institutionalization of the business, that meant thousands and thousands of diverse institutions with potentially unlimited capital came to town. Had Parry not carried that bridge, you know, what would have existed would have been far less, and I'm sure all the great development in Las Vegas would have been delayed substantially.

That one small bank, Bank of Las Vegas and then later Valley Bank, served to make that transition. But there was just so much one institution could lend. The transition that occurred was that my clients represented the financial institutions and investors of the world, not just those in Nevada.

### Larry Ruvo

I HAD AN IDEA IN 1987 THAT I WANTED TO DO A GRANDIOSE FUNDRAISER for Steve Wynn, who had been so instrumental in my career in the liquor business. My idea was to have a big event and raise money for research in retinitis pigmentosa, the degenerative eye disease that Steve suffers from.

One morning while jogging with Steve, I told him about it. I said I wanted to charge $5,000 a couple to attend this benefit. Steve laughed and probably thought I was crazy, but when we got back to the house, he insisted I tell Elaine about my plan.

They both gave me their permission, but Steve told me that $5,000 was unheard of in Las Vegas. I told him I wanted to get two co-chairs involved, Parry Thomas and Hank Greenspun, and that I thought if I could get their cooperation, we might have a chance to pull it off.

I went down to Parry's office at Valley Bank, and there was that same powerful man who'd given me that loan years before, with the same black and white chair, and I told him my plan. He immediately said, "How can I help you?"

I told him I wanted him to be a co-chair with Hank for this food-and-wine extravaganza, the best that Las Vegas had ever seen, and that we were going to have a surprise entertainer that would blow everybody away. I was also going to bring in the people from Chateau Mouton Rothschild, who would have an exhibit of the paintings that were represented on their wine bottles.

I told him I wanted this to be a memorable night for everyone and to raise a lot of money for retinitis pigmentosa research, but when I told him I wanted to charge $5,000 a couple, he was shocked.

"We just had Ronald Reagan here," Parry said, "and we couldn't raise $1,000 a person."

Despite that, Parry got Hank Greenspun on the phone, and Hank agreed to be a co-chair, and that got the ball rolling. I knew if I could use the names of those two powerful men, who were good friends, that we could possibly have a successful evening.

Elaine had the idea of getting Mikhail Baryshnikov to perform, which was terrific. He was still at the height of his talents. We managed to get two hundred couples there that evening, and it was a perfect night.

At the end of the benefit Parry and Hank came over to me and said that they were very proud of what we'd done. Hank said, with Parry standing right beside him, "When you called me that day, I thought it was a joke."

Parry said, "Well, I guess you *can* teach an old dog new tricks."

To have the friendship of what happened that night with Hank and Parry . . . to have the warmth of those two titans speaking to me in that way with accolades and compliments, I'll remember it the rest of my life."

No matter how important those two were in the Las Vegas community, to stop and listen to some kid with a dream, and to support him fully, was really something.

## Michael Milken

THERE'S A MEMORY I'D LIKE TO SHARE FROM THE DAY THE MIRAGE opened, in November of 1989.

You know *Business Week* magazine had written about how this new hotel was going to be "snake eyes" for Steve Wynn. But we knew it was going to change Las Vegas and change hotels really more than any other hotel that had ever existed. The Mirage was so different in the way that it was built, while the others were constantly having to be remodeled, and so all of us that had been involved were thinking, wow, what a hotel!

But earlier that evening I had seen Parry pull up in a Rolls-Royce and get out, and I thought, doesn't he look fantastic! He was sixty-eight years old at the time, but I thought to myself he looked like the youngest guy in the crowd. He was wearing this fantastic multi-colored flowered tie.

Now Steve was talking and explaining things about the hotel, but I just couldn't get over that magnificent tie Parry was wearing, so I walked over to compliment him on it.

Well, maybe twenty minutes later someone walks over and delivers this tie to me. Parry had taken the tie off and given it to me. I guess there may be some symbolism written into that. Anyway, I thought what a wonderful gesture that was. I've kept that tie all these years and worn it a number of times on special occasions.

Obviously, Parry's identification of Steve Wynn as a talented young man, among others, helped shaped the future of Las Vegas. And it established the foundation, I believe, for me to put my reputation on the line to finance the gambling industry. The fact that he committed to me was another positive, because I didn't feel Parry would be associated with anyone he was not comfortable with.

## Roger Thomas

I'VE KNOWN STEVE SINCE I WAS A TEENAGER. OUR FAMILIES GOT TO BE close and I would ski with Steve and Elaine up in Sun Valley, where they also had a house. Steve was even a ski instructor up there for a while and I'd ski with Dad and Steve.

In terms of role models, he was like an older brother. He was phenomenally handsome, and he did everything well. He was smarter than anyone else around and everyone wanted to know him, and it seemed that everything he did turned to gold. Just one amazing success after another.

When you meet Steve, he's just bigger than life. He's been charismatic probably since the age of four, maybe earlier. When he walks into a room, he instantly becomes the object of attention and everything stops.

We all loved Elaine as well, and there was a lot of interaction with the two girls, Gillian and Kevyn. It seems like those girls grew up in Sun Valley, and they became very close to Jane with their interest in horses and everything.

In the '70s I came back to work on the Valley Bank building and I later started my own company. Then I went to work with Charles

Silverman at Yates & Silverman and I opened the Las Vegas offices for them with this woman who was a partner. She kind of crashed and burned, and then I was introduced to the woman who was destined to be my design partner for twenty-five years, Jane Radoff.

It was sometime later that I was at a board meeting for Nevada Dance Theatre, and Elaine Wynn was on the board with me. Steve was there and said, "So what are you doin', kid?"

I'd just started working on some hospitality projects, a penthouse at the Stardust, and some work at the Aladdin and in the casino at the Lady Luck, and I was telling him how much more I liked hospitality than other aspects of my work.

Steve said, "I'm just starting a new project, and you can come and work for me."

He then told me about his current project, which was the proposed Victoria Bay Hotel and Casino, on the Strip next to the Sahara Hotel. But of course that project was never built.

It was not an easy decision for me because Charles Silverman was talking to me about becoming a partner in the firm. But I went home that night and I just had this feeling that if I didn't do this, I would always wonder what would have happened. It just sounded too good to be true, but I told myself that if I took the job and crashed and burned with Steve, Charles Silverman would always take me back. I just didn't want to pass up the opportunity and wonder what would have been. So I took the job.

I was joining Atlandia Design, which had been formed to build the Golden Nugget of Atlantic City. I didn't know then, but the potential for failure in this new job with Steve was huge. Anyway, they tried to figure out what to do with me, and they eventually told me to design and build a model guest room. They even let me have a secretary and an assistant, and off I went.

Steve liked my design so much he decided to redo all the guest rooms in the Golden Nugget downtown. Here I'd designed a room for Victoria Bay, and while I was building the model, they were looking at all the financials and realizing what it was going to take to get that project off the ground, and they decided they weren't going to do the project after all.

From there I started designing the penthouse floor at the Golden Nugget, and the offices and suites.

I met Michael Milken sometime during this period, but I really didn't know who he was. I wasn't aware at the time that like Steve Wynn, Mike was a man who was changing history as well. I was just a kid trying to design stuff. What I did know about our plans for the Golden Nugget was that we were taking dead aim at Caesars Palace as far as building a luxurious property.

One of the advantages I had was that because I had traveled so much with Dad and Mom, I knew what the really good hotels looked like. Very few of the other designers had that experience, because they had come up bootstrap, you know, so that was one of the great pluses I had to living a life of advantage.

So Steve and I decided that we didn't want to do anything like the Strip. We didn't want fake brass and fake marble. We wanted everything to be real, and we were given a budget that people weren't used to. The attitude was that we were going to develop a special pied-a-terre here in Las Vegas, and we would keep it for you whenever you wanted to come back.

Those suites at the Golden Nugget were highly themed, just as whenever someone designed a house they'd say, "I'm going Victorian," or "I'm going French Provincial," or "I'm going Modern."

So we did six different themed suites, and a suite of offices, and that was the start. And then I was doing work in Atlantic City and then all of a sudden there was this thing called The Mirage. I was told I was going to do just the guest rooms at The Mirage, and that there were two other designers. One of those designers didn't cut it, and I was assigned to do whatever he failed at. So that's how I ended up doing half the hotel, piece by piece.

Steve Wynn's style is that he wants you to participate in the design, but you should know you're participating in his idea. One of the designers kept saying, "No, I've got a better idea."

And Steve kept saying, "I don't like your idea better. I want my idea."

The designer Henry Conversano was a genius at the ability to take Steve's ideas and read the potential in them and make them phenomenal.

Later, when we designed the clubhouse at Shadow Creek golf course for Steve, I remember Steve telling us he wanted it to have the feel of Augusta National. He wanted these certain chandeliers and plaid carpeting. He described all these things, and my partner Jane said, "I get it. You want it to look like a club that doesn't allow Jewish members." Steve laughed and said, "Exactly."

## Parry Thomas

I REMEMBER STEVE AND I DRIVING AROUND SHADOW CREEK BEFORE it opened and I was just amazed at the beauty of it all. I asked him if there were going to be members at this course. And he said, "There are only two members. I'm the golfing member and you're the non-golfing member."

It was just another example of his ability to dream big and then pull it off.

## Steve Wynn

AFTER SO MANY YEARS, I WAS DELIGHTED WHEN ROGER THOMAS BEGAN to receive the international recognition he deserves. He's on the list of the one hundred greatest designers in America. He is not just some kind of local phenomenon. Roger Thomas' treatment of public areas is the most breakaway stuff on the planet. There's no telling the long-term impact of his interiors and his work at The Mirage and

Bellagio and The Wynn. No place looks like this place [*The Wynn Resort*]. His sense of play, combining classical materials like mosaic tiles . . . the carpets . . . he drew them.

His use of color, with his design partner Jane Radoff, and his artistic ability to distort and play with scale and composition, is the mark of a great artist. And his sketchbook will be famous some day. Roger does all his sketching in his sketchbook. He is a fabulous draftsman and artist. The drawings are beautiful line drawings, like Picasso's. To separate Roger from whatever credit I've received in my lifetime is ridiculous. It would be like trying to separate Siegfried and Roy from The Mirage. Roger's taste level and his creativity are sixty percent of the success we've had.

Those are great moments when I take Parry and Peggy Thomas on private tours before these hotels open. I point out the magical things that Roger has done, and they can't help but be amazed. Parry will look and say "Steve, that's beautiful." And I will say, "No, Parry, it's not me. That's Roger's work."

I remember showing them the restaurant Jasmine before Bellagio opened, with the yellow and silk wallpaper. Amazing. Bellagio was the first time I ever gave Roger a no-budget license to do whatever he thought we should do, and we developed the ideas together. I was the editor of what he did, but it was his book. Roger went first with his ideas, then I said yes or no. And he never let his ego get in the way. If I wasn't crazy about an idea and said I wanted to see something else, he'd show me something else. But he always came up with the ideas first and then I'd respond. I came up with the hotel concept, and I'd talk to him in terms of the ideas of the building, but the man who came up with the designs and put flesh on the bones is Roger Thomas.

It's much easier to be the editor than the creator of the work.

I'd say to Parry, "Do you realize what Roger has done here?"

And he'd modestly respond, "You gave him a great opportunity."

I'd say, "I can give a lot of guys an opportunity, and they can't create this, Parry."

What marvelous luck—fabulous—that I've struck such a great partnership with the son of a man to whom I'm so indebted. It's another one of those divine interventions.

# Chapter Four

# Family Matters

*[When this book was first being discussed, the thought was that a chapter about the Thomas family would be withheld from the larger manuscript and preserved separately for future generations of the family. But upon completion of the work, it was determined that Parry and Peggy Thomas's parenting skills were so much a part of who they were, and so helped to define their character and principles, that this chapter should be included for the book's general readership.]*

## Parry Thomas

OUR THOUGHTS ON RAISING OUR CHILDREN WERE TO PROVIDE REAL sound, solid fundamentals. We wanted to bring up all-American children, the best we knew how.

Peggy and I are both extremely proud of how all five of them turned out. They are just exceptional, amazing people.

Ninety-five percent or more of the credit goes to Peggy for raising them well, because I was so busy in my many far-flung business enterprises, and traveling quite a bit, so the real responsibility fell to her. But I think the fundamentals came down more than anywhere else from Peggy's parents, the children's grandparents. All of our children idolized them, and looked forward to their frequent visits to Las Vegas.

Peggy's biological father, a man named Chatterton, died when she was a small child, and her mother remarried, so the only father Peggy ever knew was her stepfather, Dr. Clarke Young, whose first wife had also died at a young age.

## Peggy Thomas

I CAN REMEMBER MY FATHER'S DEATH, BUT THAT'S ABOUT IT. HE DIED of asthma and he essentially choked to death right in our house, with several people trying to revive him. I was only three and half years old. My mother was pregnant with my sister at the time. At the time of his death he was the manager of the J.C. Penney store in Preston, Idaho. He was only twenty-nine. And J.C. Penney was still in charge of the company and knew my father and sent him to open a new Penney's store in California, hoping that the change of climate would help his asthma, but unfortunately it didn't. So we were there for only three or four months and then came back to Preston.

We actually moved to Salt Lake City when I was eight, because my mother's parents lived there. My mother didn't marry Dr. Young until I was fifteen. She was a single mother raising two daughters for twelve years.

I had gone to elementary school and high school with one of his two sons, and so I was kind of familiar with the family and knew that Clarke's wife had died. Clarke was a doctor, a general practitioner, and he was an amazing, outstanding man. He was a great-grandson of Brigham Young. My children fortunately were well acquainted with both of their grandparents on my side of the family and learned a great deal from them. They were terrific with our children. Clarke lived, I believe, to the age of one hundred and three.

## Parry Thomas

CLARKE YOUNG WAS A GENERAL PRACTITIONER AND SURGEON WHO
had graduated from Harvard Medical School. He grew up with a very
fundamental Mormon upbringing in Salt Lake, as a direct descendant
of Brigham Young. He was the eldest son of the eldest son of the
eldest son of Brigham. His honesty and integrity were beyond the
pale. Dr. Young was an enormous influence on our children, and he
was wonderful to me as well. I think I've appreciated more and more
as the years have progressed just how important he was to our family. And Peggy's mother, Mona, was equally outstanding. A person
couldn't have better parents than she had.

While Clarke Young was very attentive to the Mormon Church,
and he was churchgoing and enjoyed all the activities, he was also a
worldly man. He traveled quite a bit and had a great curiosity about
the world outside his community. I don't think he wanted any important administrative jobs in the church because he was too busy in his
medical practice and with military service and other administrative
positions within the military.

He was a colonel in the Army and chief of medical services under
General Lewis Blaine Hershey. During World War II he was in charge
of the situation for drafting all the American troops. He lived in
Washington, D.C., a great deal of the time, and in fact for about the
first ten years that Peggy and I were married, he and Mona lived in
Washington.

Peggy's mother had two daughters and Clarke had two sons when
they married. The two boys, Stafford and Jack Young, were also great
guys, so it was a good, solid family, and that all filtered down in a
very positive way to our children.

Living in Las Vegas and raising all our children here, we were naturally on guard for the influence of corruption from all directions. So we were cautious with the children in that regard, and we paid close attention to who they associated with, just like any good parents would do.

More than that, we insisted and made a point of their going to church every Sunday and going to mutual on Tuesday and all the other church programs until they got older.

Continually through this whole period of time—and a lot of it was Dr. Young's doing—a lot of emphasis was placed on the importance of achieving excellence in education. Our children were pretty much straight-A students all the way. It started with Peter, who was just an outstanding student.

Peggy was insistent that they all attend the University of Utah, in Mormon country, and with the boys we felt that if they met someone they wanted to marry, we would just as soon have them marry a Mormon girl. I remember I used to tell them that they could go to any school they wanted to in America, but if they chose the University of Utah, I would pay for it.

So they all went there, with the exception of Roger. He went to Interlachen, an exceptional high school in Traverse City, Michigan, which offered in-depth training in music and art, and then on to Tufts University.

## Peter Thomas

ONE OF THE MANY VALUABLE LESSONS I LEARNED GROWING UP IN OUR house was that when you have a job to do—since you're going to spend the time to do it anyway—you might as well do it in such a way that when you're done, you're proud of the job you did. We were taught that it's not that much harder to do something the right way than to do it casually. That applied to everything, chores around the house or school work and getting good grades, or whatever.

I wasn't that serious about school up through about the sixth or seventh grade, and then one day I got a wakeup call. I was talking to my dad one morning—I remember he was shaving at the time—and he asked me if I was excited about going down to Newport Beach for the summer. And I told him how much I loved it there and that I was excited.

He said, "When you're an adult, would you like the opportunity to own a summer home like that?"

And I told him I sure would, that would be pretty neat.

And he said something to the effect of, "Well, the way you're going in school, that isn't likely to happen."

I think I had made some C's in some classes or something. But that moment really had an impact on me. It was like he was telling me that I was not on a track to have the same kind of life we were currently enjoying. Shortly after that I started making friends with the smart kids in my classes, and finding out how much they were studying, so that I could make sure to study harder than them so I could get the best grades.

I felt I had disappointed my dad, and that was a horrible feeling.

There was another time that was even more dramatic. I was probably in the fifth grade, about ten years old, and living across the street from us was a kid named Bruce Claiborne. His father was Harry Claiborne, who later became a federal judge. Bruce was about three years older than me and a good friend. I remember Bruce wanted to buy a baseball glove and he didn't have the money. I wanted to impress him, so I went into the house and took ten dollars from my mom's purse. I gave the money to Bruce . . . not a very smart thing to do.

Well, my mom finds out and tells my dad, and Dad immediately has me get in the car and he starts driving. He says, "We don't have thieves in our house, so I'm taking you down to the juvenile hall."

I'm thinking I'm going to jail, and I started crying my eyes out. I could see the world coming to an end. So just as we're getting down there, he stops the car. He had made his point. I look back at that now and I'm thinking, man, that was pretty cruel to do to a kid. I mean, it was only ten dollars, not a thousand. That's only petty larceny. (*He laughs loudly.*) But he'd definitely made his point.

## Dr. Steve Thomas

AN INCIDENT I RECALL VIVIDLY OCCURRED WHEN I WAS NINE OR TEN years old. I was out in the back of our house on Alta with my friend Randall Jones, [*the son of Herb Jones*], and we were playing with matches and gasoline. By the tennis court we had some storage cupboards where Dad kept the lawn mower and gasoline for it. We started a small fire and there wasn't a hose nearby and I remember we were scooping up dirt to throw on the fire to try and put it out. We eventually got it out, but not before the flames had charred the inside of the storage cupboards and caused some damage.

It was typically at the dinner table at night when all the discipline was handled by my father, because he was gone working all day. So Mom reported on our activities that day, and there I sat, smelling like smoke with singed eyebrows. Dad asked, "Who was playing with fire in the storage cupboards?"

And I remember instinctively saying, "It wasn't me."

He gave me a stern look and said, "Are you sure you don't want to retract that statement?"

Later I remember feeling that the one thing I never, ever wanted to do again was lie to my father. Here I'd lied blatantly in front of my brothers and sister, in front of my mother, and he'd given me the opportunity to retract it.

Most of the lessons I learned from him were like that. They weren't corporal punishment, they weren't being put on restriction for three weeks. It was the idea of disappointing him that just turned my soul upside down. To disappoint him was worse than any beating. I'd much rather have been spanked or received any other punishment than to think I'd let him down.

My father's free time was pretty limited when we were growing up, and what free time he did have away from work was spent providing for us kids and taking us to the lake, taking us skiing, taking us to California for the summers. So, when you let him down, you just felt like, oh, man, how could I have done this?

## Parry Thomas

OF COURSE PETER WAS OUR FIRST CHILD, AND A VERY ACTIVE CHILD.

One of the cute stories I remember about Peter as a boy was when he was four years old. We still lived in Salt Lake, just before we moved to Las Vegas, and he had to have his tonsils out. I remember going down to the doctor's office in the hospital, and as we were walking down the aisle he looked up at me and he said, "Daddy, if you have to take some little kid's tonsils out, why don't you take out Roger's?"

That told me a lot about Peter right off. He was always thinking.

Peter was an exceptionally good student, particularly in the basics, reading, writing, and arithmetic. Because of that, he set the tone for the other children as they came along, and that made a really big difference in the whole mindset of the other children as they went through school. They had to be exceptional as well, and to shoot for the same achievement and excellence that Peter had achieved. I could go on and on about Peter.

## Peter Thomas

ALL IN ALL, I WAS A PRETTY STRAIGHT-ARROW KID, ESPECIALLY ONCE grades became a priority for me. Marijuana wasn't around when I was in high school, but there was a lot of smoking and drinking. I wasn't hanging out with the guys or girls doing that stuff. I was still active in the Mormon Church then, and that stuff was forbidden. Let's just say it's a very hard religion to live by.

## Roger Thomas

I WAS A WILD KID, DEFINITELY THE MISFIT IN THE FAMILY. I THINK being number two is a difficult position for a child in a big family. And when your older brother is Peter Thomas, it's nearly impossible. Peter wasn't just exceptional, he was super-exceptional. He was an exemplary student, with straight A's all the way through school. Initially, I was a poor student with all sorts of learning disabilities. Peter saved his money; I squandered mine.

Peter could be athletic in sports that he liked, whereas I could not be. He was popular; I was the weird kid. He was much taller than I was, and although he was a year-and-a-half older, we were just one year apart in school because I started school a year early. So of course I always had to deal with the comparisons between us. He also always lorded all these advantages over me, so of course I hugely hated him when we were growing up. Obviously, I'm over all that now, because he's made me very comfortable with who I am and we greatly respect each other. But it was difficult at the time.

## Peter Thomas

I WASN'T THE BEST BIG BROTHER TO ROGER, I'LL HAVE TO ADMIT. I wasn't protective of him. Actually, I used to tease the shit out of him. One time when I was about twelve or thirteen—and he's two years younger—I got him so pissed off at me that he started chasing after me in the kitchen and he picked up a butcher knife and came after me. I barely got inside a door on the other end of the house and he buried the knife in the door.

We have a lot of respect for each other now, but it was difficult back then because Roger and I just didn't have anything in common, and I admittedly didn't make it easy for him.

## Jane Thomas Sturdivant

OH, I REMEMBER PETER AND ROGER FIGHTING ALL THE TIME AND THEN Dad would come home and get the reports and they'd go into a room and both of them would come out all tear-stained. I was really young then, but I remember it clearly. They were just so opposite back then. I was always closer to Roger than my other brothers because he and I had the artistic bent in the family.

When I was a child Roger taught me to weave on a tiny little loom. You know, I grew up totally involved in textiles, and so with Roger always looking out for me and teaching me all the artistic things that he had learned, he could do no wrong in my eyes.

My relationship with Peter has always been totally different because Peter scared the hell out of me as a young girl. I'm almost ten years younger than he is, and so by the time I was old enough to know what was going on, Peter was driving. I remember he got this brand new Jaguar XKE when he graduated from college, and one day he found little cat footprints across the hood of it. He threatened to kill my cat. Well, my cat was like my child and he wanted to kill my cat! So of course I was scared to death of him. It's kind of good that Peter became a banker, don't you think?

## Dr. Steve Thomas

AS THE THIRD SON, AND THIRD CHILD, I DEFINITELY SAW THAT THERE was tension between Peter and Roger. They were *not* good friends. And because Peter was the more dominant of the two, I did my best to be *his* friend. Peter was the alpha dog, and if you want to survive, you stick with the alpha dog, you know. His interests when we were in California for the summers were boats and stuff and I hung right with him and tried to be like him. Roger was different and he was doing art and whatever, and we got along fine. We never had any contention between us and I enjoyed being around Roger, but definitely, if I had to pick a role model as a boy, it was going to be Peter.

## Roger Thomas

I WAS SEVERELY DYSLEXIC AS A KID. I ALSO HAD ATTENTION DEFICIT Disorder and other learning disabilities. In little old Las Vegas in those days, there was no science to identify these conditions, so you were considered either lazy or a daydreamer. The self-perception I had was that I just wasn't a good student, and this was only magnified by the high expectations that had been established in our family.

My parents always said that they wanted us to be the best that we could be. I heard it over and over, "Be the best." In fact, that was the Bank of Las Vegas logo for all those years before the name was changed to Valley Bank. The logo was two credit cards slightly askew with the words "The Best" written on the inside.

We had always been told by our parents that we were equipped to do well, and that we were expected to be straight-A students. I was the only kid in the family who didn't have straight A's. I had like a 3.4 grade-point average, and I was struggling to get that, but with everyone else getting a four-point average, my B-plus average felt to me like a failure.

I learned later in life when I made friends in high school that they didn't think I was weird, it was just that I knew so much and had a big vocabulary and had all these experiences and knowledge from my parents and my siblings from the traveling we'd done, that I sometimes made my contemporaries feel dumb. That's why they occasionally avoided being around me.

Growing up, I was very observant about the things that I was interested in. I had a fairly encyclopedic knowledge of contemporary art by the time I was sixteen. So when you have this exceptional father like I did, you tend to strive for more than other kids do because you think it's the norm. I didn't get to know how extraordinary my dad was until I was in the business world trying to accomplish things myself.

When you have a father who is extremely successful, you think everybody else's dad is successful too. I think that was one of the great awakenings as I got older, that my father was so exceptional. So one of the things we got early on in the Thomas family was that to perform exceptionally was just okay. Exceptional was the norm.

## Dr. Steve Thomas

MY PARENTS WANTED US TO HAVE A VARIED EXPERIENCE IN OUR EDU-cation, and so taking music lessons was one way of doing that. I chose the saxophone. The idea was that we should take lessons for a while and then if we wanted to drop it, we could.

I started playing in elementary school, and I enjoyed it. We were renting this saxophone and it got to the point in around the eighth grade where they asked me if I wanted to keep playing, and if I did, they would buy me a saxophone.

Well, no sooner did they buy it than I was in junior high school and I found girls more interesting and motorcycles more interesting, and I decided I wanted to give up blowing that sax. And they said something to the effect of, no, that's not a deal, because you made a decision and we bought this instrument for you, so you have to stay with it for a couple more years.

As it turned out, a couple years later I was chosen for the McDon-ald's All-American High School Band, and we performed at the Macy's Parade in New York and the Rose Parade in Pasadena. I also got in a band in high school. My girlfriend was in the band with me and we played Disneyland for three months one summer

Staying with the saxophone, which was at my parents' insistence, turned out to be a great thing for me. They had the sense that by not allowing me to quit, something good might come out of my music. That's just one example of good parenting.

## Tom Thomas

MAYBE BECAUSE I WAS THE FOURTH CHILD AND THE FOURTH SON, I didn't feel any pressure from my parents at all. I can remember my mom saying dozens of times, "It doesn't matter what you do, as long as you really like what you're doing, and then you'll be successful at it."

I didn't have a real perception that my dad was hot stuff until I was maybe fourteen or fifteen, when I heard from so many people about the respect they had for him.

When I was younger, around nine or ten, there were occasions when I was with him and we'd pull up to the hotels and I thought it was really cool that all the parking attendants knew his name. They'd all say, "Mr. Thomas, how are you today? Great to see you." And they would park his car over to the side, up front where we could get it back right away. I just figured these guys were really smart and that they knew everyone's name who came to the hotel.

I also vividly recall as a kid how I liked going to his office downtown, at the old Bank of Las Vegas on Fourth Street, and I thought it was neat that he had a secretary. Her name was Belle James and she was absolutely brilliant. Belle had a perfect memory of everything that happened at the bank, and because my dad for many reasons didn't write things down, she was invaluable. She was so critical to my dad and Kenny Sullivan and other executives that they made her a vice president of the bank.

Dad always looked very dapper to me at the bank. He was a great dresser and always had the nicest suits. He got them from New York. Although I saw him in this executive role, I just knew that he was a banker, and to me bankers were just like people who worked for the government. They represented an institution that kind of moved money around.

I didn't have any interest in that occupation growing up. I was more interested in becoming a marine biologist because when we were at the ocean at Newport Beach in the summers, I would just sit on our dock for hours studying all the marine life. My interest in banking wouldn't come until years later.

As for Roger, while maybe he wasn't a scholastic success, he was an incredibly focused and mature kid. He was painting these canvasses in oil when he was ten or eleven years old. He's five and a half years older than me and I remember as a little kid he had his own art studio at our place at Newport.

My three older brothers kind of set the stage for me in completely different areas. Because Steve was closer to me in age, just two years older, I guess I was pressured to follow more in his footsteps, because he was Mr. Everything.

While ours was by any standard a privileged upbringing, it's important to point out that as kids, work was a very big part of our lives. Dad was big on teaching the value of work, and so all of us had summer jobs down in Newport. From the time I was seven or eight years old I had jobs on our boat down there and working on the docks. Sometimes it would be chipping off the old paint, or painting the docks. A lot of it was pure manual labor.

There was a science to these jobs. Whether it was waxing the boat, cleaning the bilges, or varnishing the railings, I would write down the job I did and how many hours it took, and every Friday when dad would fly down from Las Vegas and join us for the weekend, he would go over everything I had done, inspect it carefully, and check it off a list. He'd then pay me the twenty-five or fifty cents an hour I'd been promised. I was a working kid, but the money meant nothing. What Dad was teaching us was the value of accomplishing something, and all of us kids had various jobs.

The reward for me was having him look at a wax job I'd done and say, "You did a great job on that." That was a super feeling. I just really enjoyed spending that time with him on the boat and tinkering around and working side by side with him. It was unusual in that during the summer I would never see him from Monday through Friday, and then I'd get this concentrated time with him over the weekend. We'd spend every waking hour with our parents on the weekends and it was really quality time. It more than made up for not seeing him during the week.

When I look back on it now, what is amazing to me is that my mom and dad basically let their kids go out in the world and do whatever was out there that would teach them important life lessons. They let us do things that I would not allow my own kids to do today. For instance, I would not put my thirteen-year-old kid on an oil tanker traveling around the world with a Taiwanese crew. And yet both Steven and I did that when we were that age.

I took my best friend Mark Jones [*another son of Herb Jones*] with me one summer and we worked on a tanker that my dad and Jerry Mack's United Tanker Company owned. We boarded in the Grand Bahamas and we carried hot sulfur to Grimsby, England. After working all summer on that boat, we came back across the Atlantic and docked in Galveston, Texas.

As young teenagers, we didn't get treated any differently than the rest of the adult crew on that tanker. Sometimes it was very hard work. We'd chip paint and repaint deck railings. We were also taught rudimentary quarter-mastering and navigation. Sometimes we would go up and work at the helm. Other times we worked in the engine room popping salt tablets and cleaning oil off the junk. All in all it was an incredible experience for a young kid. I grew up a lot that summer.

### Dr. Steve Thomas

DAD WAS GREAT AT TEACHING RESPONSIBILITY, AND THE WAY HE WOULD do that was by sometimes giving you more than your fair share of work. We occasionally found ourselves taking jobs that were beyond our years. It was risky at times.

For instance at Newport I learned to drive a boat when I was very young. Dad would take us out and teach us to drive around the harbor and I remember Uncle Jerry [*Mack*] thought that was too risky.

One time we had a dinner party at our house at Newport and Senator Howard Cannon was staying at the Balboa Bay Club, which was across Newport Bay some distance from our home. To save him a long drive in his car, Dad had me take the boat over to pick him up. It was a sixteen-foot Boston Whaler motorboat. I think I was eight years old at the time and small for my age, so I probably looked about six. I pulled up alongside the dock to pick up Senator Cannon, and he looked down at me and wouldn't get in the boat.

The look on his face said, Jeez, Louise, I'm not risking my life in a boat with this little kid!

Senator Cannon called my dad and he was irritated. He said, "What are you doing here, Parry?" And Dad said something like, "This kid knows how to drive a boat better than anybody you know, Howard. Just get in the boat and come over here."

Finally, the senator did. And lived to tell about it.

I went on my dad's tankers four years in a row as a teenager. I was out there taking grain or sulfur to Holland. That was quite an experience, out there on the open seas with American sailors when you're that young. And very dangerous. On one of the ships I was on, a guy got stabbed and we had to put him in the freezer because that's the only place you can store a dead body on a ship. It was a tough crew, to say the least.

## Tom Thomas

ANOTHER DISTINCT MEMORY I HAVE FROM MY HIGH SCHOOL YEARS, and early college years when I worked at the bank, was noticing the close relationship my father had with all the employees there. I'm speculating here, but Dad was a part of that Greatest Generation that we hear about, who went through the Depression and then World War II, and I think from that a sense of community existed in that generation that has been largely lost nowadays.

I know the way my dad treated people has certainly rubbed off on me. Everybody at that bank really loved my dad. And he knew every one of them and who their spouses and children were. I'd walk through the bank with him and he would rush over and grab someone to greet them, and say, "Hey, Joan, how are you doing? Is your husband feeling better?"

We'd go on our way, and then he'd bump into someone else and engage in a personal conversation. There were upwards of a thousand people working for the bank then, and later on two thousand, and it seemed like he knew every one of them.

I recall people coming up to me, and knowing I was Parry's son, and saying, "You know what? I would die for your dad. He's that important to me."

It's pretty remarkable to hear that from someone you've never met. So what that taught me was that the banking business is all about people. On the surface, it's about making money, but what's it's really about is becoming successful because you care about people. And you can't be successful with people if you don't care about them and care about their needs.

Dad never actually sat us down and said that we need to pay back the community for all it had given us. It was just ingrained in us from early on, by watching him. You don't have to engage in community service and charitable work for very long before you realize that it is a lot more important than some of the other things you could be doing at the office.

### Karen Mack

WHENEVER I GO TO AN EVENT WITH PARRY, ONE OF THESE BIG LAS Vegas affairs like Andre Agassi's dinner or Larry Ruvo's benefit for Alzheimer's research, I'll be sitting at a table with Parry and people will come up and say, "Parry, you know you started my career. Everything I have I owe to you." I mean people will walk up one after another and say things like that. It's really interesting to watch. These people don't forget and they are sincerely grateful.

## Jane Thomas Sturdivant

ONE OF THE EXCEPTIONAL THINGS ABOUT MY DAD IS THAT HE'S ALWAYS looked outside of himself to determine the right thing to do. The way he mentored Steve Wynn is just one story of so many. There are probably a thousand stories similar to that, where he saw people with talent and he helped them find the right niche. Here he started with this little baby bank [*Bank of Las Vegas*] and look what it grew into. Along the way, I have had so many people say to me, "Without your dad, I wouldn't have made it."

As his daughter I think that is what makes me proudest, because I realize how much he cares for everybody around him. I notice even around all the horse shows we attend, the horse-show people love him because he's generous to them. He's always trying to make sure everybody has what they need. And he's incredibly loyal. I've never heard of anybody in the horse business having the same trainer [*Bob McDonald*] for almost forty years. That just doesn't happen.

## Dr. Steve Thomas

DAD TAUGHT US THROUGH HIS EXAMPLE MOSTLY THAT WEALTH OF ANY kind, or resources of any kind, are a responsibility as much as a blessing. You're responsible for what you have and how you use it. There's a stewardship in a way.

As an example, I remember that about the time I was starting college the family was successful enough that there was talk about whether we should buy a plane to get to and from Sun Valley, which is not an easy place to get to.

The bank owned a plane, but the conversation was whether the family should have one. I was studying business at the University of Utah at the time. And what I heard was that from a financial standpoint, we couldn't justify it. Dad said that while it would be luxurious and convenient, the price difference between paying for a plane and the cost of pilots and everything, compared to the slight inconvenience of getting on a commercial airline, was such that we just couldn't justify it.

I would often go to my dad's office and there were these plaques from the Boy Scouts or United Way or whatever, and I eventually realized that was just his way of giving back and being a good steward of the resources he had been given.

Their philanthropy continues to this day, and it is a great example to us kids, for sure.

## Roger Thomas

AFTER ALL THE PROBLEMS I WAS HAVING IN LAS VEGAS, I WAS EXCITED when I heard about the chance to transfer to a new school out of state where I could study art. And I'll never forget the trouble my parents went through to get me accepted to Interlachen in mid-term. We had to immediately get an application, fill it out, and get it to Chicago by the next day to meet the deadline. My dad got Jake Gottlieb from the Dunes Hotel to fly it with him on a plane to Chicago. Jake owned a trucking company in Chicago, and he had one of his truckers take it from Chicago to Traverse City and to Interlachen the next day, along with my portfolio, on the very last day that I was eligible to enroll. That's how you did Federal Express in those days if you had good enough connections. I was accepted and allowed to start school there in January.

## Jane Thomas Sturdivant

ALTHOUGH I KNOW ROGER HAS BEEN VERY HARD ON HIMSELF IN describing his experiences growing up, in my vision he was *never* the bad seed. I mean he was always so creative and I saw him as a genius long before he went to Interlachen.

260

I thought it was so cool and we were proud of him and he made so many beautiful things, it was just incredible. And then after he went there, he'd come home and I remember he'd have the most beautiful shoes. He had one pair that had like lightning bolts on the side and he had another pair that was bright yellow and red. One time he came back and he had really long hair with a beard and he looked like Jesus, so I thought that was pretty cool, too.

If you understand people and their strengths, you need to work with them and not against them, especially when they are really bright, talented people like Roger. Young people with special talents or intelligence can get bored and go in the wrong direction pretty quickly. Boredom is what kills a lot of young minds.

Roger was just so creative. He was the one brother who, when all the others would go off and do their own thing, he would stay to make sure I was doing something that made me happy. He was the one who showed the most interest in me.

Well, Tommy and I did a ton together, and we had a lot of common friends, but Roger took it upon himself to always make sure as the youngest kid and the only girl that I had something to do. He taught me to weave, and he taught me about painting, all sorts of stuff.

## Parry Thomas

I'VE SPOKEN BEFORE ABOUT THE TREMENDOUS INFLUENCE OF PEGGY'S parents, Dr. Clarke and Mona Young, on our children, and nowhere was this more apparent than in the special interest that Mona took in Roger. She worked with him by the hour and taught him how to sew and draw, and do arts and crafts. And he just loved working with her, and that was very important in Roger's early days. Even in grade school his teachers looked at his artwork and were very impressed.

If Roger said he struggled in school when he was young, it was not his fault. It was mine and Peggy's fault. His birthday fell on the border line, and because he was a very bright youngster, we felt we could put him in the class ahead. He was two years younger than Peter but just one grade behind him. And that was a terrible mistake on our part. We should have waited and put him in the next class. Although he did all right academically, athletically he was always outside looking in. I've often reproached myself that we didn't hold him back a year. That would have made a lot of difference.

I didn't sense that there was that much sibling rivalry between Peter and Roger. I mean they always played together, but Peter was more athletic than Roger and so that might have created some feelings. We certainly didn't treat them any differently.

I will tell you that Roger was so exceptional in art that upon his graduation from Interlachen, they placed him in a combination of Tufts University and the Boston Museum of Fine Arts graduate school. That's why Roger today has such an in-depth training in the work he does. He's a walking history book of art, that kid. It all worked out very well for him. He's done all the major design for the biggest and most beautiful hotels in the world, so I guess you'd say that puts him right at the top as one of the best designers in the world.

## Roger Thomas

THIS MOVE TO INTERLACHEN HAPPENED IN THE MIDDLE OF MY JUNIOR year in high school, and it was such a great experience. It totally changed my life.

The way it was handled typified how my parents dealt with situations. They weren't about to let the behavior problems I was having in Las Vegas continue. And in truth I was floundering in Las Vegas. So they found a solution, and that was to get me out of there and into the proper environment that would stimulate my interests.

I found the art department at Interlachen so stimulating and so extraordinary that I spent all my time there, and I eventually graduated right at the top of my class.

Originally, I thought I was going to be a painter, but at Interlachen I discovered weaving and I took classes in metal-smithing and I learned how to work with silver and gold and bronze and copper. I was a ceramics major. I learned all about working with clay and the classic art of clay. I took sculpture. I took painting. What I was doing was getting a foundation in all of the elements that one uses to make a career in the visual arts.

By the time I left Interlachen, I was invited to go to Boston University. I went there for a semester, but they didn't have what they promised me in terms of equipment in the studios, and it was a really academic program, and frankly I was way beyond that. So I applied to the School of the Museum of Fine Arts. I just turned over the portfolio I had developed in high school, and I was accepted as a second-semester junior, when in fact I was really a second-semester freshman. The Museum of Fine Arts is also the art department for Tufts University, so in just another year and a half I received my degree from Tufts.

## Peter Thomas

IT WAS SOMETIME IN HIGH SCHOOL THAT I BECAME REALLY AWARE OF the breadth of my dad's involvement in Las Vegas. I happened to be looking through the newspaper one time, and once or twice a year they publish the tax rolls and everything, and there was a whole page of land holdings with my dad's name on it. And I took it to Dad and asked him what all of this was. And that's when he told me most of it was land he bought for Howard Hughes.

When Hughes came to town, he started buying up all this land, even before he bought the hotels, and he didn't want people knowing it was him buying it or the price would have skyrocketed. So my dad put it in his name. I found it pretty interesting to think that Hughes trusted him that much.

Of course, that caused him a lot of problems later with the IRS. The government, and particularly the Organized Crime Strike Force, well knew that Dad was everybody's banker, or at least the banker for all the guys they were after, and that he knew things about them that no one else knew, so that made him a target.

They made his life a living hell through those years. One of the things they did was come up with this guy who was a convicted felon. He told the government that Dad would find a piece of land, then talk Hughes into buying it, and then get a kickback for it. The Strike Force would then argue that he didn't pay taxes on it. Then they would try and use that leverage to get him to talk about everybody else, but of course he never would. It went all the way back to Washington, D.C., on the testimony of this guy who was a convicted felon, before it was all thrown out.

## Karen Mack

I KNEW THAT PARRY AND MY DAD WERE PIONEERS IN LAS VEGAS, AND that my grandfather Nate was a pioneer, but I didn't think of them in terms of being powerful.

I think when it hit me was when we were at the opening of the Thomas & Mack Center in 1983. That's when I realized the breadth of their contribution, but still the word "powerful" never entered my mind.

You know, when I was a girl I would stand out on the Strip with my grandfather and he would say, "I own from here to the mountain."

And I would think, it's just desert, who cares, you know? When you're a kid, you don't really get it.

I don't know even today for the general populace—because Las Vegas is such a transient community with so many newcomers—that there is a widespread appreciation of their contributions. But I think historians, or anyone who actually bothers to find out how the community was started, will remember their contribution. But that may be the same as with any town.

And I should add that the things they did for charities or civic causes were done merely because that was what a well-rounded person did. It's funny, but people are always looking for motives. With the Kennedy family, for instance, people will say, well, he or she is doing this because they are going to run for office. In the case of Parry and my father, I can say their contributions weren't motivated by much of anything other than that they knew it was the right thing to do.

## Dr. Steve Thomas

I KNEW THAT DAD WAS DOING BUSINESS WITH ALL KINDS OF DIFFERENT people, some of them with maybe not the greatest of reputations, and I do remember him being very concerned, even preoccupied, with his many business dealings.

I remember often when I was with him in the car, or on the boat, and he'd be sitting there talking to himself. I could see his lips move a tiny bit. And I know he was discussing business situations with himself. It was almost weird to see my dad sitting there having a conversation with himself. He was thinking about business deals he was putting together or how he was going to resolve a certain problem.

I was just a kid then but this was in the '60s when he was involved with so many important people in the community, and the Bank of Las Vegas was growing and the community was tight and small and Dad was extremely concerned with all the challenges he faced running the bank.

Dad hardly ever wrote anything down, and that was partly because he had such an unbelievable mind. He remembered nearly every phone number he ever needed. He'd just pull them out of his head. Eventually, after many years, he started using a little phone register but for years he would just commit to memory these phone numbers for hundreds of people. He also had a calculator in his head for numbers and interest rates. I never saw him pull out and use a calculator. He was a savant when it came to phone numbers and mathematical calculations.

I always wondered what it took to have that kind of mind. I was a business major and tried to do well in school and I did all right in medical school, but I always wished I had that kind of brain power, where I could trust my mind to do so many things simultaneously.

Dad always kept everything in such strict confidence, that even now, even though all these guys are gone or out of the business, I'm surprised he consented to doing this book.

## Roger Thomas

I THINK I FIRST GRASPED MY FATHER'S IMPORTANCE IN LAS VEGAS WHEN I was in high school, the summer between my junior and senior years in high school. While we were in Newport that summer, as my dad may have told you, he sold Major Riddle's house to Howard Hughes, and without asking my mother's permission, he moved Riddle's wife and son and the mother-in-law and dogs into our house and it quickly became unlivable.

So we moved into what was then the penthouse of the smaller tower of the Sahara Hotel. When that happened, I thought, oh, my gosh. We had lived in a very nice neighborhood, but when all your neighbors have homes as nice as yours, you don't feel special or extra-privileged. But living in that penthouse was something else again.

## Jane Thomas Sturdivant

I WAS JUST LIKE NINE OR TEN YEARS OLD WHEN WE MOVED INTO THE Sahara Hotel. It was great fun. I mean, you got to go downstairs and buy Richie Rich comic books and Nestle Crunch bars. Unfortunately, we never got to order room service because I think that was a no-no. But I'm sure some of us tried it anyway. I think it was just the four of us kids. Peter was off to college.

266

## Roger Thomas

FOR MY HIGH SCHOOL GRADUATION FROM INTERLACHEN, MY PARENTS brought all my brothers and sister back to Michigan for the graduation. There were kids from nearly all fifty states and five foreign countries in that school, but it was highly unusual to schlep a large family all the way from Nevada for a ceremony like that.

When I was looking at colleges, we went to New York where my dad had a suite at the Plaza, which was another clue that he was doing pretty well. My dad and Jerry Mack had the tanker company back then, and I can tell you I was the only kid whose father owned oil tankers. I was also the only kid at Interlachen who wore Pierre Cardin. I was very into couture in those days.

Another thing was that my mother and father went to school with a woman named Jinny Lee Snow, who later was at Cranbrook Academy of Art, then the center of design in America, and specialized in American Modernism. [*Cranbrook is located in Bloomfield Hills, Michigan.*] That was the center for all the architects and designers whose brilliant work was changing our modern world. So through her I grew up in interiors, on Mies van der Rohe and George Nelson, and the most amazing furniture and fabrics.

Jinny had entirely redone the interior of the house at the corner of Alta and Rancho, which was where I grew up, so watching her work was just an extraordinary environment to grow up in.

By the time I graduated from high school I had it clearly in mind that I was a spoiled rich kid, and that I was viewed that way by others. I also had a lot more confidence in my own abilities, because at Interlachen I had found my niche, and the family was more accepting of me as a result.

## Dr. Steve Thomas

WHEN I WAS YOUNG I WAS JUST A LITTLE BIT SHEEPISH AND EMBAR-rassed by whatever prosperity our family had. We always seemed to be ahead a little bit of my peers at elementary school and in junior high school.

The buddies I hung with came from families with successful fathers and parents, but because we seemed ahead of the curve, I was forever making excuses. For example, we would have a nice car, and I would make sure that they knew it was the *bank's* car. I would tell my friends that the bank owned the car, we didn't. Or the reason we lived in Rancho Circle was because of the bank. So even from an early age I realized that there was a part of our success that I didn't particularly cherish because it made me a little bit odd or different.

I realized very early that Dad was an important person in the community. On a Saturday when he was doing business around town, I would ask to tag along and we'd head over to the Dunes or wherever. And we'd go to the coffee shop and he'd walk in and the waitress would say, "Hi, Mr. Thomas, we've got your table ready."

We'd sit in the back of the coffee shop and there would be a telephone right there. And the phone would ring and it would be for him. And I realized that this was not your typical go-to-the-coffee-shop thing. First of all, we'd walk right past the line of people waiting there. Secondly, we're sitting at this table with a phone, and no one else here has a phone. And workers would stroll by, or executives, and say, "Hey, Parry. How ya doin'?" Everyone knew his name.

Then when I got a little older and I would go on a date to a hotel showroom, I'd show up and the maitre 'd would say, "Hi, you're Steve Thomas."

I'd sit down with my date and there was never a bill. It was back in the days of the comps, so I would just sign my name and never have to pay anything. I always had a great seat at the front of the showroom. It was a good thing on dates, absolutely. The girls were always impressed with the first-class treatment. So there was no question that my dad's connections ran deep.

I also remember going shopping with him at this place on Oakey and Decatur. I think it was called Vegas Village. It was kind of the Wal-Mart of those days. We'd go in there and shop and we'd be treated very special, and I always wondered why. I came to find out years later that my dad owned part of that business.

Finally, people would often go out of their way to tell me as his son what a great guy he was. They'd say, "Oh, you're Parry Thomas's son. Have I ever told you the story about how he helped me out?"

It was always nice to hear those stories, and they made a strong impression on me.

## Jane Thomas Sturdivant

I FELT WE LIVED A VERY NORMAL CHILDHOOD. AS FAR AS KNOWING how important our dad was. I mean, like anybody else's family, he was our dad and we loved him.

As far as realizing that he was a pretty important person, and that would allow us certain privileges, I think that light went on for me when I was sixteen years old. I got in this itsy-bitsy car crash, more of a fender-bender, on the corner of Sahara Avenue and the Strip. I sort of ran into the back of the car in front of me, although of course I thought it was the other driver's fault because he stopped too soon.

That intersection back then was all bars and strip joints and stuff, and of course there were no cell phones, so I had to go into one of those bars and call my dad.

Well, ten minutes later Dad drives up, and back then he had a 600 Mercedes, and it even had curtains in the back window. Then Uncle Jerry [Mack] drives up in his Rolls-Royce, and then Irwin Molasky in whatever fancy car he was driving. So there's this line of Bentleys, Rolls, and Mercedes all there to come to the rescue of this high school girl.

I wasn't fully aware of my dad's importance in Las Vegas until I got in college. I got caught up from an educational standpoint. I was reading the papers regularly and his name would appear in some stories, and then as Steve Wynn started going straight to the top of the business world, he was always publicly thanking Dad for all his support. I guess while I was in Las Vegas I just thought everyone had lots of friends in the casino business. I just didn't think we were all that different.

I knew Benny Binion, and he was really an interesting character. I was involved with horses and so was he, so we always had that to talk about. And Jay Sarno's daughter September Sarno was a friend of mine, and I would hear about all the big-money golf games her dad was involved in.

I remember when I was sixteen, and able to drive, I knew I wouldn't get a car until I graduated from high school. I remember Morris Shenker [*president of the Dunes Hotel*] told me that he'd buy me a nice car if Dad didn't. Of course I told Dad that he'd said that.

## Tom Thomas

MY ENERGIES SHIFTED FROM WANTING TO BE A MARINE BIOLOGIST AT the end of the summer of my junior year in high school, at the same time that I became more committed to the Mormon Church.

I knew that my dad had created a sense of placement in the community and that there were a lot of people who looked up to him, and people he had helped, and that they were grateful for what he had done. Although he wasn't a churchgoer, he was held in very high regard in the LDS community because he had helped out so many people in the church when he'd been asked, either monetarily or in helping them get jobs. If the church called Dad and said a good man needed help, he would never turn away from that.

It just became more clear to me at that time that Valley Bank was important to our family, it was important to the Las Vegas community and my church, and it was something that I could do. I was good at math, and I enjoyed people, and those are both important qualities

270

for a banker. And so it was then that I got engaged in pursuing that goal. There was even a big dinner in our ward over on West Charleston, and everyone was supposed to talk about what they wanted to be when they grew up. And I got up that night and said, "I'm going to run the biggest bank in Nevada."

Valley Bank certainly wasn't the biggest bank, because First National and Bank of Nevada had merged into First Interstate, but that's what I announced to everyone and that was my goal from then on.

## Dr. Steve Thomas

I WENT TO PORTUGAL ON MY MORMON MISSION. AND SO I WAS OVER there for two years, and at first they tried to talk me out of it, Dad specifically. He even offered some monetary rewards if I didn't go, because he thought that was a waste of two years, regardless of what my avocation was going to be.

As it turns out, when I was in Portugal, Dad came over there several times to visit me. I think when my mission was over he appreciated that it was a good thing for me.

I'll never forget a gesture Dad did that typifies how he was always thinking about what he could do for other people. When he was in Portugal once, he noticed that the mission president's wife had a scar on her neck. So later, when he was in Europe on some business deal, he bought her a Hermes scarf, which was probably a nicer scarf than any Mormon mission president's wife had ever had, and he gave it to her the next time he came to visit me. She just thought that was an unbelievably kind gesture. Knowing how dad thought, I'm sure it occurred to him that there were times this woman wished she could cover up that scar on her neck, and so he bought a scarf for her.

I should say that although Dad was not a churchgoer, a lot of how he lived his life was very much in keeping with all of the precepts of the church. There was always in my opinion more Mormonism in my father than non-Mormonism going on. The adage of stewardship and giving back to the community and living your life with integrity and taking care of your kids. Family comes first.

He was also very supportive of the church. He was always ready to write a check when they asked for help building a new building or whatever. And he always did so very much behind the scenes, without seeking any credit for it.

## Peter Thomas

THAT'S INTERESTING THAT TOM WANTED TO BE A MARINE BIOLOGIST, because my first real career goal as a kid also was inspired by our summers at Newport and a love of the ocean. For several years I thought I wanted to become an oceanographer. I took all the science classes at Clark High School that I thought would maybe lead to that, zoology, biology, the whole deal. And I did a project one time on cephalopods, which is the octopus family. I was so into the ocean that I thought it would be really cool to have a job where you worked by the ocean every day.

I eventually grew out of that and decided it would be pretty cool to be a banker, like my dad.

Another moment I remember was when I had my first serious discussion with my dad about my future goals. I remember I was just getting ready to graduate from high school and we were driving somewhere in the country. It's funny how you kind of remember the setting you were in when these conversations took place. Dad said, "What do you think you want to do?"

I told him I liked what he was doing and I thought I'd like to be a banker. He told me that he didn't know if I had the temperament to be a banker. He said that might not be the greatest idea, that I might want to consider something else.

He understood that banking could be a rough-and-tumble business. Being a banker in Las Vegas wasn't like being a banker in Salt Lake City. He once said that he would have liked being a banker anywhere else other than here, but the appealing thing about Las Vegas was that everything was moving at four times the speed as it was anywhere else in the banking business. And he was drawn to that kind of energy.

Remember, when Dad came here, the idea of trying to get credit for the gambling industry from the banking industry was an anathema. It was such an anathema that no one before him ever took the time to look under the first layer and even consider whether it was possible to underwrite gambling. The knee-jerk reaction, the first impression, from bankers was "Don't bother me with it." And that's exactly why the opportunity presented itself to him when he started out in Las Vegas.

Or maybe when I expressed interest he held up the caution sign to me as a way of using a reverse psychology to get me even more interested in banking. Whatever the case, that conversation got me focusing on whether I really wanted to do that, or not. And I decided that's what I wanted to do.

Dad told me, as he later told Tom, that if I were to come to work in our bank, I would have to get a law degree. There was the whole nepotism issue, of course, and he wanted me to know that I was not going to get special privileges because I was his son, that I had to bring more than all these other guys if I was going to join our bank.

Although Dad hadn't been to law school himself, he recognized that in the banking profession, education-wise, a law degree was probably the single most important thing you could have. The second-most important would be a CPA background, and while I didn't get that, I did take a lot of accounting classes.

When I started at the University of Utah, I had the advantage of knowing exactly what I wanted to do, so I was able to arrange all my classes accordingly and not have to scramble later by having chosen the wrong major.

I came to work for Valley Bank in 1975. I had finished law school and I was practicing tax law with George Sullivan, who was our tax attorney in Salt Lake. I was into my second year when I got a call from Kenny Sullivan at the bank. He said, "If you're going to come to work for the bank, now's the time or I'm going to have to hire somebody else."

He knew I'd always wanted to work for the bank. So I came down and went to work as a loan officer. My office was next to Bob Ruyman's, and I was able to learn a lot about lending from Bob.

I had very little interaction with my dad at the time because of the nepotism thing, and wanting to show what I could do on my own.

Well, Kenny Sullivan was the kind of guy who you'd ask a question of and get a one-word answer. He was a man of very few words. Bob Ruyman was at the other end of the spectrum. If you asked Bob the time of day, he'd tell you how to build a clock. But between the long-winded answers from Bob and the one-word answers from Kenny, I learned a lot about credit.

Dad was basically retired at the time, and he was not someone I could go to to solve a lot of problems at that point. Well, not too long after that was when the economy went in the crapper. And there were all these relationships that Kenny and my dad had forged, and a lot of them were done on a handshake over a two-martini lunch. This made my job doubly tough, because I had to be the bad cop on a lot of these loans.

This time marked a transition between doing business with the bank on a customer-to-banker relationship to where it was now a customer-to-banker-to-lawyer relationship. A lot of these loans started going south and I was the guy who had to collect them. I hadn't made the loans, but I had to collect them. And these loans were to guys like Morris Shenker and Major Riddle. And needless to say, I wasn't sitting there with the best documentation in the world.

So the way it worked was that these guys would come in and need more money, and every time they came in for more money, I'd give it to them but I'd take proportionately more collateral, things like real estate, like the Dunes Hotel, or Major Riddle's estate. It was a very tough time.

## Jon Joseph

[*At the time that Valley Bank of Nevada was sold to Bank of America in 1992, Jon was the executive vice president, secretary and general counsel of both Valley Bank and the holding company, Valley Capital Corporation.*]

In 1984, Parry Thomas, Peter Thomas, and I formed a three-man work-out department that would eventually grow to a twelve-person Loan Recovery Department.

We were on the cheeks of our ass. We had made the *Wall Street Journal* front page as one of the ten banks in American with extraordinary real estate debt exposure. Of course Valley Bank was, because of Parry, *the* lender to and banker for the casino industry. Casino credit was secured by a lien on real estate and FF&E. We also filed to perfect an interest in all credit owed to a particular casino.

Because of Southern California base closures, cuts in defense spending, the devaluation of the Mexican peso, and the opening of Atlantic City, Vegas was in deep kimchi. One could walk into a casino and see one or two tables occupied and a bevy of unemployed hookers at the bars.

At the height of this "depression," Valley Bank had five casinos in foreclosure, or owned after foreclosure. Casino licenses on foreclosed properties were held by the bank's trust department that was licensed by the Nevada Gaming Control Board. For a number of years I spoke at the gaming convention on "Managing Casinos in Chapter 11 and Thereafter." For anyone having trouble sleeping, I can provide a tape.

Amidst all this chaos, we ran into problems with the Saudi Arabian one-man CIA, namely Adnan Khashoggi. He was a notorious high-roller. He had used up credit in one casino, which was not easy to do seeing as he had nearly unlimited credit. But then he would simply move his side show down the Strip.

Khashoggi was associated with a character named "Tiger" Mike Davis, who was the inspiration for a TV show back in the '80s that I can't recall. He eventually dated Phyllis McGuire, who had once been the girlfriend of Sam Giancana. I could go on for days with other wild stories from this period, but I don't know who will eventually get their hands on this book.

Let me just say I loved working with E. Parry Thomas, and no words can adequately convey what his friendship and leadership brought to me during those years.

Parry is one of the most charismatic, humble people I've ever known. He had the ability to work with people from all walks of life and the ability to make each of them feel of consequence. I never once saw him use his success to leverage an advantage to those less fortunate.

Parry is a gentleman of the old school. One of the saddest things I heard him state was that a man's handshake no longer meant anything in a world where bankruptcy is a business strategy.

I know Parry and Jerry both had reservations about selling Valley Bank but I also believe that Parry was relieved to retire from this world rife with lawyers and litigations. In those dark days of the early '80s when the town and the bank were both struggling, Parry was the calming influence that helped us work out of our financial difficulties. He never panicked nor lost his wits. It was largely due to his efforts that we were able to recover much of the bank's bad debt and ultimately sold to Bank of America for over two times book value.

I'm delighted this book will put on the record just how important Parry was to the emergence of Las Vegas as a great American city in the twentieth and twenty-first centuries.

## Parry Thomas

PETER DID A LOT OF GREAT THINGS WHEN HE WAS RUNNING VALLEY Bank. Probably the most profitable thing he did for the bank was his ability to put automated teller machines in the casinos to give people instant cash. That had never been done before. No casino prior to the 1980s had an ATM, and with our good relationships with all the casinos we were able to get some into the hotels.

It was really no problem. We got permission from the state banking commissioner. But then VISA took us on, because we started charging one dollar for using the ATMs. VISA said we had to give the service without a charge, because VISA was getting service charge on their cards and they didn't want anybody getting into the act.

## Tom Thomas

VISA CLAIMED IT WAS A CONSTITUTIONAL VIOLATION OF INTERSTATE commerce. They argued that people were coming to Las Vegas from different states and that we didn't have the right to charge them for this service, so they sued us.

## Parry Thomas

THEY SUED US AND GOT A LOT OF POLITICAL POWER BEHIND THEM from all the other states. We were just a sitting duck. So Peter figured it out and before we could get halfway through the trial, Peter and Jon went up with some of their friends and supporters to Carson City and got the Nevada Legislature to vote that it was legal in Nevada to charge this nominal fee for a state-chartered bank.

## Jon Joseph

I BELIEVE THE BIGGEST IMPACT THAT VALLEY BANK OF NEVADA HAD IN the banking world was regarding offsite ATM locations. VBN ended up literally suing almost every bank in the U.S. for the right to sur-charge at off-site ATMs.

Because of Parry and Jerry, we were able to get a bill introduced and passed with only eight days left in the legislative session. This was about fifty days after the announced cutoff date for the introduction of bills. The end result, after litigation that went to the Ninth Circuit Court, was that we claimed anti-trust and won, which generated millions of dollars of new fee income for the bank. Two years after we beat PLUS, Visa, MasterCard, Citibank, Chase, Bank of America, etc., in court, the general counsel of PLUS was in front of Congress arguing in favor of ATM surcharges.

We wrote the law that requires a screen to come up to confirm the use of the ATM and the payment of the surcharge. This law has been copied around the world. Our little bank incurred over a million dollars in legal fees to get this on.

## Tom Thomas

WE WEREN'T FEDERALLY CHARTERED, SO THE STATE DETERMINED THE operating laws for Nevada banks. So by the Legislature giving their approval, VISA was not really suing Valley Bank anymore. Now Valley Bank was operating under the full authority of a state banking law. So then VISA had to sue the state of Nevada, saying that its action was unconstitutional. That brought the Nevada attorney general into the fray.

## Parry Thomas

IT ENDED UP IN THE NINTH CIRCUIT COURT IN SAN FRANCISCO AND they looked at this issue and ended up writing an opinion in Valley Bank's favor. We couldn't have written a better opinion in our favor had we written it ourselves.

What we'd done to show why this was good for the public was an experiment we conducted in Fisherman's Wharf, right in the heart of the Ninth Circuit. And I believe we set up a couple other mock ATMs to get the public's reaction. The question we asked through the process was: Would you pay one dollar for the right to use your ATM card to be able to remove three or four hundred dollars from this machine, whether you're a customer of this bank or not? The poll came back 98.5 percent in favor of paying the one-dollar charge. That's an unbelievable result. You can't get 98.5 percent of people to agree that the sky is blue.

## Tom Thomas

WHAT THE NINTH CIRCUIT COURT RULED WAS THAT VISA WAS TRYING to get everybody to continue using the cash withdrawal from a credit card, which at the time was like a fifteen-dollar charge to be able to get hard cash from the cage of the casino on your credit card.

Then there was the Western Union cost to transfer money. All these things were being compared and the Ninth Circuit ruled that VISA was interested only in maintaining their monopoly on extracting huge sums of money from people who wanted to get cash.

Valley Bank showed that with the cost of each ATM running about $75,000, for the bank to make these machines available to its non-customers with whom it has no banking relationship, it had to figure out some way to extract at least enough money to pay for the services.

That ruling opened up the whole system. At the time VISA was one of the main owners of the Plus system, which was the largest network of ATMs in the country. So they had a huge stake in this, and the minute Valley Bank won that ruling, every bank across the country started receiving money for their ATMs. At the time Valley Bank had over three hundred ATMs that were not located in our branches. They were in casinos, they were in grocery stores, they were all over the place. The bank then owned a company called Casino Cash. So it didn't say Valley Bank on any of the ATMs at the casinos.

When The Mirage opened in 1989, that was the crowning test for those machines. We put something like six ATMs in The Mirage and loaded them with hundred-dollar bills. And the amount of money over the first three days of the hotel's opening that came out of those machines was something like $3.5 million. They had to restock them with $250,000 canisters over and over, about four times a day.

They did a test and it was discovered that around eighty percent of those hundred-dollar bills went back through the cage in the casino. The reaction from the hotel people was: We want these machines. Because the machines showed an increase in gaming because they allowed people access to their cash from back home.

## Parry Thomas

I GIVE PETER AND JON CREDIT FOR MAKING THAT HAPPEN. IT CHANGED the whole business, and within the first year those service charges added about a quarter million to our bottom line at the bank. It was really a brilliant maneuver.

Getting back to an earlier point, there was no question in the late '70s and early '80s, when Peter was at the bank, that I had one hell of a drinking problem.

When I first moved to Las Vegas in the '50s, I'd have maybe two or three cocktails in the whole week. I had been a social drinker in Salt Lake when I worked for the Continental Bank, because I was on the road a lot getting business and there was a lot of social activity that went along with that. That was okay. I never had any problem with drinking then. I could handle it.

But when I started buying companies outside of Las Vegas, particularly when we bought United Tanker and Continental Connector, both based in New York, and other companies Jerry and I got interested in, it got to the point for management that I had to spend more and more time back East. We had our money in these companies and they were big investments, so we had to manage them or it wasn't going to work.

So most weekends I'd be on an airplane. The drinking problem snuck up on me. I'd get on an airplane and by the time I got to New

York and had lunch and maybe two martinis or two drinks, then go out with some of the staff and whatnot, and have a couple more drinks . . . well, it just kept on for over ten years and finally it got to where I was addicted. No question about it.

I first realized the problem after I'd been subpoenaed to testify as a witness after Major Riddle died, and there was a real showdown between the heirs to his estate and some of the creditors. And when I read the transcript of my testimony, I realized what a sloppy witness I'd been. I think this was in late 1979. So Jerry Mack and I talked about the problem and we talked about it some more.

## Tom Thomas

I GOT A CALL FROM PETER, AND IT WAS PETER AND UNCLE JERRY WHO basically set up this intervention. The whole family came down to Las Vegas on a weekend. I think it was early in 1980. I'd been back from a mission in Colombia for about a year. It was a Sunday morning. We all met early in the morning over at the house on Rancho Circle. Dad came in and looked around and said, "What's everybody here for?"

We all talked, and said how much we cared for Dad and how concerned we were for his physical health. My brother Steve talked about the medical aspects and what goes on with the liver and the other dangers Dad faced by continuing to drink. He said that Dad basically had a ten-year life expectancy, if that.

And Dad said, "I'll do whatever you guys want me to do."

There was no contention, no resistance at all. He just told us he appreciated us all being there for him and that he would do whatever it took.

Jerry knew the guys down at St. John's and he went down there and got in the rehab program.

## Parry Thomas

I STAYED THERE SIX WEEKS. THEY HAD EDUCATIONAL CLASSES EVERY day, and they really got into the vicissitudes of drinking. It wasn't too hard, but I remember it was really tough the first three or four days. I had a hell of a time. Everybody else did, too. You know, you just stop drinking and go cold turkey when you're used to drinking maybe a half a fifth a day, or something like that. You're simply addicted, and your body requires alcohol.

## Joyce Mack

JERRY STUDIED UP ON ALCOHOLISM AND LEARNED ABOUT IT, AND WHAT he discovered is that you get the whole family to do an intervention. So that's what he did.

When the drinking starts interfering with the business and the friendship and all that, then of course you've gotta do something.

It was very hard for Parry to do. They had him go down to a facility in Santa Monica the first time, and it didn't work.

## Parry Thomas

THE FIRST TIME I TRIED A PROGRAM, IT DIDN'T TAKE. JERRY TOOK ME down to St. John's, in Santa Monica. But when I went to Scripps, it worked.

## Joyce Mack

TALK ABOUT BEING A GOOD FRIEND, JERRY SAID ON THAT SECOND TIME that he didn't want Parry down there all by himself. He said he wanted to be available in case he wanted someone to talk to. So what Jerry and I did—both of us being from UCLA—we had heard about a healthy enhancement program going on that was excellent. We enrolled in that and stayed there for six weeks while Parry was in the hospital there. He almost died in those first days going through withdrawal. It was really difficult. We almost lost him, and I remember it as a very, very painful thing.

## Parry Thomas

I THINK EVEN IF I HADN'T GONE THERE, I WOULD HAVE BEATEN IT eventually, because I had the mental process to do it. But when we had that family meeting, I knew that was the end of it. One way or another, I knew I had had the last drink for my whole life. And I haven't had one since.

I went to about one AA meeting after that, but I didn't follow up with any others. I didn't want to sit around with a bunch of drunks.

## Tom Thomas

WITH ALL OF THE MANY THINGS I COULD MENTION THAT MAKE ME proud of my dad, I think right at the top of the list was the way he addressed his problem with alcoholism and beat it. I know from talking with people and reading about it how difficult that is to do. And he just took it head on and whipped it.

## Dr. Steve Thomas

HERE'S ANOTHER EXAMPLE OF MY DAD'S WISDOM, AND HIS GENEROSITY. It had been my dream since I was a boy to sail across an ocean. And I was able to do that, and take a full year out of medical school, with his permission. Dad agreed to fund our buying a sailboat to indulge in this great adventure. It was to be me and my wife, Karen, and Tom, who was taking a year out of college, and Jane, and two of Tom's buddies on the trip.

When I went down to buy the boat for the trip, I picked out a nice boat that was reasonably priced. It was, I thought, safe enough. Dad came down to okay it, because we were using his funds. He looked at the boat I had chosen and said, "Let's look around a little more."

He called up a broker and they did some research and found a boat that was twice as expensive, but probably three times safer than the one I had chosen. It had a steel hull instead of fiberglass. It had been built in New Zealand, where the one I had chosen was built in California and designed for short trips to Catalina or thereabouts.

So we sailed the boat from Newport Beach to Bora Bora, and down through the entire South Pacific. When we first departed, we went twenty-one straight days without once sighting land. We essentially sailed across the Pacific, from north to south, and that boat saved our lives a couple of times. When we hit ground, we were hitting it with steel, not fiberglass. And we got hit by Hurricane Lisa in the South Pacific. I'm pretty sure it saved our lives then. Bottom line is that if Dad hadn't gone to the expense and trouble of making certain we had a safer boat, who knows what would have happened. He was willing to let three of his kids take a daring trip across the ocean, but he wasn't about to take a chance with us doing it in a boat that wasn't as safe as could be.

## Brian Greenspun

WITH ALL PARRY THOMAS HAS DONE IN LAS VEGAS, I'D SAY HIS GREAT-est contribution to the city is his family. He and Peggy have raised bright, hard-working, responsible, ethical people who are still working and sharing his legacy in this town. So where one person was doing it before in Parry, you've now got Peter and Tommy and Steven and Roger and Jane contributing in a big way. When parents raise good, honest, devoted members to a society, that's a much greater gift to a community that anything else they could do, because the ripple effect of those good works reaches so many others.

## Dr. Steve Thomas

I REMEMBER ONE TIME COMING TO DAD AND ASKING HIM ABOUT A business deal I was offered that sounded really good to me. What I got from his answer was he thought I was getting a better deal than the person who was offering it to me. He said, "That sounds really great for you, but if it isn't as good for the guy you're doing business with, then it's not going to last. It's not a good business deal unless you both end up better off."

His point was clearly that the idea of getting ahead by getting more than the next guy would usually come back and shoot you in the foot. Business arrangements need to last, and if after a time one party feels he got the short end of the deal, then the deal will fail for both parties.

CHAPTER FIVE

# Other Ventures, Other Times

## Parry Thomas

MY TRAVAILS WITH THE IRS STARTED SOMETIME AROUND 1971, WHEN three agents came to my office at the bank when we were still located on Fourth Street. It all came about on a ricochet from the Hughes people and the government going after Bob Maheu once Howard Hughes had left town and Maheu was at odds with the people still around Hughes.

The Hughes folks had hired this company called Intertel, which was formed by former agents of the IRS and the SEC and I believe the FBI. And when this big war broke out between the opposing sides of the Hughes empire, they were really on to Bob. They wanted to get anything on Maheu that they could, and because I had handled all the property for Hughes through Maheu, they thought by trying to get something on me, then I'd in turn blow the whistle on Maheu. But of course I never would do that.

So these Intertel guys who used to be bosses at the IRS got their buddies who were still at the agency to try and come up with anything they could on me. They focused on the acquisition of the Sands Hotel by Hughes that I had put together. I had taken a big commission on that sale—it was $275,000—and the IRS argued that the commission shouldn't have gone to me, but instead should have gone to the bank.

The IRS didn't know it, but at the time I had the attorneys draw up an agreement with the whole board of directors of Valley Bank and the Sands Hotel board of directors that I was to be paid directly on that commission, and not the bank, because I had worked for years on helping Hughes with that acquisition—not to mention all the others—and that the bank had been more than compensated because the Sands had been the bank's biggest customer. In the agreement it was written that should this money for any reason be challenged, the commission would go back to the Sands. It was all documented. I was advised by my tax attorney, George Larson, not to show that agreement to the IRS when all this started, and in hindsight I wish to hell that I had because maybe the whole thing would have ended right there. But for whatever reason, it didn't.

It ended up with my having a regular agent and two special intelligence agents on my case for about three years, chasing me around to get whatever they could. It just made a mess of my life during that time. Practically everybody who ever did business with me was contacted and interviewed.

I particularly remember that at that time we still owned United Tanker in New York, and we were just about to enter a huge contract with the five biggest utilities in New England to ship liquefied gas from Algeria. We were going to have three kinetic ships built, a very expensive deal, with over a hundred million dollars for each ship to do it.

I had all the financing set with Morgan Stanley, and just before we were ready to close the deal, these agents went down and interviewed the guys at Morgan. Bob Greenfield was handling this deal for them, and he called me one day and said he was sorry to tell me but that they'd heard some disquieting news about my situation in Las Vegas and they were not going to do the financing. So we lost the deal.

As it turned out that was a blessing in disguise because another company took on the contract to build those ships and they never did work. That company lost millions of dollars, but no one could have foreseen that at the time.

I tell that story to illustrate how my life was turned upside down during that period. The IRS was looking over my shoulder at everything I did. And the way it worked in those days was that when the IRS had finished its investigation, they would charge you locally and you had the right of appeal at your state office, which was in our case in Reno.

They wouldn't even tell me what the charges were, just that I was being charged with income tax evasion.

Eventually, the case went to the regional office, in my case the Twelfth District in San Francisco, and if we were turned down, the protocol was that we would get a one-hour hearing in Washington, D.C., where the hearings were conducted by a three-lawyer review board from the Department of Justice.

In San Francisco, I had Charlie McNellis, one of Ed Morgan's top attorneys, and George Larson, from Salt Lake, representing me, and I remember waiting at the St. Francis Hotel for them to come back and tell me what my fate was. I was sweating blood that whole time, wondering what was going to happen to me.

While they were in the San Francisco office, the attorney who was handling the review could see that I was getting railroaded, and that this was a big setup. So he did a very honorable thing. Because we didn't even know what I was being charged with, and this attorney sensed how unfair this was, he did a very noble thing that he certainly didn't have to do. He wrote four names on a piece of paper on his desk. He then turned it a quarter of the way toward George Larson, so with little effort George could read the names. The attorney then stood up and told my lawyers that he had to leave for a few minutes and report to his boss. He looked down at the piece of paper and he looked at George, giving him a clear signal, and he walked out. Of course, George copied the names he'd written down, and now we at least knew where to go to start work on my defense.

One of the names was the Collins Brothers, who had built our house at Rancho Circle. The other was a guy who owned a chain of restaurants in Los Angeles. Those were the two most important clients on the list.

I got the Collins Brothers to bring down their spreadsheets on the construction of our house so I could study them and see what the hell the IRS was shooting for. In the process of going over those, I could see from the spreadsheets chart that they had about ten jobs going at the same time as our house, and ours was number two. And then they had the plumbing, the framing contractor, the electrician, and so on listed vertically with the names of the clients listed horizontally across the top.

When I saw the framing charges on my house, the total on the sheet was about $150,000 more than it could possibly have been. On a square-foot basis, you could build the Taj Mahal for what they were charging me for framing. It came out to something like six dollars a square foot for framing the house, when the average cost for even an elaborate house was just $1.50 a square foot.

So I hired a private detective to look into it, and he found that the Collins' bookkeeper was in cahoots with the framing contractor. They had padded the books, so that when the government studied it, it appeared as though the Collins had charged me $150,000 less than the actual cost, so the IRS interpreted that as a $150,000 gift I had received that I didn't pay taxes on. So at that point it was easy for us to disprove the charges on the Collins Brothers matter.

Then with the guy in Los Angeles who said I took $250,000 from him when I bought a piece of land from him for Howard Hughes, I was able to show that he was hiding a gambling problem. He was a degenerate craps shooter, known all over town. I was told I could call any pit boss in town and learn about him. So I called Harry Goodheart at the Hilton, who was a good friend of mine, and he gave me all the spreadsheets on this guy. Harry shouldn't have done it, but he was doing me a favor because he was my friend. And I saw where this man had lost $250,000 on the very same day that he said he'd given it to me. Turns out he had a new wife and he was lying to her about what happened to the money. Plus, he'd already been convicted for tax evasion, so he was trying to curry favor with the IRS by putting this bogus rap on me.

So by the time we went to this hearing in Washington, D.C., we were armed with all this information, including the board agreement on the Sands fee, and were more than ready to disprove the IRS charges.

But there was another tactic that the IRS used during this time that was so stupid and unethical that it's hard to believe. It occurred right before we went back to the hearing in Washington, and it illustrates how desperate they were to pin something on me as a way of getting to Maheu.

Bob Kaltenbourne was one of my best friends in Las Vegas, going back to my first years in town because he had been Nate Mack's business partner in some ventures. One day Bob came charging into my office and shut the door. He sat down across from me and said, "Are you under investigation by the IRS?"

I said, "Yes, how did you know?"

He said, "Well, I have quite a story to tell you."

Kaltenbourne went on to tell me that he had owned a farm out in Overton, Nevada, and that during the Depression he'd had a Mormon family working out there sharecropping for him. He kept them going during that rough time. They had two sons that Bob had put through college, and Bob was very proud of them. One of the boys had gone on to become a CPA and was working for the IRS. This young man had gone to Bob the day before he met with me and told him that his conscience was bothering him about a plan the IRS had put together to get at me.

The government had worked out a scheme to get my son Tommy, and a good friend of his who was the son of one of my attorneys, involved with marijuana, and then use that leverage to squeeze me. Tommy and his friend knew a kid from school, and his older brother was a known drug dealer. The government was going to try and get this drug dealer to give our sons marijuana as a way to lessen his sentence. The dealer was working as a double agent, setting up guys that the government would then arrest.

So my attorney and I sat down with our sons and told them about this plot to involve them. We actually held them out of school for a couple of days. I then went to my friend Ralph Lamb, who was the sheriff of Clark County, and told him all about it. He knew this particular drug dealer, and what his game was, so he had the guy picked up and brought to his office.

Now Ralph was a good friend of mine, and a tougher sheriff you'd never find. He was bone-hard tough. Ralph wrote out an affidavit for the dealer to sign, admitting that he was involved in this plan to frame our boys. The thug initially wouldn't sign it, because it would blow his own deal with the government. So Ralph pointed over to a jail cell, which was full of a bunch of dope fiends. He told him, "I'm going to tell them that you're a snitch for the government, and that you set up people for drug busts, and when they hear that, I won't be able to pick up with a blotter what's left of you. Now do you want to sign it, or do you choose the tank?"

That made the dealer's choice pretty easy.

So then we went to Washington and the Justice Department for this hearing, and we had answers to everything the government had cooked up over the previous three miserable years.

It turned out my attorney Charlie McNellis knew one of the attorneys on the government's review board from a previous stint at the Justice Department, and that attorney could see right away that the government didn't have a case. He said, "I think we're going to pass on these charges."

The review attorney then asked us if there was anything else we wanted to tell them, and George Larson took that opportunity to explain what the government had tried to do to our two young sons in Las Vegas. He told the whole story of this phony frame-up the IRS was planning. Well, it turned out that a hearing that was supposed to last one hour lasted for two days while they looked into it. They were very concerned that I'd bring charges against the government for their behavior, which I damn well could have. But I didn't want the notoriety that all of that would create in the press and everywhere else.

I just had my attorneys say that I hoped the government would transfer these agents or work something out so they wouldn't do to someone else what they had done to me. And that put an end to a three-year nightmare.

But can you imagine what would have happened to me if I hadn't had the benefit of knowing all these Las Vegas people, and being able to investigate the bogus case the agency had worked up against me? It would have had a much more dismal ending.

We did so many deals, especially in the early years, where you'd make a verbal agreement with someone on a loan or whatnot, and you'd look them in the eye and shake hands on it and that would be that. I learned that from the gamblers, because that's the way they operated. The most important thing in the world for those old-timer gamblers was their word. You had a lot of tin-horns you had to separate out, but the real honest-to-goodness gaming people—their word was their bond.

I hadn't been in Las Vegas too long, maybe three or four years, when I started getting subpoenas to federal grand juries. And at the very first grand jury I ever went to, they wanted to see all my records, my diary, my daily memos, anything at all in writing. That's what grand juries do. They dig down deep.

Fortunately, I didn't have anything at all regarding that case, which was regarding one of the Sands owners, Aaron Weisberg, investing in a company called Scopitone.

The Mob owned Scopitone, which distributed these jukeboxes with a movie tape running on a screen, so that as the music played, you could see the people dancing and this and that. The Mob put them in every bar, whether the bar owner wanted the machine or not. That's the way they worked.

I had loaned Aaron a couple hundred thousand dollars to invest in the company, and I used his stock in the Sands as collateral, as I remember. I'll never forget going to that first federal grand jury. It was in New York, in Foley Square.

They have a witness room outside the jury room and you're not allowed to take an attorney with you, so I was sitting there with all these witnesses. I looked around and all these guys were reading books. And the second time I looked around most of the books were upside down [laughing].

The famous New York District Attorney Robert Morgenthau was in charge of that case. It was a pretty big deal. So they asked me how I could run a bank and not have a diary or appointment calendar of anything in writing that they could see. Well, I don't remember how, but I somehow wiggled through their questions and told them I just didn't have those things.

When I got back to Las Vegas, I told Belle [James], my secretary, that from that point on I would keep no memos, no calendar, no anything. I told her we would have to keep everything in our heads. And from that day forward, I didn't keep any notes. It's probably one reason I developed a pretty good memory.

Whenever afterward I went before a grand jury and was asked those questions about why I didn't keep appointment books or calendars, I always gave the same answer. I said, "In Las Vegas we just don't have them and the reason I don't have them is because you subpoena them." I was right upfront with them.

∞

One of the many interesting people I met through the years was Adnan Khashoggi, the billionaire arms dealer and jet-setter. It was an unusual set of circumstances and personal contacts that got us together.

When Adnan lived in London, his wife, Soraya, got involved with Winston Churchill II, who I knew because his mother married a friend of ours, Averill Harriman, in Sun Valley.

So Adnan and his wife were getting divorced in the early '80s and she moved to California. The divorce proceedings were taking place there. Adnan was advised not to go to California, and mainly through my friend and attorney Ed Morgan, who was advising him, Adnan got a hold of me. As you can tell from his network of contacts, Ed Morgan had an incredible client list because he was such a brilliant attorney.

At the time, Adnan also had a case in litigation against an airline contractor in California. Evidently he had bought a lot of airplanes for the Saudi Air Force, and he had an enormous commission owed him for the sale of these planes. There was a dispute over the amount of the commission. With this multimillion-dollar suit with the contractor and the ongoing divorce proceedings, Khashoggi needed to avoid California, so Ed Morgan asked if we could lease Khashoggi some office space in Las Vegas while he was going through all the depositions and meetings with attorneys over these matters. We gave him space at our new Valley Bank building downtown at Fourth and Bridger, and he stayed there for a couple of months working through these situations.

Khashoggi was an interesting man. He spoke perfect English. He was a Stanford graduate and the son of a doctor to the royal family of Saudi Arabia. Being well-connected and well-educated, Saudi sheiks and other wealthy people were always calling him and asking him to buy things for them. That eventually took him into the import/export business, and that became his calling. He started buying bigger things and sending them back to Saudi Arabia and taking commissions from both the buyer and the seller. And then the Saudi government, through his father's influence, started using Adnan to procure the really heavy stuff, like tanks and airplanes and armament. Through those dealings, he became an extremely wealthy man, one of the wealthiest in the world at one point.

I got to know him pretty well and had a nice, enjoyable relationship with him early on. A few years later, Khashoggi invited me as a guest onto his world-famous yacht, the *Nabila*, which he named after his daughter. My reason for accepting his invitation was to explore the port of Antibes, in the French Riviera, which was a better and deeper port than Monte Carlo. It could handle the mega-yachts that all the Saudi princes owned, boats that were over two hundred feet long. At the time Antibes had decided to convert itself from a commercial port to a yacht basin, and Khashoggi thought it might be a super place to build a gaming hotel.

I talked to Steve Wynn about this prospect and he encouraged me to take a look at it, but he said to be careful. Steve knows this business better than anyone. So I accepted Khashoggi's offer and went over to France for about ten days to examine this port. I flew into Paris, and then on to Nice, commercially, and I was met by a fellow who represented the commissioners who were in charge of the port rehabilitation at Antibes. I looked at the property with this gentleman for several days and stayed in Nice at the Negresco Hotel.

This was a fantastic location for a hotel-casino, seven acres right at the end of the harbor, located along the main highway, with about 220,000 cars a day passing by it. The opportunity was just mind-boggling if you had the right operation. But as I recall in studying the regulations, the French government had a tax on gaming of seventy-five percent. That was just an impossible tariff. You couldn't survive in that business paying a seventy-five percent tax. Additionally, they didn't allow slot machines in French casinos, because slot machines could be audited better than *chemin de fer* and other table games.

It might be okay for French insiders to be in that business, but we could just imagine that if Americans got in the gaming business there and were caught cheating, they were going to the Bastille in a hurry. It wasn't worth it, so we passed on the opportunity.

Khashoggi then sent his helicopter and flew both myself and the port manager out to his yacht in the middle of the Mediterranean. We traveled on the boat for about a week and it was very pleasant, as you might imagine. We went to Sardinia and met many other prominent people.

Adnan invited me back a second time when they had a big ceremony to dedicate the port at Antibes. He was hosting a party and serving food out of the kitchen on his yacht and there must have been around one hundred and fifty people there, and many celebrities and a lot of politicians. I remember there were two U.S. congressmen among the group.

By coincidence, my buddy Merv Adelson was at Antibes staying at the Eden-Roc, a very famous resort which I had been through once before on leave from the Army. Merv was on his honeymoon with Barbara Walters. So I took one of the tenders from Khashoggi's yacht *Nabila*, and even those were thirty-eight feet long. Merv was in the middle of negotiating a television deal with George Hamilton and some woman he was seeing, so we brought him along and went over to Marguerita, an island off the coast of Nice, and went swimming and had lunch. Obviously, when you were with Adnan, everything was as first class as it gets.

I introduced Adnan to Barbara Walters along the way, and they got along really well and she subsequently got some private interviews with him. He was a publicity hound, so he wanted to get as close to Barbara as he could get. In fact, about three weeks after that party on the yacht, I got a call in my office in Las Vegas, and it was Merv Adelson. He said, "You'll never guess where I am."

He told me he was on Khashoggi's private DC-8 and Barbara was interviewing Adnan all the way to Europe. Both Barbara and Khashoggi got on the phone and we chatted, and that interview later aired on ABC. It was a big coup for her.

Years later, Barbara and Merv divorced, which is too bad, because he's a good friend and I liked her a lot, too.

Even after he moved out of our offices, Khashoggi came to Las Vegas often. He stayed at the Sands, and he was probably the biggest gambler in town at that time. He always had an entourage and there were always a lot of beautiful women with him. His favorite casino host in town was Carl Cohen, because Carl really knew how to take care of high-rolling gamblers. He was the best at that. I think the Sands got wealthy off Adnan. I bet he lost anywhere from ten to thirty million there, and this is in the early 1980s. Imagine the value of that today.

He also spent a lot of time at the Dunes Hotel. Morris Shenker was really working on him then. They even built a special building for him. Shenker was really going after the big players at that time, so he built a whole suite of rooms for Khashoggi and his entourage, and Adnan spent several months there. There were all sorts of crazy stories about the goings-on there. You can only imagine.

In the early '80s, Khashoggi was building a big industrial center in Salt Lake City next to the airport. It was a well-thought-out plan, but it didn't turn out to be financially sound. It ended up in a bankruptcy and some friends of mine got wounded in the deal. It was a bad situation for my friends in the Eccles family and First Security Bank. They got hung out to dry pretty badly, and I was upset the way Adnan handled that credit. I eventually interjected myself into the situation to collect on their behalf, and I did get some of the money back. I just voluntarily went in and tried to do everything I could because I knew more about Khashoggi than they did.

I was disappointed in Khashoggi because he could have stepped up to the plate there, but instead he left a lot of good Salt Lake people hanging. And so my respect level for him changed a great deal because of the way he handled that situation.

A few years later, the damnedest thing happened. The last time I saw Adnan Khashoggi was when he and Imelda Marcos of the Philippines got indicted over a three-building transaction in New York and were standing trial at a courthouse in Foley Square. Lo and behold, I got subpoenaed to that damn trial. And the reason I got subpoenaed was because the government knew that I had a helluva time collecting some bank loans that we'd made to him.

At the height of his debt to us, Khashoggi owed about two million dollars, but by the time of the trial it was down to about a couple hundred thousand.

The government subpoenaed me to be a government witness, thinking I'd testify against him. And as I recall I was the last witness in that trial, or so they tell me. I was on the stand for two days, and Adnan was sitting there as pale as could be. It was an interesting observance. I knew that if I was helpful, I had a better chance of seeing the bank get paid. But I just very honestly told the prosecution about my relations with Khashoggi and that I had no ill feelings toward him. Adnan had always been very cordial to me and was always solicitous of my friendship with him. I did testify that in fact I had to chase him all over Europe to get paid, until I finally figured out that he had a secret system for getting paid in Switzerland. There was a secret code, it was a clever situation, and it took me a little while to figure it out, but I was finally able to crack it. And our bank got paid.

Both Khashoggi and Imelda Marcos got off on the charges, and I was told by his attorneys that it was my testimony that leaned it in his favor. So I was pleased to hear that.

Another business that took up quite a bit of Jerry's and my time was our purchase of the United Tanker Group. It ended up being the biggest asset we owned at the time.

The way it came about was that Jake Gottlieb, who owned the land the Dunes was on and was a friend of ours, owned a company called Western Transportation in Chicago. It was a truck line that operated through Iowa and Ohio and Illinois.

Jake told me some time around 1968 that Bob Smith, who was the top man at Walgreen's Drugs, had told him that they were having nothing but trouble getting their merchandise into Puerto Rico and the Virgin Islands. And that the only shipping line that they could work with was a little company called SACL, or South Atlantic Caribbean Line. So Jake Gottlieb passed the information on to Jerry and me and suggested that we meet with Smith. After meeting with Smith and with the president of SACL and doing our homework, we found out that SACL was owned by a company called United Tanker Group out of New York City.

United Tanker was owned by a Chinese shipping magnate, one of the top tycoons in China, whose name was Y.M. Chen. He had a problem because the company owned both foreign flag and American flag ships. But under the law, only Americans could own American flag ships.

What Y.M. had done when he formed United Tanker was to shill up his board of directors with some professors out of Boston—Harvard and Yale and others—and he got by with it by having a charitable foundation own the ship line. But our government had eventually caught up with him and discovered that he was the real owner. Y.M. had to divest himself of it, so Jerry and I threw what we thought was a real low price at him.

It just looked like a good opportunity, and even though we didn't know anything about the tanker business, we figured we could learn what we needed. To our surprise, there were no other offers for United Tanker, and so Y.M. took our lowball offer and suddenly we were in the shipping business.

We retained Carter Hamill, who was the chairman of the board, and Jack Coakley, and Paul Yu, a Chinese man who was the executive vice president and a very smart and honest guy. He was the most outstanding man in the company, and definitely the smartest. Another outstanding man was Ken Milla, who years later worked with us at Valley Bank.

We came to find out that Carter Hamill was playing games through his SACL subsidiary because he was the owner of the cranes and charging United Tanker a helluva price for them. He had no competition for that business and he was taking full advantage of it.

A second problem was that we found out during some trips to Florida that the head of the Maritime Union down there was giving us nothing but a bad time.

The third thing that finally caused us to sell the company was the thievery in the Virgin Islands, but particularly in Puerto Rico. No matter how you physically handled the product in these containers, the workers would somehow get into them and steal the merchandise. They would also steal everything on the trailers. Walgreen's was just one of hundreds of customers using our ships, but the stealing was rampant. They'd take everything they could pry loose, even the reflectors on the trailers.

That said, overall United Tanker was a good and viable business. It was a business we learned to like, but it took a lot of our attention and a lot of our time. We were spending one week in New York and one week in Las Vegas and the next week in New York, back and forth. At the end of our ownership—I guess it lasted for about nine or ten years—we cashed out and made a lot of money in that business.

We were fortunate in our timing. What happened was that crude oil went from six dollars a barrel to thirty dollars a barrel almost overnight, and there was confusion. It was like a Chinese fire drill throughout the whole industry. And the ships became very important and very valuable. We could charter our ships for enormous prices. So, Jerry and I sat down and talked about it. We could do whatever we wanted with our ships because we had them all booked on short-term charters and we were in a position to make a move. We made the decision that instead of chartering the ships and going after high rentals, we were going to sell the ships and sell the entire company. It made good business sense because we were never going to see another time like this in our lifetime that was more opportune for getting out of the shipping business.

I also didn't want Peter or Tommy to have to inherit the shipping lines. It was too tough a business. I mean, in shipping you're dealing with some pretty rough guys. This was never more clear to us that when we were selling off the company.

We made a deal with Keystone Shipping in Pennsylvania to buy United Tanker. They had a lawyer who was handling the deal, and we had the documentation all set and ready to go forward, and then this lawyer for Keystone busted the deal. He said that I was involved with the Mafia in Las Vegas, and that it was a well-known fact, and a bunch of other garbage. And he told the Keystone executives that there was no way of knowing what they were buying, or what kind of hidden interests I had behind me that they would not want to live with. So they canceled the deal.

Well, in no time that word was all over the street, and the fraternity of shipping people was very small back then. There were only about six other companies that you could sell a company like ours to. It wasn't like you could go to your nearest brokerage office and sell your shipping line. Plus, ours was the biggest shipping company in America at that time. So instead of selling the entire company, we decided to sell off the ships individually.

Through a combination of factors, we learned that Keystone had made a deal where they had to have three handy-sized tankers that could travel through the Panama Canal. Those were tankers that carried a capacity of 40,000 tons or less. The agreement had been reached. So when Jerry and I decided that we would sell the ships, we sold the three oldest ships first, and those went to Keystone. We sold them the Eagle Courier, the Eagle Voyager, and the Eagle Traveler. With the oil markup and all the ships getting big charters, you just couldn't find ships and we knew that Keystone was desperate.

I told Jack Coakley, our president, that when he dealt with Keystone, he was going to have to deal with the same attorney who had called me a gangster. My advice was to let that attorney run the show, and not to have our lawyers open their mouths at all or offer any information. He and Paul Yu were not to add anything to the deal or subtract anything from it.

Well, about two weeks later, Coakley got a call from Keystone's president, who said, "You sold me those ships, but you didn't sell me the parts."

And I remember exactly what we told him. "We purposely let your attorney run the show, and that's because he's such a smart-ass. He's such a smart-ass that he didn't even know that the ship had parts."

Now you can't just go to the nearest drugstore and buy ship propellers or shafts or generators or pumps or anything like that.

"We've got a whole warehouse full of shafts and generators and pumps and everything else over at Hoboken," Jack Coakley said. "And I'm going to let you have those parts at our cost. We just don't do business that way. But I hope you'll fire that damn lawyer who called Parry a gangster. I want you to know he's only half-right."

We felt that Jack needed to leave a little doubt in their minds.

The president of Keystone said, "You're on!"

And that's exactly what happened. He bought the parts and fired that attorney.

Eventually we sold the sulfur ships to Mexico and the foreign flag-ships to the government of Taiwan, and the rest of the ships in the company to Ogden Marine Company out of Boston and made a lot of money.

All in all it was a good business, but it took me away from Las Vegas more than I would have liked.

Another Strip hotel that had quite a history was the Dunes, which as everyone knows was imploded in 1993 to make way for Bellagio.

I consider what happened to Jerry Mack and me at the Dunes to be the worst mistake I ever made in my business career.

In the early '70s, we got ambitious to build a corporate complex of companies, and so Jerry and I bought control of a company called Continental Connector. It was a little company that was listed on the American Stock Exchange, and it had been very successful in making microscopic electronic equipment for work in outer space. It was an ever-improving company with good management. Our idea was to branch out and have a holding company that was already listed on the exchange, because that was much easier than starting from scratch, and then we could add to it.

I was very close to Jake Gottlieb, who owned the property the Dunes was on. He was a good customer and a good guy, and we liked going to New York with him and socializing. So we merged the Dunes into Continental Connector and we were hoping it was going to work out, and that we would be able to buy the Golden Nugget, which we thought to be the most attractive downtown property by far, but about six months into it the SEC came down hard on Continental Connector, saying that the CPAs for the Dunes, Siedman and Siedman, had done an inaccurate audit at the Dunes and that therefore the financial statements weren't correct and we therefore couldn't go through with the merger. The timing couldn't have been worse for us because we had our purchase of the Golden Nugget locked up in escrow at the time and we were going to merge that in to Continental Connector.

That turned out to provide the opening for Steve Wynn to come in and eventually take over Golden Nugget, so it probably worked out for the better for Las Vegas, but it was a big blow to us at the time. That was the beginning of the end of our relations with Continental Connector.

At that point Morris Shenker got together with a guy named Cohen from San Diego, and a couple of other friends and they stepped in and started buying Continental Connector stock and got control of it. Eventually, we sold our interest and Shenker took over the Dunes.

Shenker was basically a nice person, as was his wife, Lillian. He was orphaned as a kid and came up the hard way. He worked his way clear through law school and came out of that right into the Depression. The only business he could attract was defending the Mob guys when they got in trouble in St. Louis. He became an expert in criminal law—in Mob law, you'd have to say—sort of like Oscar Goodman was in this part of the country.

For a while, Shenker was a good operator at the Dunes. He had Sid Wyman, who knew the business inside out, and his partner Kewpie Rich,, and George Duckworth was a very good floor man. And they had Big Julie Weintraub running the junkets from New York.

When we had the Dunes early on, I just made a major mistake in thinking I could merge the Dunes in with the holding company and straighten them out. We'd show promising earnings for a while. You'd go along and have two really good months in a row, then all of a sudden the third month would come along and they'd say, "We got beat bad by somebody from Texas."

Well, you knew damn well you were getting ripped off in the casino and there was very little you could do about it.

I lost track of Shenker after a while. I don't know what finally busted him. I'd guess what happened is that he started to expand the Dunes, and he just expanded too fast. That's happened to others through the years.

Another interesting entrepreneur who made his mark on Las Vegas was Bill Bennett. He first came here as an employee of the Del Webb Corporation. He had been working up in Lake Tahoe for them, and he was a good friend of L.C. Jacobson, the president of Webb. L.C. was really impressed with Bennett's work, and they soon brought him down to run the Mint Hotel when Sam Boyd left there to open Sam's Town.

Bennett had formed a slot operation up north with Bill Pennington, and they had done very well with it and expanded it quite a bit, to where it became about the biggest in Nevada. They were placing slot machines in everything from gas stations to mini-marts and any other outlets they could find. They would pay the landlord a certain amount per machine, and they were doing great. They got large enough to where they were able to cash out Circus Circus from Jay Sarno in 1983.

The genius of Circus Circus is that it was perceived as the one place in Las Vegas where families were welcome, and people could bring their kids. They always had nearly full occupancy there, and good floor traffic, because of the novelty of the place, with all the circus acts and arcade games. But it worked mainly because Bill Bennett was a good operator and ran every department correctly.

Our bank did a lot of loans with Bennett and Pennington together. We financed their slot route when that was really going well.

Although years later the place got a little rundown, Bennett put a lot of money back into the hotel in the '70s and '80s, and he clearly understood his market. He went for the opposite market of so many other Strip hotels, which were always looking for high-rollers. He understood that in terms of volume, there were a lot more small-time gamblers, and so he went for the lowball end of the business. At one time Circus Circus was the darling of Wall Street. Their stock price rose steadily and made gaming stocks a lot more appealing for the broader market of investors.

I recall he got into a debate at one time with Henri Lewin at the Las Vegas Hilton about the value of conventions to our city. Bennett felt that conventioneers didn't gamble enough, and that too much emphasis and money was being spent on bringing large conventions to Las Vegas. Of course, I think he was wrong on that score, because filling hotel rooms is about the most important thing we can do for our economy here. Conventions saved this city. But all in all, Bill Bennett was one of the smartest operators we've had in Las Vegas.

While I'm thinking of him, there's a funny story about the first time I met Bill Bennett. After we'd sold the Sahara Hotel to the Del Web Corporation, there came an opportunity to purchase the Thunderbird Hotel, which was right next door. I called Del Webb and his president,

L.C. Jacobson, and told them they ought to look at this deal. I met with L.C. in the penthouse of the Sahara, and he had two guys with him. One was sitting in on the meeting, and the other was serving drinks behind the bar. The guy who was serving drinks turned out to be Bill Bennett. He was a bright young guy in their organization and they had him there to secretly listen in on the meeting.

Del Webb decided to buy the Thunderbird, and they brought a fine operator named Bud James up to run it. About six months later they moved Bud over to the Sahara, where over the years we became very good friends. Shortly thereafter, they sent Bill Bennett downtown to run the Mint. It's kind of funny that Bill Bennett, who years later was in *Forbes* magazine as one of the wealthiest men in America, was first introduced to me as a bartender.

Another great operator was Jackie Gaughan. Along with the Binions, he was one of the most successful downtown operators ever. We mainly did straight banking with him, but Jackie did borrow a little money from time to time. Nothing really big. He just worked hard every day and kept nickel-and-diming, chugging along.

I know he's very proud of his son Michael. Michael's as smart as they come.

We did all the financing for the Barbary Coast when that hotel came along.

## Michael Gaughan

I THINK THE FIRST TIME I MET PARRY WAS WHEN I WAS JUST A TEENAGER. With my dad. It was probably around 1959.

When I built my first hotel, the Royal Inn Casino, Parry was the only guy to go to for a loan. That was around 1971. I borrowed between fifty and a hundred thousand, just for equipment. After that, I went to him every time, for every loan. Mr. Thomas never said no to me. He never even asked me questions. I know he was friends with my dad, and our family had a good reputation.

When we built the Barbary Coast in 1979, Tito Tiberti wanted me to get the money from First Interstate Bank, and I wasted nine months waiting on them. They kept putting me off. Tito was the contractor and he wanted to get paid. Finally, I got desperate and I went to Parry and I'll never forget what he said. "So where ya been?"

It took Valley Bank all of fourteen days to fund it. Every hotel we did was funded by him. I went from Bank of Las Vegas to Valley Bank to Bank of America to Nations.

Parry was the first and only banker you could get money from in the gaming business. When I went in with Steve Wynn as a partner in the Golden Nugget in 1974, I got the money to buy the stock from Parry.

I was easier than a lot of the guys to work with because I never asked for a lot of money. And make no mistake, he didn't just give to everybody who asked for it. He wasn't automatic, and he didn't throw his money away. He made very, very few mistakes. Parry said for a long time that they never lost money on a gambling loan, but I think they might have had one or two losers. Let's just say his batting average was terrific.

## Parry Thomas

THE BARBARY COAST IS AN INTERESTING STORY. IT SITS ON A PIECE OF property that used to be the old Empy Motel. Phil Empy came from Ogden, Utah, and he was my Sunday school teacher when I was a kid in the Twelfth Ward in Ogden. Long before I ever hit Vegas, Phil came down here and bought some property and put up a motel. He was a good Mormon guy and followed the religion very high up in the church.

Years later, when our children were baptized, he was in charge of the local church. He was a bishop and later a stake president and a very religious man.

Anyway, Phil used to come to me and we'd talk from time to time. He'd get offers from people who wanted to buy his motel. And I kept telling him, "Phil, this is your only asset. Don't ever sell it, just lease it."

I explained that he'd always draw a nice income from it, and that the property would only increase in value and sooner or later he'd receive an offer that he couldn't turn down, but for the present he needed to hold onto it. His property was directly underneath the power company's right of way, going down Flamingo. He had to build his motel underneath all those wires.

The same problem existed when Steve Wynn bought the property next to Caesars Palace. They had all those wires and power issues to contend with. In the case of the Barbary Coast, when it was built, they paid for moving the power poles to the north side and back around and under the ground. They went under the Strip and reappeared on the other side on those 135 feet that Steve bought from Howard Hughes, which I helped him buy. And then Caesars worked something out, because after they bought the property from Wynn, they built a big vault underneath that whole area and buried all the cable. Anything of that size, with that much voltage, you had to build a vault. And the vault had to be like twenty feet square where you could walk and work and drive equipment into it. It was a major undertaking to handle that much electricity. I'm not certain exactly how they managed it, but somehow they worked it out.

Before Michael Gaughan bought the property, someone else had bought it from Phil Empy. That person made a big offer to Phil, and Phil was getting old and wanted to leave his family with the money instead of a gambling joint, because it was against his religion to have a gambling joint anyway. After he sold it, he moved to St. George, Utah, and worked in the Temple until the day he died.

I always paid very close attention to political races in Nevada, because the people who got elected were obviously important to the bank and to Jerry and me in a number of ways, but I never got too closely aligned with any one candidate. Being in the banking business, I didn't want to come off as being too partial to anyone. You had to be like Caesar's wife because we had customers on both sides of the fence. And many times, I knew both people running for the same office, so I just had to maintain a level of neutrality.

When Paul Laxalt ran against Howard Cannon for the U.S. Senate in 1964, it was a real problem for me. [*Laxalt was Nevada's Republican lieutenant governor at the time, and Cannon was a Democratic senator.*] I liked Laxalt very much, but there were several reasons I supported Cannon. First, my partner, Jerry, was treasurer of his campaign. Jerry was very involved in politics and a dyed-in-the-wool Democrat. I was Republican, which is probably another reason we got along. We were able to look at both sides of every issue.

Another reason I supported Cannon was because when I was first coming down to Las Vegas from Salt Lake City, and working on loans and real estate on my own, Howard was my attorney. And the reason he was my attorney was that my older sister's brother-in-law married Howard Cannon's sister. So there was a family connection dating back to around 1951 or '52. Howard became my close friend through those years and I think he was an excellent senator.

Hank Greenspun and his newspaper always took strong stands on political races, and usually had an impact on the outcome. I give Hank full credit for getting Grant Sawyer elected governor in the election of 1958. He really took a hold of Grant, who was an unknown lawyer from Elko, and he marched him right through. I remember

Hank bringing Sawyer into my office one day and lecturing me right in front of Grant.

"This is going to be your next governor," Hank said. "He's a very talented man and I want you to support him."

So we did. Jerry and I threw our weight behind Grant Sawyer. It really paid off for us, too. When Sawyer was elected, I got appointed to the Nevada State Board of Finance, Jerry got elected to the state Insurance Board and a new state treasurer was elected, and we could finally get people to listen to us.

As I said earlier, the state constitution said that all demand deposits had to be kept in Nevada banks *in Carson City*. And I couldn't get that changed through the Legislature because the North controlled all the votes. So when I was on the state board, I kept studying that law, and I finally focused on the words "demand deposits." The law didn't say anything about time deposits. Well, on time deposits, interest is paid. So I had the state treasurer analyze how much money he was keeping on demand deposits and how much he was keeping on time. The answer was nothing on time.

So through the state board we made a policy to lower all the demand deposits at First National and pro-rate all the money to the banks through the state on a pro-rated basis determined by their size. Whoever wanted to take some, and to pay the state treasurer a rate of interest, was free to do so. Our Bank of Las Vegas took all we could get, and boy, there was some hollering and screaming coming out of First National. We lowered their balances down, and we took quite a few million and put the money on time deposit. The state won in the end because they started earning interest on their excess money.

∞

The Paul Laxalt-Harry Reid Senate contest in 1974 was very close. Jerry supported Reid strongly, but I don't think I supported either one. I stayed on the sidelines for that one. Harry was and is a very decent fellow and he was head of our Gaming Control Board and then became chairman of the commission, and he did a darn good job in those capacities. There was no particular bond created because we were both Mormons. I tried never to let religion enter into my politics, but I suppose in minor local politics, I have done that a few times.

If I were to talk about important politicians in Nevada, I would certainly point to Howard Cannon and Senator Alan Bible. Cannon because he was in the Senate so long and he interceded on our state's behalf numerous times when we had federal problems of intervention, particularly when Bobby Kennedy had Nevada in his crosshairs. We had no end of federal interference then. Bible helped a lot during that time also. Howard was chairman of the Commerce Committee, which was about as important as you could get in the Senate outside of the Ways and Means Committee, and Alan was on that one.

There's no question that Las Vegas will keep growing. You could double it in size from what it is today, except for one thing, and that's the logistics in transportation of getting people here. We don't have a big enough airport, and we'd have to have a six-lane freeway clear to Barstow or beyond to make the road travel work.

Our biggest weakness right now in 2008 is transportation. Particularly on weekends, the I-15 freeway just can't handle the traffic as it is now.

The biggest thing that should happen, and it should have happened twenty or twenty-five years ago, is a bullet train between Los Angeles and Las Vegas. If we'd ever get that fast train, bar the door. God knows how big Las Vegas could get. The sheer weight of this destination will force a train like that to come, but like everything else, it keeps getting more expensive as time goes on.

I still cringe when I think of the time I had a monorail system all approved and going up and down the Strip, all the way from McCarran Airport to the Golden Nugget. It was all set and with a total budget under ten million dollars, but we got defeated by the taxicab drivers' union. We had to have a referendum on the bond and the drivers defeated the referendum.

This happened in the late 1970s. I had gone down to Rohr Aircraft in San Diego, where they were going to build the cars. This was a company that built fuselages for airplanes. They had the contract to build the cars and we were going to run it down the middle of the Strip. Each hotel would have the expense of building their own platform out to the center of the Strip, and it was all set and the design was beautiful.

A guy by the name of Jerry May, who owned two of the taxicab companies, Checker and Yellow, put on a helluva campaign with television and newspaper advertising. I give the guy credit. He did a helluva job and they killed the vote for the bond issue. We were looking for a $6 million bond issue and we were narrowly defeated. I worked like heck on that thing, too, off and on for at least a year.

On another issue, I'm totally against the teachers union proposal to add an additional tax burden on the gaming industry. I agree with [*former MGM Mirage executive*] Terry Lanni that in the long run it would be a bad thing for Las Vegas.

The biggest problem you run into is that if you let the teachers come in for one, two, or three percent of taxes on gaming revenue, pretty soon you're going to have all the hospital people come in for one or two or three percent, and then pretty soon another group will ask for it and eventually you'll destroy the industry. You end up killing the golden goose that provides such a large percentage of the revenue and job opportunities for the community.

This proposal has been brought up time and again over the years and I couldn't count all the times we had to chop its head off. You just can't let it happen. The gaming industry is a business and it's one of the most productive businesses in the world, but certainly it's critical for Nevada and especially Las Vegas. And that business is entitled to pay a real healthy tax.

At the same time, it has to be recognized by the public that eighty percent of the employment in Las Vegas is connected directly or indirectly to that industry—the whole chain of command, all the way from the suppliers to the labor, to ancillary businesses and everything else involved. So it's not as simple as just saying, oh, they're the fat cats and they should pay more.

## Kitty Rodman

MY THOUGHTS GO BACK TO 1954 WITH THE BEGINNING OF THE BANK of Las Vegas and its temporary headquarters in the Huntridge District of town, and then to 1955 when Parry Thomas arrived and became the bank's chief executive officer with new headquarters at 113 South Fourth Street.

From the beginning, Parry's faith in the gaming and hotel industry and his courage to finance their projects made an impact on the whole town, especially those of us in the construction business. Without his vision and confidence, there would be no Las Vegas as we know it today.

Parry's personal trust in me and my partners, Gus Rapone and Bill Koerwitz, placed us on many lists of preferred contractors to bid on hotel projects that his bank and others were financing.

We were fortunate to have built many of these hotel projects, as well as the Valley Bank Plaza Tower at 300 South Fourth Street (now known as Bank of America Plaza) and most of the Valley Bank branches from Las Vegas to Tonopah, Moapa, and even Pahrump.

I can never thank Parry enough for opening doors that gave me the opportunity to work hard and earn enough wealth to be able to afford his advice.

314

CHAPTER SIX

# Horse Sense

## Parry Thomas

AS I'VE SAID, IT WAS THE FACT THAT PEGGY LIKED HORSES THAT GOT my friend Dick Stine to think of her as a possible blind date for me when I came back from the war. He told her that I was something of a star polo player and that caused her to agree to go on the date, because Mormon girls just don't go on blind dates. She was taking a leap of faith, for sure.

We went to a dance at Saltair, the big-band dance pavilion out on the Great Salt Lake. It was owned by the Covey family, whose son Stephen Covey is the famous author and motivational speaker.

On that date Peggy and I talked about horses all night long. That was our bond of mutual interest. Over the next months we also did some skiing together, but horses were the thing we discussed the most early on.

There's quite a long history behind how we settled up in Sun Valley and acquired River Grove Farm. It's really a story of evolution. I've had a love of horses from the time I was about eight years old, starting with my father's passion for horses, and so I always had a horse from the time I was very young. My first horse was named Bess, and my best horse as a boy was named Bees and Honey. He was a thoroughbred, a wonderful horse.

Understand, it was not uncommon to have horses on a property in Ogden, Utah, in those days. Most families around us had horses. Later, when Peggy and I got married, she had a horse named Pipema, but we had to sell it because we couldn't afford to keep it. We were really struggling financially early in our marriage. She had a job as a secretary for one of the professors at the University of Utah, and that kept us going. When I did finally get a job at the bank after graduating, my starting salary was $120 a month, and then Peter came along and our finances stayed pretty lean.

All through those early years in Las Vegas, we had in the back of our minds that we'd somehow get back to horses, but we didn't have any formal plans. I'd go to horse shows occasionally, but only as a diversion.

What triggered it all was that when our daughter, Jane, was nine years old [in 1968], she wanted a horse and we wanted her to have a horse. Peggy was in charge of that and she investigated and did a super job. She found a horse called Beau Valentine, and he turned out to be a darn good horse. He was a beautiful dark black-brown thoroughbred with a perfect white heart on his head. I bought him in Las Vegas from a trainer. He turned out to be the most winning horse we ever owned early on. Jane entered jumping shows and hunter shows, and if she entered ten classes, she'd come out with ten blues. She and the horse worked together beautifully. If Beau Valentine had been a lousy horse, what we have today at our horse farm would probably never have happened.

We then bought a piece of property and partnered with a guy named Atkins and built a barn together, and we kept Jane's horse there.

We had the home in Newport Beach, so we'd go down there for the summer to get the kids out of the heat in Las Vegas, and Jane wouldn't leave, of course, without her horse. So Peggy looked all over the Newport area for a place for the horse, and she carefully studied four or five different trainers in the area to see how they worked. The trainers didn't know who she was, but she would just sit and watch their style and their manners. She came back and said there was one trainer who was just absolutely outstanding and wonderful with children. He always used proper language and was an outstanding trainer. His name was Bob McDonald. He had a setup there at the county fairgrounds in Costa Mesa.

After hearing about him, I went out and watched Bob ride and give lessons and I got real friendly with him. And that's how our relationship with Bob started, almost forty years ago.

## Bob McDonald

I WAS AT ORANGE COUNTY FAIRGROUNDS IN COSTA MESA WHEN I MET Peggy Thomas. She explained that she had been observing trainers in the area and asked if I were interested in training her daughter, Jane, who was either nine or had just turned ten, and a four-year-old off-the-track race horse. That was Beau Valentine, and he turned out to be a very famous horse.

I didn't have any idea who the Thomas family was and what they had done in Las Vegas. I just knew that they lived in Vegas and summered at Newport Beach.

## Parry Thomas

AROUND THAT TIME, PEGGY HAD GOTTEN TIRED OF NEWPORT. THE BAY had become polluted and the traffic became too much and she didn't want to live there anymore.

We had purchased a little house up in Sun Valley for skiing, and she decided to spend her summers up there. Meantime, most of the kids were involved in school and other activities or off to college, except for Jane. So she'd go up there in the summers and take the horse with her. In those first years we kept the horse at the Sun Valley stables close to our house. They had a big stable there with string horses for people who rent and ride, and there were about eight families that had private horses there. But then a bunch of bickering started, so we built a stable on another piece of private property and partnered with the Dumkys, but that didn't work well either.

I was still in the tanker business—I believe it was in 1977 or '78— when Peggy called me in New York from Sun Valley and said she had found a piece of property. A man named Dale Donnelly had subdivided his property called River Grove Ranch, and he kept the biggest lot for himself, which was about thirty acres.

He had put that property up for sale, and the asking price was $400,000 for thirty-eight acres. He had a little A-frame building on it was all. He was a real estate developer and as a hobby he raised llamas. He had also bought the property for investment purposes because it was a spectacular piece of land.

The problem was that a big real estate dealer in Southern California named Jack Franks was going to bid on the property. Well, I knew Jack Franks and he was a guy who when he bought real estate would give you a dollar-down and a dollar-when-you-could-catch-him.

I told Peggy to offer Dale Donnelly fifty thousand less than the asking price, but to tell him that we'd pay all three hundred fifty thousand in cash. That's what she did and we got the property. I met Jack later and he said he should have been smarter, that he wanted that property really badly and that he would have upped his offer. But that's how we acquired the property in 1978.

The whole subdivision was called River Grove Ranch, and there were nine lots on it. We changed the name to River Grove Farm.

### Bob McDonald

IN THOSE FIRST YEARS OF WORKING WITH JANE AND GETTING TO KNOW the Thomas family, I was just in my early twenties, and when I would come to Las Vegas I would stay at their house. I would come out of the airport and occasionally Parry would pick me up and we'd drive what seemed like ninety miles an hour down the Strip. He told me once that he wouldn't get a ticket, and he kind of winked when he said it. And he never did.

We used to go to this little Italian restaurant on Sahara [*the Venetian, owned by Lou Ruvo, Larry's father*], and I went to a lot of shows on the Strip in those years because I had nothing better to do in the evenings.

One night I remember Parry called and said that we were going to have dinner with Frank Sinatra. I believe it was at the Frontier. [*Parry recalls the dinner being at the Sands.*] And there was this long dining table and as Sinatra was approaching I kept hearing people say, "He's coming. He's coming."

Sinatra had bodyguards with him, and one guy was walking backwards, and then two of them were criss-crossing, and it was all pretty impressive. One of the guys with him was named Chile or something like that. [*Most likely Jilly Rizzo, one of Sinatra's best friends.*] So I'm sitting at this table and this tough-looking guy next to me elbows me in the ribs really hard, and asks me if I came out to Vegas with a junket.

I told him no, and he said, "Oh, so you're a member of the Purple Gang, huh?" And he laughed real loud.

I told him I was just a horse trainer, in town visiting. Anyway, Sinatra was sitting at the end of the table, and I remember wondering how in the heck it came to be that I was in Las Vegas having dinner with Frank Sinatra. I remember that like it was yesterday.

### Debbie McDonald

I'VE KNOWN PARRY AND PEGGY FOR FORTY YEARS NOW. I MET THEM when I was fourteen and I'm fifty-four. Of course I got to know Peggy first because of her love of horses. In the early years, Parry was not in the picture at all. The horses were truly just Peggy's and Jane's deal. Jane kind of went out of the picture when she was going to college, and then Jane decided to get back into competing in dressage and then before we knew it Peggy wanted a barn built up in Sun Valley, so she asked Bob and me if we would come and build it and run it.

It wasn't long after that when they started coming up in the summers, and Parry started watching more and he got into it. Gradually, he got really involved and excited about the sport. I think as his business life was winding down, the horse world sparked a whole new sense of life and purpose for him.

In my visits to Las Vegas with Peggy and Jane, going to lunch or dinner with them on the Strip, I began to realize how important he was. The hotel people always knew the Thomas name, and I knew that Parry had important ties all over town. But one time I just happened to be watching television and this documentary about Las Vegas came on. And Parry was a big part of it. At one point the narrator said that Parry Thomas was, and I quote, "the man who turned on the lights of Las Vegas."

I was really blown away to learn everything he'd done and how much he'd contributed to the city. I had no idea before that. Parry was never the kind of person to talk about what he'd accomplished or how important he was.

## Bob McDonald

I ALSO REMEMBER HEARING THAT COMMENT ABOUT PARRY EARLY ON. Someone said, "If Parry didn't throw the switch, the lights didn't come on in Vegas." I forgot exactly who told me that, but I thought the comment spoke volumes about his importance to the city.

Some years after that, I would go up to Idaho for a couple of weeks in the summer and vacation there with the family. After Debbie and I were married, in 1977, we decided that we wanted to have a child, and we really didn't want to raise a child in Southern California at that time, so Idaho started looking pretty good to us.

I liked the winter sports, and the Thomases had a piece of property and they invited me up to Hailey, Idaho, to look at it.

Originally, they had me up there not to work for them, but to put me in touch with a homeowners' development that had a stable there. I could see there were going to be problems with that, because I had been in California long enough to know if you had fifteen people in an association, you had fifteen different opinions on how things ought to operate.

Anyway, I had a meeting with one of the Thomases' partners in a piece of property, a guy named Dumky, and I could see that wasn't going to work out.

They also had a Frenchman working for them as a trainer, a very flamboyant guy with a big handlebar mustache. He was basically full of crap. The Thomases were boarding their horses at Horseman's Center in Sun Valley, and one day Peggy showed up at the arena to ride, and this trainer was impatient with her and said, "You must disappear."

And Peggy said, "I have no intention of disappearing."

With that, she must have gone home and told Parry, who then called and asked me if I wanted to take over the training. With our desire to have a child, and as well as we got along with the Thomases, it just seemed like a natural. I knew I could do a lot of different things in the horse world in that situation, so it was an easy decision to make.

Incidentally, I ran into this Frenchman again a few years ago at a horse show and he came over to me and said, "So how's Parry?"

And I told him that Parry was good. And then he said, "That Peggy, she's a little different."

And I said, "Well, she hasn't disappeared yet."

## Peggy Thomas

I DON'T REMEMBER HIS NAME, BUT I CERTAINLY DO REMEMBER THE circumstances. He was working as a trainer at the horseman's barn, and anyone who kept horses there was allowed to use the riding arena. I went out to the arena to ride my horse one day and he came over and said, "I'm using the arena now and I'd like you to just disappear." And that was that.

## Jane Thomas Sturdivant

I STARTED TAKING RIDING LESSONS WHEN I WAS NINE YEARS OLD. BACK then Bill and Diane Coulthard lived by us and their daughter Leslie was my close friend. [*Bill Coulthard was the first special agent assigned by the FBI to Las Vegas. He was killed in a car bombing in the garage of the Horseshoe Casino in July 1972. The crime has never been solved.*] Leslie was a year older than me. She had some Western horses, and I think the first time I rode a horse on my own was back at their farmhouse in Iowa. I rode a pony named Chalk and had a great time. So Leslie and I started taking riding lessons together in Las Vegas with a man named Ted Merrick. He was an Englishman and really handsome and debonair and we had a great time. Then later that year for my Christmas present I got Beau Valentine. He was a thoroughbred off the racetrack.

I competed on Beau for a long time. He was just a wonderful horse, and very easy to ride. I rode in the hunter-and-jumper world down at Del Mar and all over California, with Bob and Debbie McDonald. I was just ten when I started getting training from Bob. When we eventually retired Beau from going over fences, my mom rode him in dressage, and he was successful in that as well. He was a lovely mover, always great under the saddle, with all the equitation series and stuff like that.

As I got more interested in dressage in my late teens and early twenties, so did Mom. But her time was limited because she always put family first, so she didn't compete that much at all.

## Parry Thomas

THEN PEGGY DECIDED THAT WE HAD TO BUILD A BARN AND A FACILITY for our horses, and I didn't know a thing about building barns. But I did know from watching horse shows and seeing who was successful and who wasn't, that the horse business is a very professional business and that to do things right you had to deal with professionals. So I asked Bob McDonald if he would want to move to Idaho and take charge of the design and building of the facilities. He agreed to do it and loved the challenge it presented, and Bob just did a great job from an operational standpoint, and in designing everything for efficiency and economics. It turned out to be a superior relationship in every way, and we're still together after all these years.

In those first years we were involved in jumping only, hunters and jumpers. Hunters are jumping horses. It's a combination of going over up to three-foot-six-inch fences clean and clear, and showing great smoothness in the jumps. That's called the equitation ability of the rider and the horse. Both of those things are judged in the hunters' competitions. So that's primarily what Bob was into, the hunters more than the jumpers. Bob's wife, Debbie, who I'll talk more about, was into the jumpers.

Bob coached Jane, of course, and she competed from early on at a regional and national level as an amateur rider. Peggy was also riding, but she wasn't competing. Then she started to study dressage. [*Dressage is one of the three Olympic equestrian disciplines. It is a program of suppling, balancing, and obedience work that prepares a horse for future pleasure-riding or competition, Western or English.*]

Peggy was riding dressage and Hilda Gurney was teaching her. Hilda was the only Olympic medalist we'd ever had in America in the sport of dressage up to that point. So we formed the farm in Hailey, Idaho, and we started buying horses for Debbie and Bob to compete with. Debbie was outstanding at it from early on.

One day when I was watching Peggy take a lesson from Hilda Gurney in California, I asked Hilda if it would be possible for the Americans ever to compete against the Germans and the Europeans in dressage.

"Not unless we get their horses," she said. "So I did some more studying and that's when Bob McDonald and Debbie and Peggy and I started going to Germany to buy these horses. I quickly learned that of all the German breeds, the Hanoverians are by far the largest.

The world of dressage is that of horses executing movements on the flat, all the way from a walk to the trot, the canter, and then to the more difficult movements of piaff and passes and pirouettes and half-passes and so on. In that regard, the German warm-blooded horses have proven to be far and away the best horses in dressage competition. It's not even close between them and the other countries. That's why Hilda told us that we would have to acquire the German horses if we ever wanted to compete against them.

American dressage horses were mainly thoroughbreds that didn't make out at the track, or cross-breed horses, quarterhorses or whatnot. But we had very few imported warm-blood horses in this country.

The Germans, for instance, started breeding their horses several hundred years ago when George III of England was the Prince of Hanover. He ruled that the crown would own the stallions and the farmers would own the mares and the crown would dictate the breeding to get superior horses. And through that regimentation, to this day the state controls the berbands [*associations*] of each of the major breeds of stallions.

For instance, in the Hanoverian breed there are probably 16,000 farmer members, and they have their own directors and they run it. Out of those 16,000 farmers, they produce between seven and eight thousand foals a year, and the regimentation and the systems are so strict that they start testing those foals when they're just two or two-and-a-half years old. Then they select the best ones to go to what they call their elite auction. They then roll it down to about the best ten percent, and they cull that number down to about 120 or 150 horses. And that's what you're looking at when you go to the German Hanoverian auction.

The same thing holds true with the Oldenburgs, the Westphalians, the Holsteiners, and the Trakaners. I think the Hanoverian line is probably more than twice as big as the next breed, which is probably Oldenburg. But the Trakaners used to be the most prominent.

At the Hanoverian auction they will auction only Hanoverians. We found out that the Hanoverian line was the biggest and the best, so we decided some years ago, around 1984 or '85, to go to that auction.

I'll never forget, at that first auction I met a German national who had become an American citizen and he was a trainer in Southern California. He was there buying horses for some of his clients, and I went over and introduced myself. His name was Herman Meiser. He was keeping notes on a big yellow pad, and he wouldn't let me see the notes.

I told him we didn't know anything about dressage, but that I wanted to get a decent horse for my wife and I needed his advice and I was willing to pay for it.

He said, "Well, there's one horse here that none of my clients can afford, but he's the best horse here. I'm not going to bid on him."

I promised Herman I would never bid against him, that I just needed some help because we were so new at this.

"Willie the Great is the best horse here," he said, "but you'll have a hard time buying it because the German Olympic Committee is here and they are determined to buy the horse."

He told me that the most ever paid for a horse at the auction was 90,000 Deutschmarks, and the German committee had made a decision where they were willing to go up to 100,000 for it. That equated to around $30,000, a lot of money in those days.

So we started bidding and sure enough there were about four or five guys over there from the German committee talking. They were pointed out to us so we could watch them. The bidding got up to about 75,000 or 80,000 Deutschmarks, and I knew their limit was 100,000. I figured I better throw a Las Vegas Sunday punch at them, so I got the auctioneer's attention and said I wanted to bid 120,000. A wonderful Australian woman who was advising us, named Annabelle De Jurenac, told me I couldn't do that, that it had never been done before. Anyway, we made the bid and the auctioneer announced that we'd bid 120,000. You should have seen the commotion around this committee. They went nuts. So we got Willie the Great for 120,000 Deutschmarks, which was around $36,000.

When we got the horse back to River Grove Farm and Sun Valley, we realized that we had more horse than we had rider. Peggy wasn't trained well enough or equipped enough to ride him, so we gave the horse to Hilda Gurney, and she competed on him all the way to the Olympics.

Meantime, we kept going back to the auctions and buying horses, and the second horse we bought for Peggy was named Frei Lieben, which means free man. He was a wonderful horse and a good horse for Peggy for many years, really a beautiful animal. We also bought jumping horses during this time.

In the first four or five years, we went to both the spring and the fall auctions. Of course, at the spring auctions the horses are six months younger and it's harder to judge what you're getting. In the fall the horses had more maturity and that took some of the guess work out of it. Even then it's a real challenge to find the best horses at that age. It takes a real keen eye to pick them out.

In recent years most of the horses we've bought for dressage competition are between three and five years old; probably only three or four horses were five years old. That would include Argentinia, a horse we bought in October 2007.

The first horse we bought for Debbie McDonald was Friedland, and he turned out to be a real grand champion. We took him all the way. And we bought him at that first auction when we bought Willie the Great.

I'll never forget. There was a guy from South Africa who had been there for months trying to buy this horse, and he was bidding up and bidding up. I finally bid 100,000 Deutschmarks and ran this guy out of money. He started screaming. You never saw anything like it. He was jumping up and down and swearing at the auctioneer for not dropping the hammer when he had the bid at 95,000. He yelled that Friedland was his horse and that I had somehow gotten it from him by not playing by the rules. It was really quite a sight.

Hilda Gurney was just tremendous to us and became a very close friend. She was the first American Olympic medalist, but of course Debbie and the American team won a bronze medal at the 2004 Olympics.

Debbie got into dressage riding literally by accident. She was initially into only jumping because she was so good at it. But she had a serious accident when a horse fell backwards on her and she busted up her ribs and shoulders and cracked her neck. She was really in bad shape. So Peggy talked Debbie into trying dressage, and we arranged lessons for her with Hilda.

## Bob McDonald

IT WAS IN THE LATE '90S, AND DEBBIE WAS JUST WARMING UP A TOP young horse named Dominant. And she was cantering down to a little warm-up jump, which was about a foot-and-a-half high, and a water truck went by and turned on the water just as she left the ground. The horse was startled and put its legs between the rails and it catapulted the rail and flipped on her. It smooshed her pretty good. It rolled all over her and she ended up with a chip in her neck. She tried to stay with the jumping for the next six or eight months, but she wasn't the same.

Jumping is like driving a car. You can't think; you have to react. And when you start playing it safe or driving safe, you're going to have a wreck.

There was a point when I told her that she needed to quit jumping and try dressage. She resisted for the first six months. Maybe resisted is too strong a word. She just wasn't wild about it. It wasn't the same. And then the more she got into it and reached the higher levels, the more she began to appreciate it. Then the love of it took over.

## Debbie McDonald

THE HARDEST THING FOR ME WHEN I FIRST STARTED TO TRY DRESSAGE was the whole different seat, the different saddle that is used. Your muscles just don't adjust right away after all those years as a jumper.

I spent a lot of time with Hilda Gurney, and she taught me how to get my feet together and schooled me on several different horses. It was definitely hard work as a professional to go back and start from ground zero. About the only similarity between jumping and dressage is that you're on a horse. It's a completely different sport, but I was willing to do it, and if I was going to do it, I knew I wanted to be really good at it, not just okay.

The reason I started dressage was definitely because of Peggy. She was the only one in the barn in Sun Valley who rode dressage. And at the time she didn't have a trainer and it was frustrating for her. She just kept picking away at it on her own. Initially, I really couldn't help her because I didn't know a darn thing about it. But Bob decided that maybe that would be a good way for me to go, so that I could help her and eventually compete myself. Peggy was clearly the inspiration for me.

## Parry Thomas

HILDA GURNEY'S NUMBER ONE HORSE IN THOSE DAYS WAS AN INTER-nationally famous horse named Keen. He was a big tall horse and retired at the time. But Hilda had Debbie ride Keen to get the feel for a horse that performed at the highest level. That was effective in getting Debbie excited about dressage, and once she was enthused, we started buying really super horses for her. The first top champion we bought her was named Beau Rivage. Years later I accused Steve Wynn of borrowing that name when he built his casino in Mississippi.

## Debbie McDonald

I THINK THERE'S A LOT MORE TO THE STORY OF THE NAME. BEAU RIVAGE means beautiful river, and I think the horse came from a part of Europe where that river existed. Beau Rivage had the name when we got him. I think the name of Steve Wynn's hotel might be just coincidental.

Beau Rivage was one of the first young horses we purchased for me to learn dressage. He was purchased more for his attitude, not for his gait. We never originally intended him to be an international horse, and a lot of people didn't think he'd get as far as he did. But he ended up in 1998 qualifying for the World Cup, which was going to be in Sweden. And we had to travel to Maryland for the U.S. Finals to see who would be representing our country in the international competition. We had only one representative for the U.S. then and it was kind of a big deal when we won, but I was really on my own. When we ended up winning the national championship, I didn't have anyone from the U.S. Federation to help me in going to Europe.

Thank goodness I had started working with Klaus Balkenhol [*an international legend in dressage riding and training*] before that, so when I went over there, he could sort of hold my hand through the whole thing, even though he spoke little English.

That World Cup was a great experience, and I look back on it now and even though I would tell someone in a similar situation that he or she wasn't really ready for it, it was eye-opening for me and a great learning experience. Someone in the European press covering me then referred to me as "the housewife from Idaho."

I mean, they're so kind to American riders over there [*said tongue in cheek*].

## Parry Thomas

BEAU RIVAGE WAS A GOOD HORSE, BUT NOT QUITE OF THE QUALITY OF the very top horses in competition. That's because his mother was a Hanoverian and his father was a French warm blood. Debbie trained that horse well and we had some others come up underneath him.

We bought Donatello, which was an excellent horse, and then we bought Brentina when she was just three years old.

The number one rider in France, Margot Otto Crepin, was German by birth but lived in France and rode for the French national team. She was planning on buying Brentina, but fate intervened.

The Germans usually put one of their best horses in the first spot in the auction to prime the price and get the auction started off with a big bid. And that year Brentina was first up in the auction. It turns out that Margot was held up in traffic driving to the auction by a bad accident on the Autobahn. We were able to buy Brentina for 110,000 Deutschmarks, which had moved up in value to about sixty cents or so at that time, so we got her for a bargain price of about $70,000. When Margot finally got to the auction arena, they were already auctioning the fifth horse. Margot and her people tried to convince Bob McDonald and me to sell them the horse, but of course we wouldn't do it.

We look forward to the auction every year. It's one of the most pleasurable things that Peggy and I do. That and watching the progress of the younger horses as they advance up under proper training.

I'd compare it to watching young people progress up the ladder in banking, watching them improve from year to year. Of course, the number of horses we buy that make it to the top is extremely limited. I mean, if we can get one super horse out of four, we're lucky. But those that don't succeed at the international level are still of such quality that they're typically better than nearly anything else out there in America, so they can be sold for a good price.

It's well known in the horse world now that River Grove Farm horses have been carefully chosen and well-trained, and we're proud of that reputation.

For a horse to make a name at the international level is so difficult. There's only between twenty and thirty horses in the whole world to get to that level. And we now have two or three of them, so that's ten percent of the world's elite dressage horses. That's exactly what we tried to shoot for when we started this whole process with River Grove Farm.

## Bob McDonald

I USED TO GO TO THE GERMAN AUCTIONS TWICE A YEAR, BUT NOW WE go just once in the fall because the spring show conflicts with the Del Mar International Horse Show, which we always compete in.

I've always enjoyed the buying and selling part of the horse business. When I first started I always thought, jeez, if you could sell a horse for $2,000, that would be something, then it was $10,000 and then $20,000. I never in my wildest dreams thought a horse would ever sell for a million dollars, but we're there now.

Here's how we ended up buying Brentina: One day Parry came to me and said, "Do you think we can make the Olympic team?" I told him I didn't see any reason why we couldn't. This was in the early '90s, maybe 1993 or '94.

Parry said that we'd go to the German auction and buy three horses and just keep doing that each year until we find the one. And as luck would have it, Brentina just happened to be one of those first three we bought.

On the day we bought her, I said to Debbie that this would be the best horse she'd ever have. I saw the same thing in Brentina that I had seen in Debbie as a rider, just that tenacity and all those special qualities that make a champion.

In an auction situation, those horses are put under so much pressure, and there is so much going on, that any horse that can gracefully deal with that much in such a short period of time and still be sane is exceptional. That's number one. Everything's about attitude. You can take a horse that's not the best mover, and shape that horse if it has a good attitude. Or you can have a horse with all the talent in the world and with a bad attitude and it will never evolve. Of course, you look at the musculature and all of that, but attitude is the key.

Brentina was amazing from the very first. I've dealt with thousands of horses in my lifetime, but when you see a horse that reacts like she does, wow.

In the horse business we frequently trailer horses to shows, and if you have like five horses in a trailer and then take four of them out, the remaining horse will often freak out, because suddenly it's alone. Brentina could care less. She'll look at you like, 'Let's head on down the road. See ya, guys.' She couldn't care less.

That kind of explains her personality. She knows she's special. You see it especially when she walks in the arena. She just puffs up and sorts of tells the crowd, I know you're here for me. That's part of what makes her so far above the rest.

## Debbie McDonald

PARRY PURCHASED BRENTINA WHEN SHE WAS THREE, AT THE SAME time that I was riding Beau Rivage, in 1994. After about a year she started competing at graduated levels of dressage, and she basically holds or did hold the champion status at all those levels, pretty much through her entire career.

When we went to the Pan-American Games in 1998, and it was her first exposure to international competition and that electric atmosphere, and the U.S. team won gold and we also won the individual gold medal, that's when we realized that Brentina had an amazing ability to be at least an international horse. Of course I didn't yet realize how world famous she would become, or that it would go to where it did, but I knew then I had a special horse.

It's hard to describe how close the bond is between a rider and a horse. The only way to explain it to people outside the horse world is like a partnership you have with a dog that you've had for years and years, whether it's a hunting dog or a pet. I mean, you just develop that silent communication where you look at each other and you know what the other is thinking. I give a simple hand signal to Brentina and she'll know exactly what I mean. Sometimes I look at her and touch her in a certain way, and she reciprocates by giving me a little backrub. It's a relationship that goes far beyond just being on top of her back.

## Bob McDonald

WHEN IT COMES TO HORSES, AS IN OTHER WALKS OF LIFE, I DON'T think Parry knows how to do anything small. At these horse auctions, his favorite saying is, "You can't deal out of an empty wagon." That's one of the Parryisms I've picked up over the years.

I grew up the opposite way because I didn't have money. I'll often tell him, "Parry, this is a nice horse, but it's only worth this amount." Parry's attitude is more like, "If you want it, let's get it."

That sometimes can be a little difficult. If we overpay for a horse, I'm obligated as the trainer to make that horse produce for us.

With that being said, I can look back today at some of the horses we bought that seemed expensive at the time and can say that they were actually cheap when you consider what we got from them. So everything's relative.

## Debbie McDonald

I'VE BEEN SO BLESSED TO HAVE A HORSE LIKE BRENTINA. EVEN AT seventeen she still loves to come to work out every day, and never gives me an argument about it. There have been so many high points in competition with her, especially when our U.S. team won a bronze medal at the Athens Olympic Games in 2004, and Brentina and I finished fourth individually.

The 2008 Olympics were spectacular, but things didn't go the way we'd hoped. It was a combination of things that worked against us in Hong Kong. First, it was a very electric atmosphere. In one corner of the arena, they had the Olympic torch that was going. In the other corner they had a huge jumbo screen, really an enormous television screen, and it showed you in the riding arena. And the horses had several movements that went towards that screen, which was kind of a frightening situation. But even though I practiced a few minutes in that arena on a previous night, Brentina was bothered and a little tense from it, but certainly nothing that I thought was going to be a real problem. The night of the Olympic competition when we went into the arena, the wind was blowing a little bit more towards the middle of the ring, which made that sound of the torch more like a jet engine. Brentina is completely terrified of big trucks, to the point where she'd do absolutely anything to get away from them. That Olympic torch sounded like a big truck that night.

Also, the stands were full and all the people were carrying these fans and waving them. So you'd look up in the stands and it was like a whole bunch of butterflies up there. Whatever the case, something definitely had her freaked out that night. It was disappointing, but for a seventeen-year-old mare to have qualified for the U.S. team and to be there at that last Olympics was still a fitting tribute to an incredible career.

### Peggy Thomas

BRENTINA IS USUALLY JUST SO DELIGHTED TO BE IN THE ARENA. AT the Olympics you could tell she was just so excited to be back at horse shows after being off for a year. You could tell when the very first show was getting under way that Brentina was wondering why our groomers weren't braiding her right then for the competition. She was just so anxious to get out there.

But I think it was definitely that tremendous flame that spooked her. You could hear it all across the arena, like the sound of ten bonfires, or maybe a hundred blow-torches.

## Parry Thomas

THE NOISE FROM THAT FLAME WAS SO LOUD THAT SIX HORSES WOULDN'T even go in the arena. Here they were at the Olympics and when the time came, they refused to perform.

## Peggy Thomas

THERE WAS ALSO A HUGE, BRIGHT TELEVISION SCREEN, BRIGHT RED IN color, on the border of the arena. As the horses entered the ring, that screen was right in front of them. Some horses react differently to certain stimuli, and Brentina was just not herself with the noise and the big screen. It's a shame because her score was so low after that first performance when she was not herself that she did not qualify to advance to the next two rounds. The same horses that did advance were all horses that she had competed successfully against many times in the past.

## Parry Thomas

ALL THE HORSES COMPETED UNDER THE SAME CIRCUMSTANCES, SO you can't complain. But I'd rather talk about all the great things that Brentina accomplished.

In 2006 the United States Equestrian Team and the United States Horse Show Association merged and became the United States Equestrian Federation. It now goes by USEF. That is now the organization for all sport horses in America, regardless of the venue or the discipline they're in. And they named Brentina that year the most important sport horse in America. That's a terrific honor.

Debbie McDonald, of course, has just been outstanding and we're so proud of her. She's been judged by the U.S.E.T. and the United States Equestrian Federation as the number one American dressage rider in America for several years. In the horse world, that puts Brentina in the company of a legendary horse like the race horse John Henry, who won that honor a couple of times.

The problem with John Henry was that he was a gelding, not a stallion. Imagine what that cost his owners, when the stud fee for a horse like that can be as much as $500,000. Gelding that horse cost them millions and millions of dollars.

While our love of horses could be called a hobby, it's also become a business for us. although it's difficult to turn a profit buying and training these dressage horses in America. If you're from Germany, it can be a profitable business. In America, you're doing really well if you can turn it into a business that pays for itself. It's nearly impossible to make it profitable. There's not the resale value of horses, there's not the audience, you don't have thousands of people coming to horse shows, and particularly dressage and jumping shows, like they do in Germany or France or Denmark or Sweden.

In Europe it's a big-money sport. Not to mention that it's an extremely expensive sport to operate. You not only have these super horses to maintain, but you've got to maintain the riders and the trainers and the vets and the grooms. You have to buy or build a farm, and that is like building any other complex. It's very expensive. It takes a large initial investment, and then how do you get your return on that investment? In America, the prize money in these shows is very low. If you're lucky you win $500 or $1,000. That will barely feed the horses. Let's just say that if you can break even in America in this business, you're a real winner.

Horses have become our passion and our retirement business. Peggy and I graduated from being proud parents of a wonderful young daughter and a super horse, and what they did together rejuvenated our love for horses and that has given us great pleasure in our retirement.

## Debbie McDonald

ONE THING THAT PARRY HAS DONE FOR THE SPORT OF DRESSAGE IN America is that he never bought any "made" horses. All the horses he's bought were purchased as young horses and were trained to compete at whatever level they reached. It's not like somebody who bought their way onto a team. Even though he had the money, Parry didn't ever want people to think that he'd bought his way onto anything. He earned it. And he's been very adamant about that.

He bought good horses to start with, horses with potential, but it has been good training and good managing and everything else that goes along with that, and a lot of luck on top of it, that makes success happen.

## Dr. Steve Thomas

I LOOK AT MY DAD'S INTEREST IN HORSES A LITTLE BIT DIFFERENTLY than maybe others do, and I could be wrong because I have a great love of boating. But I always thought my dad's bigger interest was in boats and the ocean and the sea. We always had a boat on Lake Mead, and then we had the Newport Beach home and he would take us to Catalina Island, and he always had boat journals around the house. Growing up, I didn't see horse journals around the house ever. I saw him flipping through *Yachting* magazine and *Sea* magazine. We'd often go to boat shows, and he'd talk with Uncle Jerry about his latest boat.

## Joyce Mack

WHENEVER SOMETHING ABOUT PARRY AND HIS SUN VALLEY RANCH would come up, Jerry would say something like, "Those damn horses!" I think Jerry had always envisioned that he and Parry would grow old on their boats in the ocean.

## Dr. Steve Thomas

THEN AT SOME POINT I REALIZED THAT DAD WAS STARTING TO GRAVI-
tate toward Sun Valley and the horses. Before you knew it, the Newport place was sold and the boats were all gone. My impression was
that he was teaching us another lesson as our dad. And that is that
when your wife and companion loves something as much as our mom
loves horses, it doesn't matter if you like boats more or golf or tennis
or whatever else. You do what she wants you to do. A—you owe it to
her, and B—that's how you're going to keep her happy and thereby
yourself happy staying with her.

So my impression in watching him make that changeover was not
that horses were the love of his life that he was returning to, but that it
was a major concession to Mom. I don't know when the last time was
that he rode a horse. He doesn't ride them. She does. Sure, he loved
polo at one time, but it's Mom that has the great passion for horses.

I always felt he put his energy toward the horses also because he
had a daughter that he wanted to keep safe from boys, and so he got
Jane involved with horses in her teenage years. And he had a wife
who had enjoyed horses her entire life. Now maybe I'm not correct on
that. Maybe he truly loved horses and it was just my own prejudice
towards boating and the ocean that makes me feel that way.

# ABOUT THE CONTRIBUTORS

**STEVE WYNN** BEGAN HIS CAREER IN 1967 AS PART-OWNER, SLOT MAN-ager, and assistant credit manager of the Frontier Hotel. He is now chairman of the board and chief executive officer of Wynn Resorts Ltd. He has developed Wynn Las Vegas and Wynn Macau and Encore. Wynn was previously chairman of the board, president, and chief executive officer of Mirage Inc., where he built The Mirage, Treasure Island, and Bellagio.

**ELAINE WYNN** HAS WORKED SIDE BY SIDE WITH HER HUSBAND SINCE 1976. Since 2000, she has served as director of Wynn Resorts, where she oversees everything from the selection of staff uniforms to the lux-ury shops and spa amenities. She is a former chairman of the UNLV Foundation. As a philanthropist and children's advocate, she plays a key role in special events and the company's charitable involvement.

**PEGGY THOMAS** HAS BEEN MARRIED TO PARRY THOMAS SINCE 1947. They met on a blind date in Salt Lake City immediately after Parry returned from service in World War II. They have five children, and divide their time among their horse farm in Hailey, Idaho; Las Vegas; and Southern California. "Peggy deserves all the credit for the good things that have happened in our family," Parry says.

**BILL BOYD** IS THE EXECUTIVE CHAIRMAN AND CO-FOUNDER OF BOYD Gaming Corporation. As executive chairman he serves as the primary liaison of Boyd Gaming with customers and employees, and takes a leading role in shaping the company's strategic direction and vision. Bill's father, Sam Boyd, came to Las Vegas in 1941 as a dealer. He later was a stockholder in the Sahara, Mint, and Union Plaza hotels. Bill Boyd practiced law in Las Vegas for more than fifteen years and was a partner with his father, among others, in the Union Plaza and the Eldorado Casino. In 1973, Bill Boyd and his father co-founded Boyd Gaming Corporation, whose first property, the California Hotel and Casino in downtown Las Vegas, opened in 1975. At that time, Bill left the practice of law and began his full-time career in the gaming industry.

**ROBERT MAHEU** (1917-2008) WORKED FOR THE FBI AND PERFORMED special assignments for the CIA before he became Howard Hughes' "alter ego" in 1957, as he wrote in his book *Next to Hughes*. Maheu's work in his investigative company, Robert A. Maheu and Associates, which he formed after leaving the FBI, included a failed assassination attempt on Cuban dictator Fidel Castro for the CIA. Maheu was responsible for every major business decision Hughes made in his Las Vegas years, 1966-1970, and it was he who arranged for Parry Thomas to advise and structure all of Hughes' hotel-casino and real estate investments during that period. He died shortly after being interviewed for this book.

**IRWIN MOLASKY** IS CHAIRMAN OF THE MOLASKY GROUP OF COMPANIES and for more than fifty years has played a significant role in the growth of Las Vegas. As a developer, he was responsible for many of the city's firsts, including the private 730-bed Sunrise Hospital; the 17-story high-rise office building now called Bank of America Plaza, previously known as Valley Bank Plaza, where Parry Thomas was CEO; the high-rise luxury condo project Park Towers at Hughes Center; and the Nathan Adelson Hospice, which serves the terminally ill and their families. He was also a key figure in the development of the University of Nevada, Las Vegas through a land donation, and was the founding chairman of the UNLV Foundation.

**JON JOSEPH** JOINED VALLEY BANK AS VICE PRESIDENT AND GENERAL counsel in 1981. He managed Valley Bank and Valley Capital's Legal and Loan Recovery Departments, and at the time of the merger with Bank of America in 1992 was executive vice president and general counsel of both companies' respective executive committees. Joseph moved to San Francisco in 1992 post-merger to manage Bank of America's Bankruptcy Department. He is retired and living in Bend, Oregon.

**DR. ROBERT MAXSON** IS THE PRESIDENT OF SIERRA NEVADA COLLEGE in Lake Tahoe. Previously, he was senior vice president for academic affairs at the University of Houston, and then president of the University of Nevada, Las Vegas from 1984-94. Maxson also served as president of Cal State Long Beach from June 1994 to January 2006. During his time in Las Vegas, he served on the Board of Directors of Valley Bank of Nevada.

**BRIAN GREENSPUN** IS THE CHAIRMAN AND CEO OF THE GREENSPUN Corporation, and president and publisher of the *Las Vegas Sun*. Greenspun is responsible for his family's varied business interests that include ownership of American Nevada Corp., the developer of Nevada's first master-planned community, Green Valley; and the Greenspun Media Group, which publishes local magazines, weekly newspapers, and national niche publications. His father, Hank Greenspun, who founded the *Las Vegas Sun*, was a close friend and business associate of Parry Thomas, and a major benefactor of UNLV, where two institutions bear his name: the Greenspun College of Urban Affairs and the Hank Greenspun School of Communications.

**PETER M. THOMAS** IS THE FIRST SON AND CHILD OF E. PARRY AND Peggy Thomas. He is an attorney by education and a member of the Nevada, Utah, and District of Columbia Bar Associations. He became a managing partner of the Thomas & Mack Company in 1995 after serving as president of Valley Bank of Nevada and its successor, Bank of America Nevada, for fifteen years. Peter is married to Nancy Paxman, and they have four children.

**ROGER THOMAS** IS THE SECOND SON IN THE THOMAS FAMILY AND was born in Salt Lake City. He is executive vice president design for Wynn Design and Development and has designed resorts for Steve Wynn for twenty-nine years. He resides in Las Vegas with his partner, Arthur Libera, and has one child.

**DR. STEVE CLARK THOMAS** IS THE THIRD SON OF E. PARRY AND PEGGY Thomas. He is an orthopedic surgeon practicing in Las Vegas. Steve is married to Karen Parker and they have three daughters and two sons-in-law.

**THOMAS ADAM (TOM) THOMAS** IS THE FOURTH SON AND CHILD OF E. Parry and Peggy Thomas. An attorney by education, Tom has been the managing partner of the Thomas & Mack Company. since its formation in 1992. Tom is married to Leslie Goodman and they have four daughters and one son. Tom functioned as the family's liaison on this biography of his father.

**JANE THOMAS STURDIVANT** IS THE FIFTH CHILD AND ONLY DAUGHTER of Peggy and Parry Thomas. Since an early age, Jane competed in equestrian events, winning many junior competitions in hunter and jumper shows. She graduated with a degree in political science from the University of Utah. Jane and husband, Peter, make their home in Hailey, Idaho, where she continues training with Debbie McDonald and competes as an amateur in national dressage competitions. Jane is an accomplished textile artist and avid gardener. Jane has one son and three stepchildren.

**JOYCE MACK** HAS BEEN A RESIDENT OF LAS VEGAS SINCE 1949, WHERE she and her late husband, Jerry, raised their three daughters. She received her education at UC-Berkeley and UCLA. Joyce is a leading philanthropist in the Las Vegas community and serves on numerous charitable boards.

**KAREN MACK** IS A NOVELIST AND FORMER TELEVISION PRODUCER AND the second daughter of Jerry and Joyce Mack. Her first novel, *Literacy and Longing in L.A.*, was on the *L.A. Times* bestseller list for fifteen weeks, climbing to No. 1. In her television career, she won two Golden Globes, including one for Best Motion Picture for Television for her film *One Against the Wind*. She formerly served on the Board of Directors of Valley Bank of Nevada.

**KITTY RODMAN** WAS A DRIVING FORCE BEHIND SIERRA CONSTRUCTION Corporation for fifty years. She was a shareholder, director, and secretary-treasurer from the company's formation in 1953 to its liquidation in 2003. Before her company built many Strip hotel projects, it built many local banks, schools, UNLV buildings, and even projects for the Atomic Energy Commission and Nuclear Rocket Development Space Agency, and even facilities at the mysterious government testing ground known as Area 51. Steve Wynn's Mirage Hotel towers were among the last major projects Rodman oversaw. She is involved with many Las Vegas charities, most passionately with Opportunity Village.

**HERB JONES** (1914-2008) WAS A FOUNDING MEMBER OF THE LAS VEGAS law firm now known as Jones Vargas. He graduated from the University of Missouri in 1940 and served in the Army during World War II. Following the war, he earned his law degree from the University of Arizona and was admitted to the Nevada bar the same year. He was a founding director of the Bank of Las Vegas (later Valley Bank of Nevada) and wrote the bank's charter. He was a close friend of

Parry Thomas's for more than fifty years, and his sons remain close friends with the Thomas family. Herb Jones died four months after his interview for this book.

**LARRY RUVO** IS THE SENIOR MANAGING DIRECTOR OF SOUTHERN WINE and Spirits of Nevada. In 1970 he partnered with Steve Wynn to open a wine and spirits distribution company. Ruvo has guided Southern Wine to become Nevada's largest wholesale liquor, wine, and beer importer and distributor. He also is heavily involved in the Alzheimer's Association, both locally and nationally, and has overseen the construction of the Lou Ruvo Brain Institute, a planned research center that will be a national resource for the most current research and scientific information for the treatment of Alzheimer's, Parkinson's, and Huntington's diseases. The institute was designed by renowned architect Frank Gehry, named by *Time* magazine the "world's greatest living architect."

**MICHAEL MILKEN** IS CHAIRMAN OF THE MILKEN INSTITUTE, A NON-partisan economic think tank; chairman of FasterCures, which seeks improved efficiency in the medical-research process; and co-founder of the Milken Family Foundation, which since 1982 has recognized outstanding educators and supported a broad range of medical innovation and breakthroughs against many life-threatening diseases. *Fortune* magazine called him "The Man Who Changed Medicine" for his three decades of work to accelerate medical solutions. As a financier, Mike is often said to have revolutionized modern capital markets, making them more efficient and democratic by innovating a wide range of financing techniques previously unavailable to smaller entrepreneurial companies. *The Washington Post* said he "helped create the conditions for America's explosion of wealth and creativity." This financed the growth of 3,200 companies in such fields as cable television, cellular phones and other industries, and created millions of jobs. He had a profound impact on the growth of Las Vegas by financing many gaming, publishing, and home-building companies. A graduate of UC-Berkeley, he earned his MBA from the University of Pennsylvania's Wharton School. Mike and his wife of forty years, Lori, have three children and three grandchildren.

**MICHAEL GAUGHAN** COMES FROM A LONGTIME LAS VEGAS GAMING family. His father, Jackie Gaughan, has owned several downtown casinos, including the Union Plaza, the Las Vegas Club, the El Cortez, and the Showboat. Michael opened the Barbary Coast Hotel and Casino in March 1979, on what was then the most prominent and busiest corner of the Las Vegas Strip. That property became the foundation for Coast Casinos. In 2004 Michael sold Coast Casinos for $1.3 billion to Boyd Gaming. In July 2006, Boyd announced that it was selling the South Coast to Michael for an estimated $576 million. It is now known as South Point. Gaughan won the Mint 400 off-road race in 1966, and his son Brendan has been a nationally prominent race-car driver since the early 1990s.

**JACK BINION** IS A PROMINENT CASINO OWNER AND ENTREPRENEUR and the son of the legendary Benny Binion, who owned the Horseshoe Casino in downtown Las Vegas. Jack became president of the Horseshoe in 1963 at age twenty-six. The Horseshoe was known worldwide as the purest "gambling joint" in the world, and was famous for accepting any wager with the stipulation that the limit was established by the gambler's first bet. After selling his interest in Binion's Horseshoe to his sister Becky Behnen in 1998, Jack acquired the rights to the Horseshoe brand outside of Nevada. He went on to form Horseshoe Gaming Holding Corporation, which developed and operated several highly successful riverboat casinos under the Horseshoe name. Along with Doyle Brunson, Jack Binion is considered the founder of the famous World Series of Poker. Binion was named to the Poker Hall of Fame in 2005.

**DEBBIE MCDONALD** IS AN AMERICAN DRESSAGE RIDER WHO HAS COMpeted in the two Olympic Games and many international competitions. She and her husband, **Bob McDonald**, who live most of the year at River Grove Farm in Hailey, Idaho, on the Thomas estate, have had exceptional careers since they started their relationship with the Thomas family forty years ago. Bob designed and runs the training facilities at River Grove, coaches Debbie and other talented young riders who compete in national and international competitions, and attends the German horse auctions with the Thomases every year. Debbie was part of the U.S. Olympic bronze medal-winning team in the 2004 Summer Olympics in Athens, riding the world-famous mare Brentina, and also competed on Brentina at the 2008 Olympics in Hong Kong. She has won a silver and gold medal in team dressage at the World Championships, and won both the team and individual dressage gold medal in the 1999 Pan American Games.